Alexander W. M. Clark Kennedy

To the Arctic Regions and back in six Weeks

Being a Summer Tour to Lapland and Norway

Alexander W. M. Clark Kennedy

To the Arctic Regions and back in six Weeks
Being a Summer Tour to Lapland and Norway

ISBN/EAN: 9783337192815

Printed in Europe, USA, Canada, Australia, Japan

Cover: Foto ©Andreas Hilbeck / pixelio.de

More available books at **www.hansebooks.com**

TO THE

ARCTIC REGIONS AND BACK IN SIX WEEKS.

BEING

A SUMMER TOUR TO LAPLAND AND NORWAY.

WITH NOTES ON
SPORT AND NATURAL HISTORY.

BY

Capt. ALEX. W. M. CLARK KENNEDY,

F.R.G.S., F.L.S., F.Z.S., ETC.;

LATE COLDSTREAM GUARDS,
MEMBER OF THE BRITISH ORNITHOLOGISTS' UNION; AUTHOR OF
"THE BIRDS OF BERKSHIRE AND BUCKINGHAMSHIRE."

MAP AND NUMEROUS ILLUSTRATIONS

London:
SAMPSON LOW, MARSTON, SEARLE, & RIVINGTON,
CROWN BUILDINGS, 188, FLEET STREET,
1878.

[*All rights reserved.*]

LONDON:
GILBERT AND RIVINGTON, PRINTERS,
ST. JOHN'S SQUARE.

TO

MY FELLOW TRAVELLER,

THESE PAGES,

DESCRIPTIVE OF THE SCENES WE VISITED TOGETHER,

ARE AFFECTIONATELY

Dedicated,

BY

HER HUSBAND,

THE AUTHOR.

"Up, up! let us a voyage take;
　　Why sit we here at ease?
Find us a vessel tight and snug,
　　Bound for the Northern Seas."
　　　　　　　　　W. HOWITT.

He. "Dost thou love wandering?
　　Whither would'st thou go?
Dream'st thou, sweet daughter,
　　Of a land more fair?
Speak, mine own daughter
　　With the sunbright locks!
To what pale banish'd region
　　Would'st thou roam?"
She. "O father, let us find
　　Our frozen rocks,
Let's seek that country
　　Of all countries!"
He. "Why, then, we'll go."
She. "On, on! Let's pass the swallow as he flies!"
　　　　　　　　　BARRY CORNWALL.

PREFACE.

This portion of a book is read, I am well aware, by the public with less interest than any other part of the volume; and I believe it is quite true that one third of those who peruse a work, never turn to the preface at all! This being so, the shorter the preface is, the better.

My only excuse for adding another volume to the already long and ever-increasing list of Scandinavian travels, is my belief that comparatively few of our fellow-countrymen, and more especially of our countrywomen, who, year after year, "take their pleasure abroad" by returning each successive summer to the familiar Continent, are aware what a splendid field is open to them by paying a visit to the glorious scenery of Norway, or by pushing still further northward across the Arctic Circle to the wilder land of the Laplanders, and the regions lighted by the rays of the midnight sun.

I do not imagine that anything new is described in this book, as I have merely endeavoured to truthfully record our daily life in a most interesting land, where it must certainly be the traveller's own fault if he is not delighted with what he sees.

Such a tour as that described in the following pages lies, as far as the question of money goes, within reach of all who travel abroad; and certainly there could be found no country so near home, which combines the advantages of good fare, glorious scenery, pleasant modes of conveyance, entire novelty, and last, but not least, a remarkably health-giving climate, with a moderate expenditure, as does this part of Scandinavia.

It being generally admitted that every one is entitled to have a "hobby," and to ride it, no apology is needed for the notes on natural history which will be found scattered here and there throughout this little book.

I will only add, however, that if an interest

in the wonderful and ever-attractive works of the Creator is a component part of the nature of travellers—whether journeying for the purpose of sport, health, novelty, or merely in search of the picturesque,—they will speedily develope a taste which will afford them fresh delights throughout the changing scenes of life, and they will lay up for themselves an endless source of enjoyment, which will last long after the so-called "pleasures" of the world have begun to pall.

Such, at least, is the sincere belief of

THE AUTHOR.

LONDON, *April*, 1878.

CONTENTS.

CHAPTER I.

Attractions of Norway—Shooting and salmon-fishing—A paradise for the artist—Pleasures of carriole-driving—Novelty of the country and life in Lapland—Different routes to Norway—The first train from Stockholm to Christiania, in 1871—Disregard of time amongst the natives—Civility to inferiors—Guide-books—Useful hints—What may be seen in six weeks 1

CHAPTER II.

Start from Hampshire—Accident on the railway—Our luggage—Arrive at Hull—We go on board the "Hero"—Scene in Hull docks at night—We leave the Humber—A northerly gale—Frequency of storms in the North Sea—A select dinner—Splendid sunset—A rough night—Cod-fishing on the "banks"—Birds at sea—The Naze—Fishing-boats and seagulls—Christiansand and sport to be had there 18

CHAPTER III.

The Skager Rack—We sight the Swedish coast—The Færder lighthouse—The Christiania fjord—Its beautiful scenery—Northern divers—Mackerel and porpoises—Rifle practice—A seal in sight—Arrival at the capital—The Custom-house—A fish supper at the hotel—Brightness of the nights—We engage our carrioles—Oscarshal—The castle of Agershuus—Hoyland, the robber—Sights of the city—The discomforts of Norwegian beds . 34

CHAPTER IV.

We leave Christiania for Eidsvold—Slowness of trains—Sport near Dahl, a reminiscence of 1871—A crowded boat on the Mjösen—The lake in summer and winter—A rush for lunch—Our "crew" fire a salute at Hamar—Arrive at Lillehammer—Geology of the Mjösen—Wild flowers—Trout-fishing—My otter hunting horn—We start in our carrioles—Useful advice for driving in Norway—Lovely scenery in Gudbransdalen—Enormous trout—Colour of the Logen—Fishing in Gudbransdalen—A fox—Holmen—We pass the night at Skaeggestad—Norwegian jams . . 59

CHAPTER V.

An early start—Irrigation in Norway—Laziness of the peasants—Great altitude at which trees grow—Cattle and their drivers—The old station at Storklevstad and its mistress!—Magpies, and mode of capturing them—Kringelen—Invasion of Romsdalen by the Scotch—Fate of Colonel Sinclair's band—Delay at Moen—Laurgaard—The pass of Rusten—Toftemoen and its master—His proud lineage—An angry bull—Dombaas station—In bed above the clouds!—Wolf and fox skins, and old silver ornaments—We leave Dombaas—The lemming—Its habits, migrations, and enemies—Exorcism used in ancient times against the lemming—A sæter—Price of cows and ponies—Fokstuen on Dovre 84

CHAPTER VI.

Great cold on the Dovre fjeld—Fishing at Auflus Bridge—The ancient station at Hjerdkin—Wildness of the Dovre-fjeld—Sneehætten Mountain—Its crater—Richness in colouring of the rocks and mosses on the fjeld—Arrive at Kongsvold—Trout—Eagles and owls—Excellency of Kongsvold station—The Dovre a splendid field for botany—Abundance of flowers—Reindeer moss—Shooting on the Dovre-fjeld—A snowstorm—Beauty of the drive from Kongsvold to Drivstuen—The "leap of the stomach"—A girl postboy!—The hawk-owl and its habits—Bjerkager—We join a wedding procession—Great heat at Engen—Hopgardens in the Guul valley—Salmon-fishing in the Guul—We go by rail to Throndhjem—Midsummer's night on the shores of Throndhjem fjord . . 115

CHAPTER VII.

Great heat in Throndhjem—Herr Bruun's fur stores—Eider-down quilts from Greenland—I purchase presents for the Laps—We leave Throndhjem for the Arctic regions—St. Han's eve—Monkholm Island and its legend—The "Nordland" and her officers—Jelly-fish at Besaker—Porpoises and bottle-nosed whales—The Namsen fjord—Excellency of the Namsen for salmon-fishing—Seals—Terns and gulls—Curious appearance of Apelvær Islands—"Haycocks" of cod-fish—The cod fishery of the Loffoden Islands—Sleepless birds of the Arctic Seas—Torghatten—Splendour of the sunsets on the western coasts of Norway—The Seven Sisters' Mountains—Crossing the Arctic Circle—Scenery near the Polar Circle—Our first view of the midnight sun . . 113

CHAPTER VIII.

Bodö—"Jagts"—We cross the Vest fjord—Vast flocks of sea-fowl—Grand scenery of the Vest fjord—The Müelström and its history—Everest's description of the whirlpool—The Isle of Flakstad and its whales—The Loffoden Islands—Fishing from the ship—Cod and "lythe"—Stocknarknæs—Swarms of eider fowl and sea-birds near Stocknarknæs—The trade of the poor fishermen of Loffoden—Extraordinary wildness of the scenery of these islands—In the Arctic Ocean—Sea-fowl in the And fjord—Vast flocks of eider ducks—The

"Nordland" reaches Tromsö—Schmidt's hotel—
Midnight fishing in Tromsö fjord—The cuckoo in
the Arctic regions—Precautions against fire—The
midnight sun is "put out" . . 169

CHAPTER IX.

We pay a visit to the Laplanders on Kvaloe Island—
Our lazy crew—Wintry scenery—Eider fowl in
their breeding haunts—We find nests of the eider
ducks—Eider down and its value—Habits of eider
fowl in Lapland—Strict protection of these birds
in Iceland—Bishop Pontoppidan's account of the
eider—Dreary scenery at the Lap encampment—
Difficulty of distinguishing the male and female
Laps—Ugliness of the Laps—Their tents—We
are welcomed by the Laps—Dirty habits of the
Laps—Their babies—Their cradles described—
"Hush-a-bye, baby, on the tree top!"—The Lap
family at dinner—Linnæus on the felicity of the
Laplander's lot—King eiders . . 193

CHAPTER X.

Drawbacks to the felicity of the Laps—Lapland not to
be recommended to an anxious farmer—Extraordinary growth of crops north of the Arctic Circle
—A Tromsö harvest—Effect of the Gulf stream
on vegetation—Discrepancy of temperature—
Reindeer-horn spoons—"Kosnager"—Lap women
"spinning"—Religious observances of the Laps—

Healthiness of these people—Love of the Lap for smoking and drinking—Their food—The reindeer the source of riches to the Lap—An opulent Laplander—Reindeer moss—Uses of the hide, horns, sinews, and flesh of the reindeer—Reindeer hams and tongues—Lap women—Milking the tame deer—A Lap's larder—The glutton—" Fisk Lappar "—The reindeer as a steed—Description of the Lap sledge—A winter "family move"—Harness of the tame deer—Fractious behaviour of these steeds—Instinct and habits of reindeer—The reindeer a plucky animal—We bid adieu to the Laps—A golden eagle—A Tromsö shop and its contents—I purchase reindeer-horns and walrus tusks—Uses of walrus ivory . . . 220

CHAPTER XI.

The sights of the Arctic Ocean—The polar bear—Digestive powers of the white bear—Shooting a bear—A large bear—Lamont's books on Arctic sport—Russian whalers at Tromsö—The chase of the walrus—Shooting and harpooning walruses—Fondness of mother walruses for their young—We are visited by Laps with their deer—The cuckoo in Lapland—The watchman in Tromsö church-tower—Lap dolls—" Rein " grass—A novel barometer—Good fishing—We re-embark on the "Nordland"—The midnight sun—Prosperity of Tromsö—Table of the midnight sunshine—Immense quantity of sea-birds in Finmark—The puffin—Amongst the Loffodens again—A weasel on deck—The white fox—Mode of capturing Arctic foxes by the Greenlanders—The silver fox—Amusements of the Laps—A noisy congregation—Lap cures for sickness—Lap funerals . 254

CHAPTER XII.

The Vestfjord at midnight—Grand scenery of Loffodens and the Bodö coast—Our last view of the midnight sun—Bodö—Absence of sands on the Norwegian coasts—Glaciers—Serrated mountains—Kerry cattle in the Polar regions—The last of the Arctic Seas—Crossing the "circle"—A "right" whale in sight—A private whaling expedition—We are unable to join it—The luxuries of amateur whaling—Sunset south of the Arctic regions—The Isle of Torget and its "hat"—Wild scenery—A rough day—I catch a large cod—Little auks—The little auk as food—"Red" snow, and its cause—Return to Throndhjem—A wedding in low life—An ancient church—The beauty of the graveyard of Throndhjem Cathedral—The interior of the cathedral—St. Olaf—St. Olaf, the champion of Christianity—Death of Olaf—Shrine of St. Olaf—The legend of Olaf and Tvester, the wizard 281

CHAPTER XIII.

Great heat in Throndhjem—We go to the cathedral service—A tea-garden—Cheap drunkenness!—

Walrus-tusk knives—Bruun's fur shop—Sights of the city—The Lierfossen—Smelting copper ore—Fruit in Norway—On board the "Nordland" again—We sail for Bergen—Emigrants for America—A beautiful sunset—King Olaf's saga—Hitteren and its red deer—Christiansund—picturesque situation of the town—Abundance of flowers there—The fish trade of the town—The sea eagle—Eagles conquered by fish—A spread eagle!—Rough sea off the Molde fjord—Molde and its fruit-trees—The Romsdal valley—Sport in Romsdalen—A grand panorama of the Romsdal Mountains — The Romsdalshorn — A "spring-whale"—Sharks on the Norwegian coasts—The shark fishery—The black shark—Harpooning the basking shark — A bagman from the Arctic regions!—Aalesund and its lobsters—Associations of the Vikings—Longfellow's saga of King Olaf . 315

CHAPTER XIV.

Rollo the walker—The cliff of Hornelen—The Nord fjord—The Islands of Losmoë and Sulen—"Jagts"—The Sogne fjord and its attractions—We arrive at Bergen—Rainfall at Bergen—Description of the jagts—We bid adieu to the "Nordland"—"Early to bed" the motto of the inhabitants—Precautions against fire in Bergen—A disturber of our rest—The sights of Bergen—The museum—The story of a bedstead—History and trade of Bergen—The skating soldiers of the

Norwegian army—Old silver at Bergen—We leave Bergen—The sea-serpent—The evidence for and against the existence of the "Kraken"—The description of leviathan in Job—Blasting rock near Bolstadören—Curious salmon traps—Arrive at Bolstadören—The Evanger Vand—Courtesy of all classes in Norway—Vossevangen—Midnight trout-fishing—Woodcock in their nesting haunts —The lament of the birds of passage . . 350

CHAPTER XV.

An early stroll in Vossevangen woods—The black wood pecker and northern nightingale—Blackthroated divers—Habits of the golden-eye duck—The Vöring-foss—"Fläd-bröd"—The Tvinde-foss— Stalheim station — The engineering of the Stalheims-cleft—Wild scenery of the Nærödal— Romantic situation of Gudvangen—A splendid panorama of waterfalls—We arrive at Lærdalsören —Service in the old church of Borgund—Its history—Maristuen on the Fille fjeld—Bears—A cold drive over the Fille fjeld—Lemmings—Wild scenery—Nystuen station—Costume of the peasants—Attractions of Nystuen—Desolate aspect of the fjeld near Skogstad—Reindeer—Fine trout at Oiloe—Story of a peasant attacked by wolves— The "little" Mjösen—Mosquitoes at Fagernæs —A charming station—A moonlight drive to Odnæs—Fine timber at Odnæs—A midnight supper of fieldfares and redwings—By steamer down the Randsfjord—The legend of the swallow, the crossbill, and the peewit—Hönefos and its history—By train to Christiania—We leave Norway by the "Albion"—Wenham lake ice—Christiansand—Bloodthirsty mackerel—A North Sea fog—We nearly run down a fishing-boat—Back to the Thames—A Norwegian national song—Au revoir 381

Appendix 419
General Index 423
Index to Scientific Names of Animals, &c. . 415

LIST OF ILLUSTRATIONS.

Exterior of Throndhjem Cathedral .	*Frontispiece*
Little auks or "rotchies"	17
The icy Arctic Ocean .	33
Carriole and Norwegian pony .	58
Pair of long-tailed ducks or "harelds" .	111
The fulmar petrel	112
Seals "at home" . .	168
A hungry Arctic fox at a trap .	192
Pair of king eider ducks .	219
Head of the reindeer . . .	250
Boat approaching a walrus . .	283
Carved stonework in Throndhjem Cathedral	314
Fishermen hauling their herring-nets	319
The old church of Borgund . . .	389
Map of route of Captain and the Hon. Mrs. Clark Kennedy . . .	*At end*

TO THE ARCTIC REGIONS AND BACK IN SIX WEEKS.

CHAPTER I.

> "Thou hast sail'd far—
> Permit me of these unknown lands t' inquire;
> Lands never till'd, where thou hast wandering been,
> And all the marvels thou hast heard and seen."
> CRABBE.

"HAVE you yet been to Norway?" is a query that I have often put to numerous friends, on being asked to help them to decide where to take their annual holiday; and if their reply be in the negative, as is generally the case, then my answer is, "You have not seen the most glorious country in Europe; by all means go next summer."

The chief attractions of this northern land may be summed up in a very few words. It

possesses splendid scenery, in the shape of
magnificent mountains, with glaciers and
eternal snows; forests of dark pine and waving
birch, where the axe has never yet been wielded
by man; quiet valleys, with many a little
village snugly buried among the fir-woods,
each with its quaint old church, and picturesque
wooden farm-houses are dotted here and there
on river-bank and hill-side. Its waterfalls and
streams are among the grandest in the world
for rugged beauty, while its "fjords" and
"fjelds" afford the most picturesque scenery
one can imagine.

The sportsman will always find in Norway a
fairly good stock of winged game in autumn or
winter, though bears are very scarce nowadays,
and even reindeer less numerous than of yore,
and hard to obtain.

The angler can always find employment for
his rod in almost every river or lake, and may,
if he takes sufficient trouble to find out for
himself the choice waters, obtain excellent
sport with both trout and grayling, though it
is quite a delusion to suppose that every one

can kill a salmon in Norwegian waters, as
(though there are plenty of those fish in the
rivers) they are well protected wherever they
are found, and a stranger would find it most
difficult to obtain permission for even a day's
salmon-angling. And I may here remark that
most of the best rivers, and several of the
inferior ones, too, are let year after year to
Englishmen; and yet travellers are constantly
complaining that they find it impossible to
obtain leave to fish in such a river, and at once
put down the lessee thereof as a selfish fellow,
quite forgetting the fact that the said lessee,
probably as keen a fisherman as they are themselves, has left England on purpose to enjoy his
salmon river, and finally, that he has a perfect
right to keep for himself and his friends that
sport for which he has to pay a good round
sum!

For the artist, of course, the variety of subjects for the pencil is endless; and I should
imagine the principal difficulty would rest upon
a careful selection of the *most* beautiful objects
of scenery in a country where fresh charms for

the eye meet one at every turn of the road, at each winding of the river or the fjord.

Not least among the attractions of Norway, especially to ladies, is that of being able to drive oneself along roads, magnificently engineered, in one's own "carriole," than which mode of travelling any lady who has spent a few weeks in the country will agree with me there is none more agreeable. There is certainly a delightful feeling of freedom about this carriole driving. You are entirely your own master; your ponies are, as a rule, excellent, and very sure-footed; you are not bothered by having the bewigged and powdered head of your coachman ever in front of your nose, nor need you fear your conversation with your friend in another carriole being overheard and commented on by the footman behind. You can drive as slowly or as fast as you like, and can stop at any part of the road to rest or explore for as long as you like; and you are pretty sure of fresh relays of good ponies to speed you on your journey from "station" to "station."

However, I must not longer dilate on the marvellous attractions of my favourite country; but it is no easy matter to know where to stop, once having begun to sing the praises of "Gamle Norge," as the peasants love to call their native land. One more word, and I have done. If you like novelty, a thorough change of scene, and diversity from any other part of Europe, go to Norway. Turn your affections and your steps thither also, if you are in search of good health, for it is one of the most health-giving lands on the globe's surface; and the author is quite sure that if you once set foot in the country, you will be very sorry when your time bids you return home; and having visited it once, you will often long to go back again.

It has been the fashion for many years to go abroad every summer, and very few are their numbers nowadays who cannot boast of being foreign tourists! The reader knows the Continent proper, perhaps, very well. He has doubtless long since "done" France, the German Spas, and the familiar Rhine. He may have many a time crossed the Alps, and sailed on the bosom of the lovely lakes of northern Italy. He may have explored the ruined beauties of Roman architecture, and sought for relics of bygone times on the plains of classic Greece. He probably has wandered among the mountains of the Bavarian highlands, and he may be a constant "migram" to the valleys and hills of Switzerland. The quaint churches and curious cities of Belgium may no longer please him; and the china-stores or the old-world costumes of Holland may have long since lost their charm of novelty. Why then do the same people year after year, as regularly as summer returns, revisit haunts of which they are often heartily sick, merely because it is the "proper thing to do"?

Turn your steps, I pray you, this summer to the North; to old Scandinavia, the land of the mountain, lake, and river, the home of the brave Vikings, the land of rich legends, where some of the most splendid scenery in the world is to be found. Or if you are more adventurous, pack up your small portmanteau for a trip to the Arctic Regions, and accompany us in our six weeks' travel to distant Lapland, the haunt of the white fox and the reindeer, the home of the little Lap, the land where throughout the long summer nights you can see the blood-red orb of the sun shedding his splendours o'er fjord, fjeld, and ocean!

A tour to Norway is—notwithstanding the statement in the previous pages that comparatively few travellers attempt it—a regular summer trip for many, and its beauties are becoming better known and appreciated every year. A considerable number, however, of the English annual visitors are what are familiarly termed by the captains of the steamers "old Norwegians," which means that those so called have been in the country several times, generally for purposes of sport; for, as before mentioned, not many who have once become acquainted with Scandinavian rivers, fjords, and fjelds, are able to resist the pleasant temptation of another visit.

So many varied routes from this country to Norway are now open, that the traveller has several lines of march from which to select the one that pleases his fancy most. He can, for instance, make Hull his starting-point, and proceed by steamer to Throndhjem, Bergen, or Christiansand direct, and from the latter port go on to Christiania. If he happens to live in or near London, he can save time and trouble by sailing direct from the Thames to the Norwegian capital. Should he desire to make Scotland his starting-point, a steamer will take him from the harbour of Leith. But if it happens to be his sad case that to brave the dangers of the deep is not only no pleasure to him, but verily pain and torture to body and mind, as is, I fear, the plight of many who take their pleasure on steamers, he has a pretty route open to him *viâ* Dover and Ostend, which will only give him the half-dozen hours' misery of the short run across the Channel, instead of the three days or thereabouts which would otherwise be spent on the North Sea. If not in a hurry to reach their ultimate destination of Christiania, those who decide on this route (which the author travelled by in the spring of 1871) have the opportunity of seeing several interesting places on the way, which if they are not already acquainted with them, are worth seeing. Among towns one passes by this route are Bruges, Ghent, and Brussels, in Belgium; Hanover, Hamburg, and Kiel, in Germany; and, more interesting than any, Copenhagen. Having spent as much time as he wishes in Denmark, the mail steamer will take him over "The Sound" to a small town called Malmö, in the south of Sweden. Thence he can either take the railway to Göttenburg, and by steamers through the lakes to Stockholm; or by rail all the way to the capital of Sweden, where he will find some magnificent hotels, and several museums, and other objects of interest. The traveller can then journey on by the railway to Christiania, passing by Carlstad and Arvika, a pretty line of country.

The author happened, curiously enough, to travel by the first train that ever ran over this line of railway, in the spring of 1871. I had been in Stockholm, attending the funeral of the Queen of Sweden and Norway, who had just died. The funeral procession was very imposing; and the various crown jewels, which were kept in Christiania, had been brought from that city to be " present " at the ceremony. The escort for these valuables consisted of several of the high officers of state, and owing to their great kindness and to that of the British consul at Stockholm, I was taken, free of expense, from that place to Christiania by the train conveying back the jewels and officials. I well remember the immense saloon carriage, in which we made ourselves very comfortable; and the weather being very cold at that time of year, the carriage was well warmed. The officials, mostly grey-haired old gentlemen, were very happy playing whist uninterruptedly for the one and a half day's time which the journey occupied. Whenever our train arrived at a bridge, these old gentlemen took great care of themselves, stopping the train, and getting out, when we all would walk leisurely over the bridge, and the train slowly followed. After the bridge was duly examined, a few pipes smoked, and " good luck " drunk to the safety of the bridge and prosperity to the new line, we would get in again, and once more proceed on our way. We slept at Carlstad that night, and the bridge scene and consequent delay was often repeated during the day. Next morning the officers were rather sleepy, as the game of cards had gone on to rather a late hour on the previous evening, so they did not choose to "embark" again until mid-day, and the "first train" at last arrived at the Norwegian capital just as it was getting dark; thus accomplishing the distance of some four hundred miles in thirty-four hours. I only mention this day's travelling to show the utter disregard of *time*, which is the case with the people—both rich and poor—throughout Scandinavia.

Any traveller must bear in mind that the custom of the natives is *never* to be in a hurry; so that he is much more likely to be promptly and civilly attended to if he is careful to give his orders for horses, food, or what not, in a considerate tone of voice; civility, even to inferiors, *costs nothing*, and the tourist may rely upon it that he who gives his orders at an hotel or roadside "station" in a rough or domineering voice, will not be served with what he may require with either the same willingness or civility as would one who takes care to give no offence to the poor peasant by speaking kindly, and not appearing to be in too great a hurry. This advice is most important, and the result of non-compliance with it costs many an Englishman the annoying delay of perhaps several hours at a "station" before horses (which are all the time probably in the stable) are supplied to him, even if he is sufficiently lucky to obtain any at all!

After this digression, I must resume the question of the advantage of the route from Dover to Ostend, and through Germany and Denmark, as previously described. The principal advantage of course consists in the avoidance of the long sea voyage which must be taken by any other line of travel; but the disadvantages are that it entails a loss of time (unless one thinks that the various cities passed compensate for this), and nearly three times more expense than by direct steamer. This little work is not intended by the author for one moment to be thought of as in any way supplying the place of a "Guide Book;" and care has been taken, as far as possible, to avoid useless repetition of facts and information easily found by reference to "Murray," which I unhesitatingly affirm to be by far the best book to take with one to both Norway and Sweden, and without the latest edition of which no tourist should leave home.

The author, at least, has never been without these invaluable guides when abroad; and on all parts of the European continent, and in Northern Africa and in Asia also, I have found in countless instances comfort, advice, and help, by reference to my beloved and often much-begrimed "Murray," when all other assistance had failed!

Although almost every information that can be required is to be found in the above-quoted guide, and in Mr. Bennett's "Handbook," the following hints I think may be found useful to the traveller, and will not be out of place here.

Firstly.—Take as little luggage, consistent of course with comfort, as you possibly can;

one fair-sized portmanteau for each person, together with a *small* bag, and a bundle of rugs, ought to be sufficient. This amount of luggage can be readily carried upon one carriole, whereas, if you have much in addition to this, you will find it the cause of terrible delay, and often of extra expense, at every station where you change horses, which on the average is every eight or nine miles.

Secondly.—If you purchase heavily in old silver curiosities, carved wood, the skins of animals, and the like, as almost all travellers are wont to do, you will find it by far the best plan to fill small but strong wooden boxes now and then; and when at places on the coast, such as Bergen or Throndhjem, have them sent round by a coasting steamer to Christiania, where the landlord of your hotel or Mr. Bennett will gladly take charge of them until your arrival. Photographs, old silver ornaments, &c., get terribly damaged by being knocked about the country while the traveller is on his carriole journey.

Thirdly.—Every one should be careful to take

a *few useful* medicines from England, as one may be taken ill at some very out-of-the-way spot in the mountains, and good doctors in Norway are extremely scarce, whilst in Lapland they hardly exist at all.

For all other information the author refers the traveller to "Murray," whose "knapsack" edition is bound in a flexible cover, and will be found less bulky than the larger guide, and it answers all practical purposes. He must be sure also, on his arrival in Christiania, to obtain the inexpensive little volume published every summer by Mr. Bennett, and which contains such a mass of local notes (especially referring to the proper payments for horses from one "station" to another, all which places are mentioned by name, with the government scale of charges from stage to stage), that the traveller would often be at a loss without the well-known "Bennett's Handbook."

The reader will understand, I trust, that it is utterly impossible to see one quarter of the beauties of Norway in a few months' travelling, and we should have many a successive summer to cross the wild North Sea before we became acquainted with half the interesting and beautiful nooks which the country possesses.

The tour described in the following pages was necessarily rather hurried, but the routes we took were as varied and interesting as could well be; and the districts through which we passed were a combination of some of the most wild and rugged, with many of the most homely and peaceful scenes in the land.

By following our line of march, or by striking out one somewhat similar for yourself, you can travel—making London or Hull your starting and returning point—about five thousand miles in the six weeks we place at your disposal. If you can spare more time, you of course can easily travel over far more country, or can linger as long as you choose at any place that takes the fancy.

The object, however, of the present volume is to give a rough sketch of what can be accomplished with ease in the short space of time above mentioned, with the ultimate intention of seeing a little life and scenery within the Arctic Regions.

The most convenient way of relating our story is perhaps in the form of a journal; we will therefore commence with our departure from England in a new chapter.

LITTLE AUKS OR "ROTCHIES."

CHAPTER II.

" And now in our trim boats of Norroway deal,
We will sport through the waves
With the porpoise and seal,
And the breeze it shall pipe—
So it pipe not too high,
And the gull be our songstress
Whene'er she flits by."

SONG OF CLAUD HALCRO.

Thursday, June 8th, 1876.

THE day we have fixed for our start to the lands of the midnight sun is indeed a lovely one; and as we leave the pretty Hampshire park behind us, a full chorus of birds salutes our ears as we pass through the bright green woods, as if to wish us good-bye and a pleasant journey!

The short run up to London was quickly accomplished, and without mishap to our train, although a large portion of the tunnel under the "Hog's back" (well-known to the good people of Surrey) took the opportunity of falling in just as a luggage-train was passing through the tunnel during the forenoon, but we heard that no one was killed.

The only interesting incident to myself was the hurried glimpse I caught, as we dashed past the Aldershot "North Camp" station, of the familiar white jackets of a detachment of my old regiment, and also some of the Grenadier Guards, who were employed, with the questionable assistance of half a gale of wind and a glaring sun, in endeavouring to make bull's-eyes at eight hundred yards' distance on the faces of those well-known targets, pounding away at which I have spent many a day!

We made a few small additions to our kits to-day, consisting of a broad-brimmed straw hat for L——, to keep off Norwegian suns, and grey gauze veils to enable both of us to keep at bay the mosquitoes; and this is a very necessary armament for one's face and neck in hot weather, when those little pests positively swarm, especially if one is fishing, or walking near a

river or lake. A couple of pairs of *really*
strong, thick laced boots, well studded with
large nails, are what I would recommend every
lady to take with her to Norway. Ordinary
English ladies' walking-boots, with their ugly
high heels and absurdly thin soles, would last
but a very few days on a Norwegian hill-side;
and if a lady has to walk through wet grass or
on muddy roads, as she sometimes is obliged to
do, she will soon see the advantage of thick
boots over thin ones, as carriole-driving with
cold wet feet is by no means a pleasant or
healthy amusement.

Our amount of baggage is by no means large,
and this will save us a world of trouble and
delay during our travels. It consists of two
portmanteaus, one for my wife and the other
for myself, a very small hand-bag apiece, and a
good bundle of rugs and waterproofs, while one
salmon-rod and gaff, and a couple of trout-rods
tied up with the umbrellas, completes the list.
There is also a small trout "creel," which,
when not filled with its legitimate occupants,
will serve to carry our luncheon.

We have taken care to keep sufficient space in our portmanteaus for some sheets, two pairs of towels, and a couple of pillow-cases, and, from my experience at the road-side "stations" in Norway in 1871, I fancy we shall find these articles very useful.

Friday, June 9th.

The weather in London was so dreadfully sultry last night, that we were only too glad to find ourselves rushing through the heated air in the 10.35 a.m. express for the port of Hull, whence our steamer sails this evening. The extreme heat soon changed into rain, which we had expected from our rapidly falling barometer; and by the time we reached Peterborough, its fine old cathedral could scarcely be distinguished through the mist. On sped the train through the dreary fen country, with its flat green meadows, long lines of gaunt poplars, and straight canals, looking doubly dismal in the tremendous downpour,—on past Grantham and past race-loving Doncaster, till the two hundred miles were accomplished, and our destination reached at four o'clock.

On the platform we found an individual who told us the unwelcome news that we could not go on board our steamer at once, as the cargo was not yet completed, and the captain stated that he would not sail until six o'clock to-morrow morning.

Having disposed of a capital and remarkably cheap *table-d'hôte* dinner at the station hotel, I walked down to the docks, where an enormous assemblage of shipping belonging to all nations was congregated; and after a considerable search for our steamer, the "Hero" by name, I found my way on board and down to the cabin, which we had engaged six weeks ago, and which turns out to be a very snug one, and almost in the middle of the vessel.

As we shall sail early to-morrow, the captain advised us to come on board this evening and sleep in our cabin, instead of passing the night on shore and having to get up at five in the morning, which was too good advice to be thrown away. Returning, therefore, to the hotel, I soon saw our baggage off on a truck to the ship, where it arrived at the same time as

L—— and myself. After settling our small cabin as comfortably as we were able, we took a stroll round the docks, which, although the hour was late, being past nine o'clock, still presented a very busy appearance. The rain had now ceased, and there was a bright full moon shining, and the night was warm and pleasant, but a rising wind howling through the rigging of the numberless ships around us does not hold out very sanguine hopes of a calm day in the North Sea to-morrow.

The whole of the vessels in the same dock as that where our steamer lies sail on their respective voyages during the next few days, and some at the same time as we do in the morning. Most of these ships are steamers of a large size, and are destined for Copenhagen, Hamburg, Norway, and other European ports. Several belong to Russia also, and we particularly noticed one vessel whose decks were being crowded with quantities of traction-engines and steam-ploughs from Suffolk for Riga, where we hope they may be as useful as the cargo of sewing machines, on board another large steamer destined for Archangel. It is now 11.30 p.m., and our crew are making the most awful noise it is possible to conceive in their frantic endeavours to complete the cargo by 6 a.m., as if they don't we shall lose the "tide," and more delay will ensue.

Saturday, June 10th.

It is really wonderful how loud and continuous noise on board ship tends to send one to sleep; and though I am told that the hideous commotion over our heads went on all night long, we certainly were utterly oblivious to things of the outer world until we awoke at seven o'clock to find that the "Hero" had sailed more than an hour ago, and that we were steaming away down the tideway of the Humber.

Our first breakfast on board gave us the opportunity of seeing what our fellow-passengers were like in appearance; and although the principal part of them — thirty-five in all — paraded at the feast spread for us in the saloon, comparatively few of that number were to be seen towards the end of the meal. At about nine o'clock we got clear of the Humber; and the breeze, which had been freshening all night, soon began to make itself felt. Being, luckily for my own pleasure on board ship, a good sailor, I could not repress a smile as those who had set to work with such a hearty appetite only a quarter of an hour ago, whose conversation had been so energetic, and whose cheeks bore a few moments since the rosy hue of health—one after another cut short their *déjeuner*, and with trembling hands, pallid visages, and shaky legs made the best of their respective ways to "enjoy" the privacy of their cabins.

Going on deck, I found the wind very strong from the north-east, and in consequence the sea was "short and chopping," as indeed this stormy North Sea generally is. It is not often that a voyage to or from Norway is calm, even in summer time, and the reason given for the frequent storms in the North Sea is, that being so extremely shallow, in a comparatively short time a very nasty rough sea is stirred up from, as it were, "the very bottom." The captain of the "Hero" tells me that in no part is the North Sea believed to be over than thirty fathoms in depth, and in general it is not over twenty fathoms. L—— was, unfortunately, soon in her berth, quite *hors de combat*, but not suffering much.

The delay last night was very annoying, as after all we hear that a great deal of the cargo we were to have taken was left behind, which is unlucky for us, as it consisted of iron sleepers for a Norsk railway, and would have proved a valuable ballast, and saved us much rolling to-day. The wind being north-easterly is also unfortunate, as it is dead ahead of the vessel and very strong, and we are progressing at present only nine knots per hour, which is terribly slow, and the ship being narrow, and so lightly laden, rolls terribly. By eleven o'clock, the flat shores of the coast at the mouth of the Humber had disappeared from view, and we have seen the last glimpse of old England for some weeks. A few seagulls still follow the ship, and continued to do so long after the land had faded from our sight.

The storm continued all the morning, but the sun shone brightly throughout the day, and a cloudless sky made the heaving sea look less cheerless. We saw no vessels to-day, after we were out of sight of land; and, indeed, it was not easy to see very far, for such clouds of spray surrounded the steamer as to wet one through if one remained long on deck. A "tent," constructed of sail-cloths and boat's-oars, was rigged up for our benefit by the captain's orders, but no sooner had I gone beneath its shelter, than it was blown down, and the wind being still very strong, we left it where it fell, to be put up again when the storm abates.

Luncheon, or rather dinner, at 2 p.m., was by no means the sociable meal that breakfast was in the morning; only one passenger besides the captain and myself appearing at the table, where the wooden "fiddles" did not prevent several breakages of plates and glasses, so much did the vessel roll and pitch.

The force of the wind lessened towards evening, but the waves broke over our decks and deluged me very often. By 9 p.m. the wind veered from the eastward to due north, and in another hour's time it became due west, and sails were then hoisted, which steadied the ship considerably. L—— was much better in the evening, but could not leave her cabin. The change in the length of the day, as we proceed northward, is already observed to be considerable, and I could read my book on deck with perfect ease at half past ten o'clock to-night. The sun itself actually set at 8.25 p.m.; and I amused myself by timing it from the instant that the lower part of the ball of fire appeared to touch the water till the tip of its upper rim finally disappeared from sight below the horizon. It took exactly four minutes and a half, which could not fail to make one's thoughts dwell on the rapidity of the flight of time. It was one of the most splendid sunsets I ever saw; the western sky having a glorious appearance for an hour after the sun had set over the stormy waters.

Sunday, June 11th.

Last night was dreadfully rough, and the pitching of the ship made sleep quite out of the question, as our entire time was occupied in doing our best to prevent being thrown out of our respective berths at every roll. The wind lessened very much towards morning, and by mid-day it was so much calmer that my wife was able to come on deck, and remained there the whole afternoon. The crew were now able to erect the "tent" again, and as the sun was very hot, its shelter was acceptable. When about eighty miles distant from the nearest land we passed a small fishing-boat, whose crew of a couple of men were engaged in taking up their deep-sea lines, which are set principally for cod: these lines are sometimes half a mile, or even more, in length. Many English boats come out to these northern "banks," as the fishermen term them, to fish for cod, but it often becomes perilous work in a small boat, as these seas are, as before stated, subject to very sudden gales. I noticed a pair of black guillemots (*Uria grylle*) this morning close to the ship, diving away, and bringing up little fish in their bills each time, and we were then nearly one hundred miles from any coast, a long distance for so small a bird.

The atmosphere was beautifully clear all day.

and we first sighted land with the naked eye, about sixty miles distant, at six o'clock in the evening. This land proved to be the Naze, the most southerly promontory of Norway; and we could almost distinguish, by the aid of a glass, the lighthouse which is built on the summit of its awful cliffs, where it is much needed to keep vessels from approaching too near this dangerous headland.

Several of the passengers began to appear on deck towards evening, but they were all very unsteady on their legs. We again saw a most splendid sunset, promising fine weather tomorrow; and as we entered the Skager Rack, which divides the Naze from Denmark, we noticed great numbers of fishing-boats of all sizes making for the open sea from the various towns along the coast. Most of these boats had a perfect cloud of seagulls, both small and great, hovering over them; nor will the birds leave the fishermen until they have had a share of the fish to whose whereabouts those small gulls yonder are directing the boats, and many of the birds have already commenced fishing on their own account. The night was so fine and warm that we did not turn into our berths until past eleven o'clock, and the land was still several miles distant.

At two a.m., on *Monday, June* 12*th*, we were awakened by a tremendous noise, which was occasioned by the arrival of the ship in the harbour of Christiansand, and by passengers landing and others coming aboard. Although the hour was early, it was quite light, and we had a charming peep of the picturesque little town from the cabin port-hole.

Christiansand, which was founded as long ago as 1641, and which possesses a cathedral and an excellent harbour, is a most striking place to an English eye. Beyond the harbour, we could see many a pretty-looking wooden house snugly nestled amongst dark fir-trees, and painted in different colours, principally white and red, and one or two bright green. Contrasting with these picturesque buildings are huge rocks, many of them rising to a considerable height behind the town, with fir-trees scattered here and there; and large boulders of a grey stone, apparently granite, line the edge of the water of the Topdals Fjord, where we are now anchored. L—— was so sleepy, that on seeing from the port some huge rocks close to the water's edge, which had evidently been lately whitewashed (no doubt to point out some safe anchorage), she immediately drew my attention to the *snow*, which certainly was not to be expected in the middle of the merry month of June!

Some very fair shooting is to be had near Christiansand, provided you know where to go; and good salmon fishing is to be obtained in the Torrisdal river, under a picturesque waterfall; but for all the author knows, the angling there may now be let, as is the case with nearly every river worth fishing in the country. There are but few Englishmen out here yet; but I was sorry to miss an old brother-officer (Cathcart), whose steamer left the harbour for Throndhjem, as ours entered it.

After a stay of a couple of hours, and a great deal of noise and wrangling about some iron, a quantity of which a merchant in the town

wished to have put on board for England, as it
did not suit him to wait until the steamer
touched again on her return from Christiania
next week, we left Christiansand, and again
stood out for the open sea, which was now so
calm that not even a ripple was perceptible on
its surface.

THE ICY ARCTIC OCEAN.

CHAPTER III.

TO NORWAY.

"Where'er I roam, whatever realms to see,
My heart, untravell'd, still returns to thee."

EVERY ONE was fortunately able to remain on deck throughout the whole day, as there was a dead calm and a cloudless sky, and the warmth of the sun made it most enjoyable for those who had suffered from the effects of the rough voyage. From 4 a.m. until 3 p.m. we were still in the Skager Rack, which is open sea, and occasionally is extremely rough; but being so calm to-day, the "Hero" kept nearer to the Norwegian shore than is usual, and we were thus enabled to see many a little town half hidden among its overhanging fir-woods, and pretty villages, mostly built upon small bays, which indent this wild-looking coast at frequent intervals. Although the sun was very bright,

the horizon to the eastward was not very clearly
to be seen; and about an hour before we entered
the Christiania fjord, we obtained our only
view of Sweden, which was so distant as to
give one the idea of its being quite a flat
country, which of course it is not. The
entrance to the beautiful fjord which leads
direct from the open sea to Christiania, and
which in consequence is named after the capital,
is guarded by a fine lighthouse, built upon
Færder Island—a large mass of bare rocks—on
which, however, there are one or two small
buildings; but the spot seems very desolate for
a winter "residence," though as our vessel
steams close past the island to-day it looks
picturesque enough; and those gulls and ducks
scarcely seem to move on the slight swell
which the screw of the ship sends slowly in
little waves towards the rocks. It is not easy
to imagine that the calm, deep blue water which
we gaze on to-day can be hurled in foaming
masses over those bare rocks, and dashed
against the lighthouse with fearful violence,
during the dark nights of the Norwegian winter.

The length of the Christiania fjord is about seventy miles, and its scenery, although not quite so striking as that to be met with on many of the mountain-girt fjords on the western coast, is very beautiful, the pretty towns and country seats dotted about upon its wooded banks having a peaceful look about them difficult to be described. The fjord is, in many parts, especially as we near Christiania, studded with numerous islands; some of these are of large extent, and are covered with patches of waving birch or woods of the dark green pines; while others are merely rounded masses of barren granite, or gneiss, rearing their gaunt forms here and there from the blue waters. The small farms that strike the eye of the traveller upon both banks of the fjord are, as a rule, merely little "clearings" in the woods, and the buildings composing each homestead are painted some bright colour, perhaps red, light-brown, or green; and we could hear distinctly on the summer air the tinkling of the bells round the necks of the cows which fed among the trees near the water's edge, or grazed

in the bright green fields, which now and then
appeared amongst the woods.

I could not help noticing the remarkable
absence of bird-life to-day during our voyage up
the fjord, as I remembered what vast quantities
of ducks and other sea-fowl I used to see here
in the spring of 1871. The reason for their
absence, I presume, is that they are mostly
away breeding upon the more rocky and less
frequented parts of the coast. We noticed
only one pair of the well-known Eider ducks, a
few cormorants, and a pair of the Great Northern
Diver *(Colymbus glacialis)*, which, with a shot
from a Henry-Martini rifle belonging to the
captain, I considerably astonished by sending a
ball just between them as they sat in the water,
at about six hundred yards' distance! They
at once dived, and we never saw them again.

Fishing-boats without number were observed
just as we passed the town of Frederikstad, all
congregated in the same spot, busily engaged
in netting mackerel, of which fish there was
apparently a vast shoal, many of them taking
little leaps from the calm sea to escape the

porpoises, which were very busy amongst the boats, swimming round and round, and following the direction the fish were taking.

The detailed description of this fjord is of course to be found in the guide books. Suffice it, therefore, to say, that the principal place that took our attention was the town of Horten, where most of the vessels for the navy are built, and which, in fact, corresponds to our Portsmouth; and the "straits" of Dröbak, where a strong fortress guards the approach up the fjord towards the capital: at the latter point, the passage for a vessel is very narrow. From Christiansand to the upper end of the fjord, where Christiania is situated, took us sixteen hours to accomplish; and time hanging rather heavy on our hands during the afternoon, Captain D—— had an empty tar-barrel thrown overboard, and we had excellent rifle practice from the stern with his Henry-Martini as long as it was in sight.

The heat became very oppressive during the afternoon, and although only just 8 p.m. when we came in sight of Christiania, the sun was quite obscured by most curious heavy clouds, which hung over the city like a canopy, the heat being terrible, and we could scarcely breathe. The approach to the head of the fjord is very fine, but its effect was rather marred by these thundery-looking clouds, which obscured entirely the surrounding hills. Just before we reached our moorings at the quay, L—— and I were standing forward, when a large seal raised his head and shoulders out of the water within about twenty yards of the ship, took a good long look at us, and then disappeared. I merely mention this to show how inquisitive these curious creatures are, and how close they will often come to a large city.

No passports being required in Norway, we quickly were able to get ashore, and but a very slight examination of our baggage was made by the Custom-house officials, who I always think are more civil in Scandinavia than in any other country with which I am acquainted. We were not even asked to open our portmanteaus, but an officer most courteously inquired if we had anything liable to duty, and on our answering in the negative, he merely scratched a letter with a piece of chalk on each trunk, after which our luggage was at once taken on shore, placed upon a handbarrow, and trundled away to the Hotel Victoria. Landing at a Norwegian port is conducted with so much quietness and absence of bustle, that it cannot fail to strike the traveller very favourably when he calls to mind the many annoyances attendant on the arrival of the mail-boat at Ostend, Calais, or Boulogne, where porters, both authorized and unauthorized, quarrel over the unfortunate passenger's luggage, and where animated, not to say angry, disputes so often take place within the precincts of the noisy *douane*.

There are several good hotels in Christiania, but the Victoria has always been the favourite with travellers; although its charges are decidedly high, I think that the excellence of its cuisine and the civility of the attendants make up in extra comfort for one's bill. L—— and I walked to the hotel in company with Mr. J————, who has a good fishing-station on the river Gaul near Throndhjem, one of the best salmon streams in Norway except the Alten and a few other large rivers farther north. The heat was suffocating; and, though the distance from the quay to our hotel was only about a quarter of a mile, we were all very glad to sit down in the large, well-ventilated dining-room, where a capital supper was speedily placed before us. Such a supper it was never before our fortune to see, and that meal cannot ever fade from our memory! The feast consisted of all kinds of fish, and L—— was soon able to recruit herself after the fatigues of the voyage upon such delicacies as fresh salmon, lobster-salad, prawns, and hashed beef, assisted by cooling draughts of the excellent Norsk ale, which is a very mild beverage, and immensely patronised by our countrymen. Such a spread of fish was surely seldom seen. Besides the head and shoulders of a splendid newly-caught salmon, there were dishes of both fresh and fried trout, smoked salmon, boiled salmon, mackerel, anchovies in various forms, shrimps, salmon kippered, sardines, and cheese in various stages of decomposition (which is usually preferred in this country), and of half-a-dozen different kinds. Over one of the cheeses, or rather covering what remained of what *once* was cheese, we noticed a small, dome-shaped glass; this apparently is used to prevent the remnants of this delicious morsel literally *running* off the plate! Add to this long list cold meat, and most excellent rolls as fresh as could be wished for, bread and capital butter, and coffee to finish up with, and picture three persons seated at the small table which was groaning under this mass of good things,—for all the above delicacies were upon the cloth at one and the same time,—and it will give you a good idea of an hotel supper in a Norwegian city. You need not expect, however, the same choice of food to be placed before you during your travels in the interior, for you will not get it, and must rest content with the good but plain fare which you will find.

The "Victoria" was very full, as the Storthing or Norwegian parliament, which is elected

and meets every three years, was just breaking
up, and several members with their families
were living in the hotel previously to their
departure for various parts of the country.
However, we were given capital rooms, and
during our short stay were most comfortable.
The hotel is decorated with quantities of stuffed
birds and fine heads of elk and reindeer, while
skulls of the seal and walrus ornament the
passages, and a large marquee is erected in
the open yard in the middle of the building,
and in this *table-d'hôte* lunch and dinner is
served daily during hot weather. When wet,
a large coffee-room upstairs serves to accom-
modate some sixty or more visitors.

Before retiring we bid adieu to Mr. J——,
who starts in his carriole at 4 a.m. to-morrow
for his quarters on the Guul, as he thinks that
a few salmon will already have run up from
the sea, although it is certainly early. We
were sorry to lose a pleasant *compagnon de
voyage*, but we have promised to pay him a
visit on our journey to Throndhjem.

It is wonderful to see how great a difference

exists in the duration of light, as we proceed further towards the north, every few miles to the northward seeming to make the night so much brighter. At midnight we were able to read the smallest printed book with perfect ease.

Tuesday, June 13th.

We were awakened at seven o'clock by the appearance of rolls and coffee in our bedroom, a Norsk custom, and one to be highly commended, the coffee that one gets in this country being always excellent. The oppressive heat was dispersed by a gentle air during the night, and though it was very warm all day in the sun, the shade was pleasant enough, though far hotter than in London.

After his arrival in Christiania, the first thing for the traveller to do who intends to drive through Norway, is to see at once about his carriole; and with this object in view,— as soon as we had discussed breakfast, which consisted of fresh-laid eggs, ham, anchovies, fresh salmon, and trout,— we walked to Mr. Bennett's residence in the Store

Strandgaden. Mr. Bennett is *the* individual amongst the seventy thousand souls who live in or near Christiania, whose assistance it is most advisable to procure, and I am sure no traveller will regret having applied to him for help either as to outfit or as to the best routes to pursue. He will give you the very latest information as to railways, lines of country newly opened up, sailing of steamers, &c., or will supply you in a very short space of time with carrioles, harness, preserved meats, books, maps, a supply of small coin, or anything else you may require, and every one who knows him will agree with me in saying that he is equally courteous to the tourist who invests largely in his goods, and to him who merely comes to ask his help and advice. That this is no exaggerated panegyric on Mr. Bennett I can conscientiously affirm, and I shall not readily forget many little acts of kindness he showed towards me when I was suffering from a bad cold, caught in the severe spring of 1871, whilst sledging from Christiania to Bergen over the snowy wastes of the Fille-Fjeld.

We found Mr. Bennett at home, and as it so happened we were the first travellers this summer he was fortunately able to supply us with a couple of most excellent carrioles, which were new last year, and are neatly painted; they are both provided with first-rate springs, which save a great amount of shaking, and good waterproof aprons cover the seat and body of the vehicle. We also arranged with Mr. Bennett for the hire of two sets of strong harness, very plain but durable; the thick, leathern reins being particularly serviceable. I may here remind all travellers, and more especially the fair sex, that an immense degree of extra comfort is afforded by providing oneself with *leathern* reins, as if one does not take one's own harness, which of course has to be changed from one pony to another at every "station" on the road, the peasants will often supply you with bad harness and reins made of rough rope, which cut one's hands to pieces, ruin your gloves, if you wear any, and when wet become so slippery as to be almost impossible to hold in the hands. As we did not intend to remain more than six weeks in Norway, we found it would be much less expensive to take carrioles on hire, at a regular charge of so much a day, than to purchase the vehicles, and then sell them for what you can get when you leave the country, which is the wisest plan if your stay be one of two months or more.

My wife took her first experimental drive up and down the Store Strandgaden in the carriole we selected for her use to-day, and being well accustomed to driving, found it a very easy matter, and declared her carriole the most comfortable carriage she had ever used. The charge *per diem* for these carrioles may be thought, as it certainly was, rather high; but it is only fair to mention that they were, as before stated, almost new; and the extra comforts in the matter of good springs, and luxurious seats with cushions for one's back, made them well worth their hire to us, to say nothing of their very respectable and even smart appearance. These carrioles had only once been used, and had not been out of their sheds since last spring, when they were driven through Sweden by the son of the British Consul-General and a friend. I shall not describe this vehicle, as it must be well known to most people, and a minute account of it will be found in every guide-book.

Among the really necessary articles to take with one on a carriole journey are the following : a grease pot filled with *good* grease for greasing the wheels, which you must do now and then ; some brandy, in case of illness ; a supply of stout rope and a ball of twine, which you will find useful for tying on extra luggage or for mending broken harness, &c. ; and two or three pairs of very strong leathern straps, for attaching your portmanteau or box to the seat behind the vehicle. We were quickly supplied with the above items, and Mr. Bennett kindly consented to take charge of our portmanteaus (which were sent down during the afternoon from the hotel), and strap them firmly on the carrioles, and finally, to have the latter taken to the railway-station and placed on trucks, ready for the early train to-morrow morning for Eidsvold, whither we intend to proceed.

We purchased some pretty carved wooden knicknacks, made by the peasants in the district of Telemarken, some small silver ornaments, and a fine skin of the lynx (*felis lynx*), shot last winter near the town of Drammen. After luncheon at our hotel, we arranged to visit Oscarshal, the day being very fine; so we took a two-horse "droski," a carriage almost similar to those of the same name used in St. Petersburg, and driving down the principal street of Christiania (the Ostregaden), soon left the town and passed the new Palace, the situation of which is very fine, and continued along a most picturesque road, shaded with trees in full leaf, and between pretty villas and country houses, with gardens of great beauty, some of which were ornamented with miniature lakes, and the whole atmosphere was sweet with the scent of the purple lilacs, and quantities of laburnums relieved the varied shades of green of the latter trees. This drive is one of the most charming in Norway, as within a few minutes after leaving the noisy city, the traveller is driving along a road skirted with dark pines and clumps of the white-stemmed birch, which to-day nods gracefully to the southerly breeze, that wafts the fresh sea-air from the fjord, whose beautiful expanse, dotted with many an islet and covered with pleasure-boats, meets our eyes at nearly every turning of our road.

Oscarshal, which is only about a couple of miles from Christiania, is a country seat of the king's, or more properly speaking, it should be called a shooting-box, which it resembles in the style of its architecture. An old woman showed us over the place, the rooms of which are very plainly but tastefully decorated, and furnished neatly, but by no means luxuriously. The room pointed out to us as the banqueting-hall is decorated with a pretty series of paintings by Tiedman, intended to represent the various phases of a Norwegian peasant's life from the cradle to the grave; these are painted upon the wall itself. In the drawing-room we were shown several medallions of well-known statesmen of this country, and some statues of Norwegian kings, whose names sounded to our ears romantic enough to recall the days long gone by, when the brave Vikings filled the north of Europe with terror. The names of these four monarchs were Harold the fair, Olaf the Holy, King Sverre, and Olaf Trygvesin, who is said to have founded the city of Throndhjem.

From the lofty tower, which we next ascended, a most glorious view was spread out like a map below us, the deep blue waters of the fjord contrasting prettily with the rocky islands, the bright green woods, and the wooden houses of the city, which shone in the warm rays of the evening sun, while well-tilled meadows and snug country villas had a wild background of waving forest, and lofty mountains with many a rugged summit reared their gaunt heads to the cloudless sky.

Oscarshal, or more properly speaking the ground on which it is built, has for many years belonged to the royal family of Norway; and the castle is said to have been given to Queen Euphemia, of Rugen, by her husband, Haakon the Fifth, for her majesty to hold entertainments, and here the lords and ladies of her court were accustomed to dance on moonlight nights, each one dressed in some sylvan costume. The estate was afterwards given by this queen to a monastery, from which it subsequently reverted to the crown, and the present building was erected by King Oscar.

A pleasant way of returning to the city would have been by means of a boat; but having our " droski," we found it better to go back by the same road that we had driven before; and the sun was just setting as we reached Christiania, the peeps of the fjord and the distant mountains being even more picturesque than earlier in the afternoon, owing to the roseate hue that seemed to rest upon everything, reflected from the sky above.

Before reaching our hotel we drove past the ancient castle of Agershuus, which is built upon the fjord, and commands the harbour entrance. It is worth seeing, and the objects to interest the traveller are, among others, the Regalia of Norway, a very fair collection of armour, and two fine old curiously-wrought cannons which were captured from the Swedes, and I am told they are discharged in case of a fire to raise an alarm. A fire in a town almost entirely constructed of wooden houses is indeed a very serious matter: and scarcely a town and village in this country exists, but can boast of having been either partly or entirely consumed by fire. Part of the castle is used for a prison, and the wretched slaves, as the Norwegians term them, are generally heavily ironed. A small sort of cage, with iron bars, is also pointed out to the visitor, and in this the celebrated Norsk robber, Hoyland, whose character and doings are said to have corresponded with the English Robin Hood, was imprisoned for life. I have always thought the story of his life very interesting, so that I trust I may be forgiven if I here transcribe the account given of Hoyland in "Murray."

This account commences with the statement that this hero's principal vices were two in number,—inordinate fondness for ladies, and theft! "His robberies were, however, always confined to the upper classes, while his kindness and liberality to those in his own rank of life rendered him exceedingly popular amongst them. His crimes never appear to have been accompanied with personal violence. He was a native of Christiansand, where he began his career. On being imprisoned for some petty theft, he broke into the inspector's room, while he was at church, and stole his clothes; these Hoyland dressed himself in, and quietly walked out of the town unobserved and unsuspected. He was subsequently repeatedly captured, and imprisoned in this castle, and as often made his escape. On one occasion he was taken on board a vessel just leaving Christiania Fjord for America. Previous to his last escape, all descriptions of irons having been found useless, he was placed in solitary confinement in the strongest part of the basement of the citadel—his room was floored with very thick planks.

"Here he had been confined for several years, when one night the turnkey said to him, 'Well, you are fixed at last, you will never get out of this, and so you may as well promise us you will not attempt it.' To this he only replied, 'It is your business to keep me here if you can, and mine to prevent your doing so if possible.' The following day when his cell was opened, the prisoner was gone, apparently without leaving a trace of the manner in which he had effected his escape. After a repeated and careful search, on removing his bed, it was found that he had cut through the thick planks of the flooring. On removing the planks cut away (and which he had replaced on leaving the cell), it appeared he had sunk a shaft, and formed a gallery under the wall of his prison; this enabled him to gain the court-yard, from whence he easily reached the ramparts unseen, dropped into the ditch, and got off. No trace of him could be found. About twelve months afterwards the National Bank was robbed of 60,000 specie-dollars, chiefly paper money, and in the most mysterious manner, there being no trace of violence upon the locks of the iron chests, in which the money had been left, or upon those of the doors of the bank. Some time afterwards a petty theft was committed by a man who was taken, and soon recognised to be Hoyland. At last he hung himself in prison in despair."

As we are very anxious to start early to-morrow morning, on our journey towards the Arctic regions, we have no time to see all the sights of Christiania and its vicinity.

It may be mentioned, however, that any one who has the time to spare, will be amply repaid by ascending the Frogneraasen, which is about 1500 feet above sea level, and where a beautiful view of the country is obtained. There is a good theatre; public tea-gardens, which are pretty, and where a fair band plays during the summer evenings; an interesting museum, both of natural history and of Northern antiquities; and I would especially advise the tourist to visit the lovely Sarp-Fos, a fine waterfall on the Glommen, near the town of Frederikstad.

Many lovely drives may be taken from the city, and excursions of a few days in various directions would be very pleasant if one had plenty of time; and in a word Christiania is one of the prettiest and pleasantest summer residences in Europe, and it deserves to be far better known than it is, and more fully appreciated by our fellow-countrymen.

11 p.m.—It is an oppressively hot night, and we are just going to enjoy our last night's repose in comfortable beds for some time to come. The beds are certainly the greatest drawback to comfort in Norway; they are generally very short, and a tall man's feet hang over the "footboard," while his head rests upon the wooden "top" of the bed. Mr. Bennett advises us to remedy the shortness of the beds by taking off all the "wedge-shaped" pillows, which have the unpleasant effect of causing one to slide away from the head of one's bed; then to take the ordinary pillow and double it up to form a sort of bolster, which will enable one to lie comfortably with one's head fairly close to the top of the bedstead. This advice is very good, and I used to profit by it when in the country in former years.

As we lean out of window and glance down the street towards the fjord, all is silent as the grave in the lately noisy city, save the barking of a solitary dog; and the stars are twinkling overhead in the bright summer sky, and so light is it that they are almost invisible, and we call to mind Wordsworth's lines as very appropriate to such a lovely night.

> "Calm is the fragrant air, and loth to lose
> Day's grateful warmth, though moist with falling dews.
> Look for the stars, you'll say that there are none;
> Look up a second time, and, one by one,
> You mark them twinkling out with silvery light,
> And wonder how they could elude the sight!"

CARRIOLE AND NORWEGIAN PONY.

CHAPTER IV.

" Away, away, from men and towns,
To the wild woods and the downs,
To the silent wilderness,
Where the soul need not suppress
Its rapture, lest it should not find
An echo in another mind."

SHELLEY.

Wednesday, June 14th.

WE were awake by six a.m., and were glad to see every promise of a fine day, as on looking from our bedroom windows a gloriously bright sun poured down upon us, and the sky was azure, unflecked by a single cloud. At eight o'clock we found ourselves at the railway station, having walked the short distance from the hotel, and we now found the advantage of having Mr. Bennett's help yesterday, as the first objects that we noticed were our carrioles carefully packed upon trucks, and covered with waterproof sheeting in case of wet weather. Mr.

Bennett himself was awaiting us on the platform, and kindly got our tickets, as there was but little time to spare, and the train was very full of passengers.

At length we managed to squeeze ourselves into the only empty places in a first-class carriage, in which we found two English gentlemen, the Rev. J. T— —, and Mr. W———, who had been our fellow-passengers on board the "Hero" from Hull.

There was great delay on leaving Christiania, owing to there being more passengers and luggage than usual; but shortly after half-past eight we steamed slowly out of the terminus, and when fairly out of the town we found the heat very oppressive even at this early hour. In every first class on this line of railway are little reservoirs of iced water, with plated cups chained to the side of the carriage, for the use of the thirsty traveller; would that the same luxury was to be obtained on English lines during the hot weather.

This train was, as all trains in Scandinavia always are, very slow, and we stopped at every station between Christiania and Eidsvold, our destination and the northern terminus of the railway, and which we reached in three hours' time. As we steamed onwards through the dark pine forests near Trygstad and Dahl, my thoughts returned to the weary tramps I used to have on many a bitterly cold morning in the early spring of 1861, in these same woods, in quest of capercailzie and black game, of which there then were a fair number, and I hear there are still a good many left. As we passed the little station of Dahl, I was able to point out to my wife a pretty house, sheltered with birch and pine trees, and built just on the edge of a steep bank overhanging a little river, which turns the saw-mill which adjoins the house. To this picturesque spot I was once invited by the hospitable owner; and accompanied by a Danish gentleman, whom report credited with being a great *chasseur*, I left Christiania on a gloomy night of early spring, arriving at the miller's house by the late train. No beds were given us, as they were all occupied by the family, and we slept the sleep of the weary stretched upon the "dining-room" table, from which couch we were aroused at 4 a.m., and hurried off into the pitch-dark outer air for the "capercailzie hunt," as the sportsman from Denmark persisted in terming our enterprise. There were plenty of capercailzie in the forest, they were well preserved, and we ought to have had a fair day's sport. All, however, was ruined by a misshapen hound rejoicing in the name of "Oscar," which, much against my wishes, was brought with us, and which being under no control whatever rushed through the forest giving tongue during the entire morning. Never shall I forget that wretched day. "Sport" the Dane called it! I hope it was so to him, but it certainly was by no means enjoyment to me; and after toiling through heavy snow some four feet in depth and tumbling over buried tree-trunks for ten weary hours, during four of which it was pitch dark, getting two shots only during that time, I gave up the "sport" in utter disgust, the wretched dog continuing his *chasse* until nightfall. The result of our "hunt" was spread out on the

snow in front of the forester's cottage where
we renewed our weary bodies with the aid of
game pies and good wine; and (instead of
three or four capercailzie, several hares, and
some duck and black cock, which we ought
easily to have got if that miserable "Oscar"
had been left at home) my eyes rested on the
magnificent spectacle of one teal which the
miller had by great luck shot as it *sat* on the
ice in a bend of a small stream, the lacerated
remnants of a hare which had been captured in
the pitchy darkness by Oscar, and a brace of
magpies, which had fallen to my own gun!
That miller was a good man, a thoroughly
hearty, hospitable fellow, and I should like to
see him once more; but if I live to be as old as
Methuselah, I would not go out shooting again
with him, his Danish friend, *and* Oscar for
untold gold!

Eidsvold is very prettily situated at the
southern extremity of the lake Mjösen, which
is the largest inland piece of water in Norway.
Our two carrioles were soon taken off the train,
and were hoisted by a crane on board the small

steamer, which was overcrowded with passengers, and consequently there was a great rush for places. Several members of the Storthing were on board, with their families and servants, also about fifty saloon passengers; while some 200 or more peasants quite filled every nook and corner of the little vessel. Eidsvold is notable in the history of Norway, on account of its being the spot where Halfdan "the black" promulgated the earliest code of laws for the government of the country; and the independence of Norway was proclaimed here in 1814. The pretty little village, surrounded by bright green woods, and farmsteads dotted about near the shores of the placid lake, seems almost asleep beneath the rays of the scorching sun, and presents to-day a very different appearance to the same place when I last saw it six years ago. The mountains, so bright and sunny now, were all white on that gloomy wintry afternoon, and each wooden roof in the village had its covering of fresh-fallen snow; these forests were many feet deep in snow at spots where "drifts" had taken place, the fir-trees had mantles of hoar; and the waterfalls, which rush down to the lake with a merry noise to-day, were silent in their icy shrouds. The dark waters of the Mjösen were stirred up into a perfect sea by a bitter north-easterly gale blowing direct from the cold wastes of the Dovrefjeld, and clouds of half frozen spray dashed over me as I waited shivering on yonder bank for a chance shot at wildfowl, where it was almost impossible to keep one's legs on account of the slippery ice at the edge of the water. How different the scene to-day: summer is truly preferable to winter! And on that spot where I was almost frozen as I stood, the small Norwegian cows are to-day lying basking in the sun, enjoying the pleasant heat, and scarcely do they even take the trouble to flick away with their tails the clouds of flies which buzz around them in the summer air.

The scenery on the Mjösen has been often described, and need not here be repeated; suffice it to say that it is likened by some travellers to Lake Como, but I certainly think the views on that lovely Italian lake are very different from any fjord of Norway. The view to the southward, as we steamed away from Eidsvold, was extremely pretty. We could see the dark pine forests stretching away for many miles in the direction of Christiania, the woods being surrounded by hills varying in height, but none of any altitude; most of them were clothed almost to the summit with the bright alder, and the richer green of the birch; while several mountains to the westward covered with rugged masses of grey rocks, piled in vast heaps as if thrown one upon another by volcanic action, added a wild aspect to the more peaceful scenery of the low-lying lands.

It is well for the sportsman to know that very fair fishing can be obtained in the river near Eidsvold, and also at Minde, where grayling are more plentiful than trout, and give good sport, but we had no time to try the fishing to-day. Rare ducks are to be got on the lake in the autumn and winter; and I have seen many scarce divers (such as some of the rarer Grebes) upon its waters, which would be a good spot for forming a collection of specimens if the naturalist had only a week or so in the country at his disposal. There are no salmon in this lake, but there is said to be some fish resembling a herring, which is caught in large numbers, but what its true species may be I had no chance of determining, as we neither saw nor ate any of the fish in question, which I much regretted.

Shortly after we quitted Eidsvold, we were summoned by a bell to luncheon in the large cabin, and the rush which ensued for the best places was most amusing, and more resembled a kennel of hungry hounds being turned into their feeding-yard than a company of respectable travellers sitting down to table. We were obliged to wait for our turn for seats, as the passengers being so numerous were "turned" into the cabin in relays of twenty or thereabouts. The food was certainly not worth the hurry which every one was in to get to the table, and (though no doubt the fare is better when there are fewer to provide for) our lunch on board this steamer was one of the dearest and worst we had in Norway.

We took rather over eight hours in steaming up the Mjösen, which is more than seventy miles in length; and innumerable stoppages were made during our voyage, for the peasants to disembark, and as the towns and villages were upon both banks of the lake, much time was lost in zigzagging across the water. At the town of Hammer, our steamer met with a great reception, owing to a prominent member of the Storthing and his family disembarking there, and who it appeared had made himself very popular from being the successful mover in obtaining the grant of a large sum of money for the extension of local railways. As we sighted the place, bunting was run up on the flagstaffs on the landing-stage and in various parts of the town, while a salute of three cannon was fired from the shore; this was replied to by a small and dangerous-looking piece of ordnance on board our steamer, and which the gunner, who was one of the crew, evidently thought rather "uncanny," as he took care to conceal himself well behind the mast before applying the slow match.

Just before we sighted the village of Lillehammer, which is our destination, the weather suddenly changed, the wind becoming quite cold, and a heavy shower passed down the water; and at the northern end of the lake we saw several fine ranges of lofty mountains, the snow which still lies on their highest crests and ridges showing us that the country we are making for is truly a northern land. Towards the close of the voyage, the scenery was certainly very fine, but properly speaking more pretty than magnificent. A great many waterfalls of considerable height here and there met the eye, appearing like threads of silver as they dashed down from the rocky cliffs; most of the hills fringing the lake being covered with fir, excepting where little clearings had been made by the peasants, whose brightly painted wooden houses were often perched so far up the mountain side as to make the cattle appear to our eyes scarcely larger than lambs.

Being unluckily but very poor hands at the most interesting study of geology, we were unable to appreciate, as well as we otherwise might have done, the curious features connected with the formation of this remarkable lake.

The Mjösen is wonderfully deep, being seldom frozen entirely, and indeed it does not freeze at all until the winter is well advanced; and its depth may be better understood when it is stated that soundings taken a few years since at the Eidsvold end of the lake proved it to be in some parts about two hundred and fifty fathoms deep; and as Lady Di Beauclerk remarks,[1] the Mjösen being "400 feet above the level of the sea, it will thus appear that the bottom of this lake is about 800 feet below *the bottom* of the North Sea! Whether this profound fissure is the result of volcanic or glacial action is a question for scientific geologists to decide."

We had no trouble at Lillehammer, our two carrioles, with their respective loads of harness and luggage, being quickly transferred from the boat to the land, and they were soon trundled up the steep ascent to the town by porters, whilst we found our way to a neat, clean little

[1] "A Summer and Winter in Norway," by Lady Di Beauclerk, p. 21.

hotel, kept by one Madame Ormsrud, who with her daughter's help made us very comfortable, the only thing we could possibly object to being, that there was no bath to be had in the town, and a small wooden *foot-tub* was provided for our joint use, in lieu of the more commodious article; and only one blanket was to be obtained, to do service between a couple of beds. Baths are very seldom to be obtained in Norway, and if the weather is warm, by far the most pleasant tub is to be found in the fjord or river; and one can have the best of cold shower-baths by sitting beneath a waterfall, or " foss," as it is here termed.

After supper with our two English friends, who leave for Throndhjem at an early hour to-morrow, my wife and I took a charming walk outside the village, and ascended a steep hill, our way leading us through very pretty woods of birch and alder, interspersed with little open spaces of the greenest grass imaginable, carpetted with myriads of wild flowers, of which the commonest seemed to be the yellow trefoil, wood anemony, and the familiar ragged robin while hosts of rarer plants were seen on every side; and the little river which dashed at a great pace downwards from the mountains was edged with clusters of the handsome yellow mountain globe flower (*trollius Europeus*) and the purple cranesbill. The water in this stream was beautifully clear, so much so indeed that, though the trout rose freely at the living gnats that swarmed on the bubbling surface of the pools under each of the tiny saw-mills, which were built on the banks at every fifty yards or so, they could not be persuaded to take the small Scotch artificial flies that I carefully introduced to their notice. At least I only brought to bank two or three small fish, scarcely worth the eating; and as we turned our steps back towards the hotel, the evening sky was still glowing brightly on the calm lake beneath the town, whose inhabitants seemed to have all retired to rest, although the hour was only half-past ten, so deserted did the long silent street appear to be.

Thursday, June 15th.

This day, as it was the first occasion on

which L—— was to try carriole-driving, was an important one to us; and very glad were we to find when we awoke at six o'clock, that there was every chance of a glorious day. This promise was amply fulfilled; and indeed the heat was rather too severe towards mid-day, at which time we always found it a good plan to rest for a couple of hours, or even more, at some station-house, where we lunch, thus avoiding the greatest heat of the day. As the very antiquated-looking conveyance called a diligence, though a very sorry vehicle compared with the continental one of the same name,—left the inn-yard, I was in time to shout good-bye to our friends T—— and W—— from our bedroom window, and to give them the benefit of our good wishes by the merry notes of my hunting-horn, which caused some excitement to both the charioteer and his horses, as they rattled away on their northward road.

This horn, by the way, has hardly been used since it did me many a good day's service two years ago with my pack of otter-hounds, among the bonnie rivers of Ayrshire and Galloway; and

I have merely brought it with us to raise the cheery echoes as we drive through the mountain passes, or sail on the hill-engirt fjords of old Norway.

Whilst we were discussing our breakfast, the carrioles were prepared in the yard, and our portmanteaus being carefully secured behind the vehicles by thick leathern straps made for the purpose, my fishing-rods and salmon-gaff were tightly lashed along one of the long springy shafts of the carriole that I was to use, (by far the safest way of carrying rods without fear of accident,) each of us had our respective handbags secured in the body of the carriole between one's legs, and my wife had the bundle of rugs on the top of her portmanteau, while the post-boy, termed "skydsgut," took his seat upon my trunk, the ponies were harnessed and we "embarked."

It is rather difficult for ladies to get up into a carriole at first, but after a little practice L—— got on capitally; and she generally took care to wear a thin long waterproof cloak, to guard her dress from the wheels (which are generally covered with grease and dust) as she entered and left her carriole.

It was half-past ten o'clock when we had finally completed our arrangements, and we started at a merry pace along a capital road, soon leaving Lillehammer far behind us. L—— led the way, and I followed close behind, and although to any one unacquainted with this mode of travelling it sounds unsociable enough, it is really quite easy for two persons to converse with one another without much difficulty, excepting the slight trouble which the one who drives first has in turning his head round.

Our road from Lillehammer led up rather a steep ascent for a short distance, and we paused on reaching the highest part of the hill for a quarter of an hour to rest our ponies, which were excellent little animals, and of a pretty light fawn-yellow colour, which indeed most of the ponies here are. They are wonderfully sure-footed, scarcely ever stumble, and never fall; at least I never saw one do so during many hundreds of miles driving.

An excellent piece of advice, which was given

me some years ago, on my first visit to Norway, was this, and it is well worth bearing in mind. Never leave a "station," by which name the posting-houses are called, in a hurry; that is, do not drive away at a great pace; always drive the first couple of miles or thereabouts pretty slowly, gradually increasing the pace if you wish, and you will find your pony do far more work than if you drove him hard at the beginning of a "stage." Finally, do not let your animal appear too hot when you reach a station, which is easily preventable by driving the last half-mile slowly. If you take the ponies into the yard covered with foam, you will probably get bad horses for the next stage, instead of good ones, as the farmers very properly object to their animals being badly treated; and you will risk being put to the annoyance of waiting as long as the station-master chooses to keep you, although probably he had fresh ponies in the stable at the time you arrived. Every one who has driven in Norway will agree, I feel quite sure, with our opinion that the ponies are most excellent, docile creatures, and

those travellers (of which I fear there are too
many) who overdrive them deserve the inconvenience and incivility they will surely meet
with.

Our first "stage," by which is meant the distance from one station to another, was one of
about nine miles, and the road after leaving the
lake wound close alongside of the eastern bank
of the Logen river; but so much has been
written of these scenes that all we can say will
be merely repetition. The peaceful aspect of the
country, the overhanging mountains, the beauty
of the waterfalls which we continually passed,
the fine river by whose fertile banks we drove,
the excellency of the road, the freedom of this
charming mode of travelling, and above all the
splendid freshness of the air, sweetly redolent of
the pine woods, were each and all duly appreciated by us; and we certainly took a long time to
drive the nine miles, so often did we stop to look
around, and so charmed was L—— with the glorious scenery and the novelty of driving herself
in " an arm-chair " (as Lady Di Beauclerk says)
through the country. A large body of soldiers

were encamped in the valley at the head of the Mjösen lake, their white tents contrasting very prettily with the bright hue of the grass where they were pitched, and the darker foliage of the surrounding pine forest. Our road lay about 200 feet above the plateau, and we watched for some time the evolutions of the regiments, far below, and I conclude they were out for their annual "manœuvres." The Logen Elv, by whose banks we drove during the whole day, contains plenty of trout, some of them attaining a very large size, and the peasants state that some have been caught as heavy as thirty and thirty-six pounds each. These cannot, I should say, be the ordinary trout (*salmo trutta*), as they run far too large in size to be of that species, and are more probably the great lake trout (*salmo ferox*), common in Loch Awe and other Scottish waters; these fish would naturally ascend a large stream like the Logen for the purpose of depositing spawn. The colour of this river has ever been a matter of wonder among travellers, being of a curious white hue, much resembling London-milk.

The reason of this peculiar colour is supposed to be from the abundance of streams running into the Logen from the snow-covered mountains; but as most of the larger Norwegian rivers have tributaries coming direct off the snow or even from the glaciers, this would appear scarcely a satisfactory statement. The fishing in the valley of Gudbransdalen, which commences at Lillehammer and is some 160 miles in length, is fairly good; but when the angler looks into the milky waters of the Logen, he will wonder, as we did, how the fish can by any possibility see a fly, however large or however gorgeous in colour. I had little time, however, for fishing: but the fish in this valley, as far as I could learn, were mostly caught by bait, and indeed very few of the peasants ever use the artificial fly. There is good shooting in Gudbransdalen in the autumn, especially snipe and a fair sprinkling of wild fowl.

Our first change of ponies was at a prettily situated place called Fossegarden, and on leaving this station we drove through a very extensive pine wood, where we found our mackintosh-coats useful, as a very heavy hailstorm passed over the valley, only lasting a few minutes, but coming on suddenly. The traveller should always have his waterproof and great coat at hand, as storms come on with so little warning that if one's wraps are not to be got at immediately, one is wet through before the cloak bundle is unstrapped. During our drive through the fir wood we plainly "scented" a fox, which could not have been far off; we gave him the benefit of a little "music" on my horn, but I fear a Norsk fox would hardly recognize the cheery notes which would soon quicken the steps of the same animal in old England. Eight miles driving through the very pretty valley, here studded with picturesque wooden houses, and past numerous waterfalls, brought us to Holmen, where we had to wait for an hour for new ponies, so we took our luncheon to pass the time.

There are few statements in a book, to my mind, more uninteresting than a summary of food placed before the traveller, and it is only necessary therefore to state in one or two instances what is to be obtained to eat, so that others can judge what to purchase in the way of potted meats and the like in Christiania. We took nothing at all with us in the way of provisions, and we certainly could not complain of our fare at the roadside stations; but probably later on in the season, when of course there would have been far more persons travelling, we should have come off very badly. I therefore can advise any one driving into the interior to lay in a small stock of preserved meats and soups. Brandy is essential to be brought from the capital or from England; but the first-rate light ale of the country is to be obtained at nearly all the posting-houses, as well as excellent milk. Our lunch to-day consisted of cold ptarmigan, cheese, and white bread: the ptarmigan are of course not shot at this time of year, but were obtained in the early spring, and they keep a long time hung in a cool place, and near a lump of ice if possible. The afternoon was very hot, so that we were not really sorry when the people of

Skjæggestad station told us that all their ponies had gone with the diligence, and would not return until midnight, so we arranged to sleep at this place, where we were made very comfortable. The little inn is most picturesquely and snugly placed at the foot of a high hill; the river running between the road and the opposite side of the valley, where a fine range of forest-clad mountains are seen, their summits here and there dotted with small patches of the still unmelted snow of the past winter.

We saw, on our way from Kirkestuen to Skjæggestad, a large cleft or fissure in the side of a mountain, termed the Devil's Passage, as the little river which flows out of the hill is subterranean for some little way. Our supper was very good at the station; hare steaks, hashed ptarmigan, broiled trout fresh from the Logen, and several sorts of jam, by way of pudding, being some of the items of the repast. The best jam we have tasted yet is called "moltebær," and is made from the "cloudberry" (*rubus chamæmorus*.) Another excellent preserve is "tytebær" jam, and this corresponds to the "cowberry" (*V. vitis Idæa*). Gooseberries too, as well as little mountain strawberries, are very common, but will not be ripe just yet.

At 10.30, I went out for an hour to try for a few trout in the river, it being still broad daylight, and the sun could be seen shining upon the highest peaks of the mountains. I saw some small boys, each with a stick, on which were strung a goodly number of trout and grayling; but the fish would not rise well to my flies, and the evening began to feel very chilly, so I soon returned, and found L—— very sleepy, but delighted with her first day's carriole-driving.

CHAPTER V.

"Grey mists at morn brood o'er the earth,
   Shadowy as those on Northern seas;
The gossamer's filmy work is done,
   Like a web by moonlight fairies spun,
And left to whiten in the breeze.
The sun bursts forth—the distant hills
   Shine out, and splendid is the day."

MARY HOWITT.

Friday, June 16th.

WE slept capitally in very tiny beds, so were quite ready to rise when the good old woman to whom the station belongs, called us between four and five o'clock a.m., and after a cup of coffee, we were off once more in our carrioles. The morning air was glorious, but a little cold until about eight o'clock, when the coats in which we had wrapped ourselves on starting, were laid aside, and a hot sun suddenly bursting forth, soon told us that it was to be a summer's day, and the "gossamer's filmy work" was shining brightly on every blade of grass, which caused the meadows to have the appearance of a silvery sea.

Irrigation appears to be carried on to some extent in that part of the valley through which our way lay during the forenoon, each little farm having a series of long wooden troughs which conducts the water from the mountains downwards to the fields, the supply in this manner often being brought from long distances. The last occasion on which I had seen irrigation to any extent was on the banks of the far-away Nile, where the brown-skinned Egyptians working away at their "sakias" all day long formed always a prominent feature in the landscape; and I could not help contrasting the two countries, so vastly different from one another, and the two peoples so much alike in one respect at all events, viz. in laziness. When in the East I was certainly under the impression that not a more lazy set of people in the world were to be found than the Egyptians and Arabs of the Sinaitic desert; but for laziness in its "laziest" aspect, commend me to the dawdling idleness of the Norwegian peasant.

The valley was lovely, fresh beauties of mountain, wood, and glen bursting constantly upon our view; and we especially noticed several fine waterfalls, or "fosses," many of which were quite 300 and 400 feet in height. Many of the mountains under which we drove appeared to be about 2000 feet in height, and were covered to their summits with birches, ash, and spruce fir, while plenty of Scotch fir is everywhere to be seen. The height to which wood grows in Norway is certainly great compared with Scotland, as the following particulars will show. The Scotch fir grows on the mountains of Norway to the great height of 2870 feet above the level of the sea, whilst the common birch exists to the altitude of 3300 feet, and the juniper and many smaller shrubs flourish at even a greater height, where grow also quantities of beautiful flowers and mosses. Oak and beech is very seldom seen in Norway; but the poplar, willows of various kinds, and the beautiful mountain ash are met with almost everywhere, excepting in the extreme North, where the only woods of any extent are of Scotch fir.

Our first stage this morning was one of nearly nine miles to a pretty station called Listad, and another eight miles brought us to Byhre. We got most excellent horses at both these places, and a very short drive from Byhre of only six miles and a half was got over at a great pace, and we reached Storklevestad, covered with dust, for the morning was extremely hot, and here we were compelled to wait for two hours, there being no horses. This was rather annoying, as it was only 10 a.m., and we had intended to have stopped for lunch about midday. The diligence had as usual taken the only available ponies, and the people had to send two small boys out to the mountains to search for ponies for us while resting. We amused ourselves by looking out of window at droves of cattle, goats, and ponies, which passed by continually; all, we are informed, were on their way to a great fair near Lillehammer. The cows were very small, and looked very thin, but gave capital milk: L—— thought them something like Alderneys. The goats were in very large herds, and were driven by tiny children; while the cattle were herded by women; and the ponies, some of which were very nice ones, but small, generally were under the care of old men, whose bronzed faces, blue coats, and long red night-caps made them look very picturesque.

Part of the station-house at Storklevestad is shown to travellers as being constructed of some of the beams of an old house which was near this spot, in which St. Olaf was born. The station-mistress at this place was a very curious old lady, and was much interested in the inspection of L——'s earrings, waterproof, and other articles. She was, I fear, not brought up in a very cleanly manner, as when she took away the remnants of our lunch, she rather startled us by taking a large spoonful of each kind of jam herself, after which she licked the spoon as a child would do and replaced it carefully in the jam!

There was a remarkable absence of bird-life

in the valley through which we drove, with one exception, for there were any amount of magpies, whose continuous chattering as they flew round their nests relieved the stillness of the forests, which sometimes became almost oppressive, and their familiar black and white plumage reminded my wife of "auld Ireland," where they are (and bad luck to them, say I), almost as numerous as they seem to be here.

The peasants have rather a good plan for capturing these birds, by means of alluring them to feed on some carrion, such as a goat or sheep, on the body of which small snares of thin wire are carefully set, and by some of them the magpies are sure to be caught, when they alight to commence the luscious feast.

Our ponies at length appeared, and turned out to be very fast ones, which was fortunate, as this stage was ten miles and a half, under a scorching sun, and we found L———'s large straw hat and my pith-helmet most useful: indeed we could scarcely have driven without them, so hot was the sun, and there was not a breath of wind all day.

After leaving Bredevangen i Sels our road wound along the river, which gradually became sufficiently broad to be termed a lake, and we found ourselves passing beneath a very precipitous mountain called Kringelen, and we paused under a huge shady rock to read the romantic history attaching to it. In the year 1612, whilst Sweden was at war with the Danes, a small body of troops were sent from Scotland to assist the Danes. Gottenburg was in possession of the Danes at that time, but the enemy held the entire coast-line from the Baltic to the North Cape. "The Scotch, therefore, decided on the bold plan of landing in Norway, and fighting their way across it to Sweden. A portion landed at Throndhjem, and the rest, 900 strong, commanded by Colonel George Sinclair, landed in Romsdalen, from whence they marched towards this valley, ravaging the country on their way. At Kringelen an ambush was prepared by about three hundred peasants. Huge quantities of rocks, stones, and trees were collected on the mountain and so placed that all could at once be launched upon the road beneath. Everything was done to lull the Scotch into security, and with perfect success. When they arrived beneath the awful avalanche prepared for them, all was sent adrift from above, and the majority of the Scotch were crushed to death, or swept into the river and drowned; the peasants then rushed down upon the wounded and stragglers and despatched them. Of the whole force only two of the Scotch are said to have survived. But accounts differ on this point, one being that sixty prisoners were taken and afterwards slaughtered in cold blood. Sinclair's lady is said to have accompanied him, and it is added that a youth who meant to join the peasants in the attack was prevented by a young lady, to whom he was to be married the next day. She, on hearing that one of her own sex was with the Scotch, sent her lover to her protection; Mrs. Sinclair, mistaking his object, shot him dead." [1]

As we finished reading the account of this dreadful massacre, we looked upward at the

[1] From Laing's "Norway."

huge grey mountain, which in some parts appeared almost to overhang the road below, and one easily realized with what ease even a far larger army could have been annihilated by the same means. A small stone obelisk now marks the spot where it is said Sinclair fell. The remainder of the Scottish division landed to the north of Throndhjem, marched straight to Stockholm, and they were successful in helping to relieve the city, then besieged by the Danes.

Moen was the next posting-station that we reached. It is by no means so clean or nice as many of the others, nor are the people so obliging. Here, too, they were very unwilling to give us fresh horses; and we were treated with a good example of Norwegian dawdling, as four persons spent rather more than *one* hour in putting a single shoe on a pony, which was eventually provided for our use. The drive to Laurgaard passes through a flat valley, where I believe the wild-fowl shooting is good in the autumn, and there are a fair quantity of reindeer on the high "fjelds" near Laur-

gaard, which is prettily situated and remarkably
healthy, being some 1000 feet above sea level.
L—— was glad to be able to get a drink of
fresh warm milk here, as our drive had been
very dusty and the weather extremely hot.

One of the most magnificent stages in
Norway, to the author's mind, is that between
Laurgaard and Brændhaugen i Dovre, combining as it does splendid Alpine scenery
of every kind, including snow-capped hills
towering above the road; vast forests of birch
and pine, and masses of granite rocks, interspersed with juniper, on every side; and the
river, pent up between narrow precipitous
banks of solid stone, dashing at breakneck
speed far below.

In Bennett's handbook the traveller will find
full instructions for a very charming trip from
Laurgaard on horseback, through most romantic
scenery, to the summit of a mountain called
Formokampen, about 4700 feet high, and
whence a magnificent view over many miles
of country is obtained. There is good trout-
fishing in this river, and in other waters near

Laurgaard. At Brændhaugen we were fortunate in obtaining new ponies at once, and so wasted no time, but pushed on past the pretty village of Dovre with its picturesque church till Toftemoen was reached. It was now nine o'clock, and this station being most inviting and having such a cleanly look about it, we were almost persuaded to remain for the night, but we finally decided to push on another seven miles to Dombaas. At the village of Dovre the valley of Gudbransdal ends, and we then ascend gradually to the steep plateau of the Dovre-fjeld.

The charmingly situated station-house of Toftemoen is kept by one Herr Tofte, a white-haired and very obliging old man, who is very proud of his lineage, being able to trace his descent in a direct line from Harold Haarfager (the "fair haired"), who was the first king of all Norway, and who died in the year 933. Herr Tofte boasts that his ancestors never married out of their own family. He is a very rich man for a peasant, and his father has a large "sæter," or mountain farm, not far from the station, where he keeps some two hundred or more sheep, four hundred cows and calves, and numerous goats. Herr Tofte's daughter showed us some beautifully carved specimens of birch-wood, made during the long winter evenings by the peasants, and we purchased at this station by far the prettiest pieces of carved work that we saw in any part of Norway.

Our last stage was entirely up hill, and the ascent continued by the bank of the river, and was so steep that we were constantly obliged to stop to rest Herr Tofte's ponies, which were the best we have yet driven. As we were driving through a dense fir wood, soon after leaving Toftemoen, my wife was confronted by a bull, the smallest bull we have ever seen, but he was in no good temper, as he stood in the very middle of the road lashing his tail, bellowing loudly and throwing the earth over his shaggy head with his hoofs. However, after making a pretence of charging L——'s carriole he allowed us to pass, but we could hear his angry bellowings echoing through the forest long after the animal was out of sight.

At ten o'clock, while the rays of the setting sun were lighting up the heathery summits of the mountains, and making the snow on the more distant hills glisten with all the hues of the rainbow, we came in view of the wild-looking station of Dombaas, a cluster of wooden buildings some two thousand feet above the sea.

We have had a very long drive to-day, having traversed seventy-four miles, and L—— especially was glad to enjoy a rest. When travelling for pleasure, forty to fifty miles a day will be found quite enough for a lady to attempt. As we turned our ponies' heads from the main road into the narrow lane leading up to the station, we caught sight of the dilapidated form of the *diligence*, standing in the courtyard, so the notes of my otter-hunting horn were soon echoing through the mountains, speedily bringing every head out of their respective windows, and among which we were very glad to see the cheery faces of our old friends T—— and W——, whom we had parted from two days since at Lillehammer.

We were, for the first time since we have
left Christiania, regaled upon fresh salmon and
reindeer venison; after which we were glad
to retire to the longest and best beds that it
has as yet been our fortune to find in the
country, provided, however, with no blankets,
instead of which each bed had a pretty quilt
made of the eider down. There are no
shutters, and usually no curtains in the bed-
rooms, the consequence being that we often
find it no easy matter to go to sleep, so bright
are the summer nights that the rooms are
scarcely any darker than would be the case at
noonday.

Saturday, June 17th.

We were able to realize when we awoke this
morning, the great height at which Dombaas
stands, as from our beds snow in extensive
patches was visible all around the house, many
white-capped peaks piercing the blue sky above
us, and snow even appeared in the deep glen
some hundreds of feet below. A curious effect
was produced also by the appearance of the
country at a lower level at about four o'clock

a.m., as, though the atmosphere around the station was beautifully clear, and the sky bright blue, the whole of the valley was one vast mass of white cloud, which, as the sun's rays pierced it, gradually rolled away right and left, showing to our view in a few moments of time a large gap in which the valley with its rolling river and fir woods stood out at once in a clear frosty atmosphere, while the clouds quickly moved upwards along the rugged sides of the mountains till they rested upon the loftiest peaks far above us, and almost immediately melted from our sight into the azure sky.

It was a most odd sensation to thus feel that one was quietly resting in one's bed far above the clouds! The air is very bright but keen here, and there was a sharp frost during the night, and as we took an ante-breakfast stroll, the day had all the appearance of a fine frosty winter's morning at home.

After breakfasting with our two friends, we again bade them good-bye, and they rattled off at 6 a.m. in the old diligence, on their way towards Throndhjem, while we spent some time in bargaining about the price of some old silver ornaments and skins of animals, which the station-master, who spoke English fairly, introduced to our notice. We eventually purchased two curious neck-studs of roughly fashioned silver, about one hundred years old, costing some twelve shillings each, also a ring of the same period. I have bought several silver rings in various parts of Sweden, Norway, and Denmark, and was always much struck with the enormous size of these ornaments, as, though intended for the finger of the women, they quite easily fit a man's thumb. One inch and three quarters in circumference is the exact size of some of these rings in my own collection. A vast amount of rubbish is now sold in all the towns in Norway, a great deal of which is simply made up on purpose to tempt travellers, in exact and often in excellent imitation of the old silver, and many a novice brings home to England on his return "gamle" silver, which he might have obtained with far less trouble and expense from its original manufacturer in Birmingham! By hunting about in the out-of-the-way villages and farm-houses in various parts of the country, however, really good specimens of the *bonâ fide* ancient ornaments can be procured, at a fairly reasonable price. It is wonderful, nevertheless, how great has been the increase in the prices asked and easily obtained for silver in the towns within the last few years. The same is also the case with the skins of foxes, wolves, brown bears and other animals; while horns of the elk and reindeer fetch nearly three times as much as they did in 1871.

On inquiring the reason of this enormous rise in prices, the invariable reply was, " Yes, the price *is* far larger than we ever used to obtain; you need not buy the articles if you dont wish to; we can afford to wait till those who will give the best price come." And upon one's asking who these excellent customers may be, the answer all over Norway is the same, " The Americans." It is indeed too true that our cousins from the other side of " the pond " have quite spoilt the market.

Americans who can afford to travel are generally rich, and can always give what they are asked to pay; and I never remember seeing a Yankee in any part of Europe leave a shop for the reason that the articles he intended to purchase were too dear!

The wolf is becoming much rarer than used to be the case on the Dovre-fjeld, but a goodly number still haunt the woods in winter-time, and often commit great depredations in the farm-yard, and among the cattle at the "sæters." There happened to be two fine and very large skins of wolves for sale at Dombaas, which, as they were particularly good ones, we bought. One was shot by the son of the station-master last winter; and the other was picked up dead near the body of an animal, in whose skin arsenic had been inserted, on which the wolf had been feasting. These skins cost 2*l*. 5*s*. 0*d*. each, which is considerably less than is asked for them in the cities. We also invested in a white fox-skin, and I was glad to buy the very finest skin of the brown fox that I ever saw.

It was nearly midday when we left this wild spot, the first part of our drive being a steep ascent of some three hundred feet up the side of the mountain behind the house; this road was very heavy, and there was a great quantity of light-coloured sand upon the road, exactly resembling the sand of the sea-shore. It seems very remarkable to find it at such an altitude, and the Dovre-fjeld would be a most interesting field of inquiry for the geologist.

Our road led through a fine forest of ancient Scotch firs, whose stunted and gnarled stems showed that for many ages they had stood in this dreary bleak region, till they have become twisted into all kinds of fantastic shapes by the mountain storms, but yet not overthrown; though one cannot help wondering how they can weather the gales of winter, with their precarious foothold amongst the huge grey rocks which are scattered broadcast on every side of the rugged way.

From Dombaas one of the finest routes in the country turns off towards the west, leading to the splendid scenery of the Romsdal; but being anxious if possible to reach the Arctic regions by about Midsummer's-day, we prefer pushing on to the northward, instead of visiting this favourite and lovely valley. As we left the station-yard at Dombaas, my wife saw the dead body of a little animal, between the size of a large rat and a guinea-pig, lying upon the doorstep. It was yellow and white in colour, with brown markings, and by no means an ugly little creature. It was a Lemming, and the first we had seen; although during our drive to-day we noticed many of these curious animals, especially after passing through the pine woods, and attaining the level of 3000 feet above the sea; and they were to be seen on all sides running in and out of little burrows beneath the tufts of heather and roots of old trees, occasionally sitting up on their hind legs and "washing their hands" after the manner of the common rabbit. The life-history of these animals is so very remarkable that I shall make no apology for here giving a slight sketch of their habits.

The lemming (*Georychus lemmus*) is a permanent inhabitant of the northern parts of Europe; but so constant are its migrations that districts where it is found in large numbers in a particular year, may perhaps be entirely free of the animals all the next season. It varies much, both in colour and size, according to the various regions it inhabits. In the extremely cold parts of Northern Russia, in Siberia, and even in Lapland, the lemming is sometimes but little larger than a common mouse; whilst the Norwegian animal more nearly approaches the size of a large water-rat. In the latter country the lemming is generally of a black and tan colour, or tawny mingled with a good deal of white in stripes or blotches over the body. In Lapland its general colour is of a much darker brown all over; but specimens from both countries are of course subject to much variety.

The wonderful migrations of these interesting, but harmful little creatures have always to a certain extent been a puzzle to naturalists; many different theories having been advanced to account for the direct causes which give rise to the instinct which at certain times prompts them to take such long journeys. They appear in vast quantities every three or four years, and seem invariably to move in a westerly direction, never being observed to return to the east, the North Sea apparently being their last and only insurmountable obstacle. Their habits are certainly well worth a careful study; and it is most wonderful to think that such countless millions of tiny animals are all stirred by the same impulse to proceed in a given direction and in a straight unbroken line. They must need more than human perseverance, for no obstacle daunts this army of rodents in their migrations towards the ocean. They climb the steepest mountains, unless they can easily pass round them by traversing their lower ridges; they swim the broadest lakes, the widest arms of the sea, and all rivers that may lie in their line of march, utterly devastating the land over which they pass, and traversing in a short time immense tracts of country.

Of the various causes which lead to the wonderful migrations of these creatures, the most probable one is, I think, the temporary superabundance of the lemmings during certain winters after a favourable breeding season. As a natural consequence of the increase in their numbers a scarcity of food prevails, and they are compelled to quickly shift their quarters from the high-lying and comparatively barren fjelds, which are their summer haunts, to the more fertile, cultivated regions in the valleys.

Their enormous numbers, after an unusually favourable breeding season, can be easily accounted for when it is stated that the lemming is very prolific, the female adding to the number of her domestic circle several times during the year, and producing five or even six young at a birth. They are, one would imagine, useless animals; but in some districts they are caught and eaten by the peasants, who say that when properly cooked the lemming is as palatable as the common squirrel, which latter inoffensive little creature is a favourite article of food in many parts of Europe. As their food consists almost entirely of a vegetable diet, the lemmings may not be so uneatable when "served-up" at table as we should imagine them to be; we confess, however, that we would hardly care to try one, even if cooked by a Parisian *chef*. There is little doubt that, by one of the wondrous dispositions of Providence, some kind of instinctive foreboding of an approaching unfavourable season is felt by the lemmings, causing them to leave their summer quarters; for all observers I believe agree that their chief migrations occur during the autumn months of those years which are followed by an unusually severe winter.

Their largest moves take place as a rule about once in every ten or eleven years, but partial migratory movements occur much more frequently. What an extraordinary instinct must it be that causes them to voluntarily assemble in countless masses from a district embracing perhaps several hundreds of square miles, at some given point, and whence, having collected all their forces, they proceed towards the west. Onward they go, in one enormous battalion, like the hosts of locusts one sees in Upper Egypt, and they proceed in a direct course, turning neither to the left nor to the right.

The appearance of the country, after one of these hordes of rats have passed over it, has been compared by some writers to a ploughed field, all grass and herbage being devoured to the roots in parallel paths, like furrows. Nothing seems to deter the lemmings from following out the line of march they have chosen for themselves, and of course many thousands are drowned when crossing rivers, fjords, and torrents, which apparently are by no means accounted serious impediments by these curious animals. Should large boulders of rugged rock, up which they cannot climb, come in their road, they merely make a slight *détour* to avoid the impediment, resuming at once their straight course after it is passed. Should, however, a stack of corn or a rick of hay be met with, the lemmings will very soon eat their way *through* it; and they will often climb over sheds and houses, if the doors or windows do not happen to be open, in which case they enter at one end of the building, and walking straight through the house, effect an exit at the opposite side. Even a fire does not turn them from their course; and if, when swimming across a lake, they chance to meet a boat, they sometimes climb into it by means of the ropes that may be hanging over the side, rush across the deck of the vessel, and dropping into the water again on the other side, resume their journey.

There once existed a general belief among the lower and uneducated classes in Lapland, and in Norway also, that the animals thus migrating had been dropped from the clouds, literally "rained down" from heaven.[1] This supposition, I have no doubt, first arose from the birds of prey, which follow closely on the tracks of the lemmings, sometimes dropping these animals alive from their talons while flying at some height from the ground.

[1] A curious anecdote of a fish falling apparently down from the skies, but in reality only from the bill of a heron flying over a town in Banffshire, is given in Smiles' " Life of Thomas Edward," the Scotch naturalist.

The unlucky lemming has numerous foes to contend with; indeed, if it were not so, their numbers would doubtless increase to an alarming extent. One of the most persevering of its enemies is the Arctic fox, which follows the migrations of the lemming in great packs. The large eagle owl (*Bubo maximus*), and its showy relative, the snowy owl (*Strix nyctea*), eagles, kites, hawks of many kinds, and birds and animals of prey of all sorts, also follow the lemmings. At such a time a rare opportunity presents itself to the ornithologist, as many a scarce specimen may now be seen and added to his collection. The glutton, the weasel, and other beasts of predatory habits, may also be obtained by the collector at this time, and the crowds of birds are simply astonishing, and resemble camp-followers attending the movements of a large army.

The following most curious prayer, or exorcism, was offered up by the clergy in olden times throughout any district in Norway, which was infested with these troublesome creatures:—

"Exorciso vos, pestiferos vermes, mures, aves, seu locustas, aut animalia alia, per Deum, etc. (here the sign of the cross was made), ut confestim recedatis ab his campis, etc., nec amplius in eis habitatis, sed ad ea loca transeatis in quibus nemini nocere possitis; et ex parte Dei Omnipotentis, et totius curiæ cœlestis et Ecclesiæ Sanctæ Dei vos maledicens, quocunque ieritis sitis maledicti, deficientes de die in diem et decrescentes quatenus reliquiæ de vobis nullo in loco inveniantur; quod prestare dignetur qui venturus est judicare vivos et mortuos et sæculum per ignem. Amen."

The literal translation of this quaint prayer is this:—

"I exorcise you, pestiferous worms, mice, birds, or locusts, or other animals, by God the Father, etc., ✠ that you depart immediately from these fields, or vineyards, or waters, and dwell in them no longer, but go away to those places in which you can harm no person; and on the part of the Almighty God, and the whole Heavenly Choir, and the Holy Church of God, cursing you whithersoever you shall go, daily wasting away and decreasing, till no remains of you are found in any place; which may He vouchsafe to do, who shall come to judge the living and the dead, and the world by fire. Amen."

After this lengthy digression, I must resume our narrative. The road, when it quitted the pine-wood above Dombaas, gradually ascended until we reached a comparatively level plateau, and here began the true Dovre-fjeld, and, although the road ascended for the next fifteen miles, it was nevertheless comparatively level, and easy going for our carrioles. The vegetation upon this vast plateau is very scanty; and as we passed by one large "sæter," (or mountain "summer farm," where the cattle are taken during the hot weather to feed on what little herbage they can find), we could not help wondering what the cows, to the number of at least one hundred head, besides goats and ponies, could possibly live upon in such a stony and desolate wild. Talking of cows reminds me that a good five-year-old cow in Norway will only produce, if sold, from 3*l*. 10*s*. 0*d*. to 4*l*. Ponies, on the contrary, are very high indeed in price, and a fair animal will fetch at least 35*l*. or 40*l*., while a first-rate pony would command even double the latter sum.

The only dwelling we met with for many miles was the station-house of Fokstuen on Dovre, about seven miles distant from Dombaas, and a wild-looking place it was. There was plenty of snow on all sides, and as we drove up to the door the wheels of our carrioles broke through the large lumps of unmelted snow which was lying in the yard. This station is 3150 feet above sea level, and as the spot was cold, dreary, and uninviting, we purchased some bread, butter, hard-boiled eggs, and ale, to serve as our lunch; and, having stowed them away in our carrioles, again resumed our journey as soon as our new ponies were harnessed. The old women who kept this station had some curiously-worked woollen gloves for sale, of green, red, blue, yellow, and all the colours of the rainbow, exactly similar to the same articles which I have purchased from the fishermen in the Shetland Islands; and there is no doubt but that the present inhabitants of Orkney and Shetland, to a large extent, were importations from the "hardy Norsemen," and the original settlers may possibly have taken the patterns of their gloves with them!

PAIR OF LONG-TAILED DUCKS OR "HARELDS."

CHAPTER VI.

"I have look'd o'er the hills of the stormy north,
And the larch has hung all his tassels forth,
The fisher is out on the sunny sea,
And the reindeer bounds o'er the pastures free,
And the pine has a fringe of softer green,
And the moss looks bright, where my foot hath been."
HEMANS' "VOICE OF SPRING."

THE drive from Fokstuen to our next halting-place was a very long one, of nearly fourteen miles, and we were dreadfully cold, constantly driving through snow lying on the road, and which was frozen so hard that our post-boy, whom we desired to pick up a piece of snow for us, found it a hard task to cut through it with his long knife; whilst the air of this high region was very keen, and pierced our thickest wraps. About half way between the two stations the road crosses a pretty stream by a bridge, called Antin's Bridge, and as the place looked a likely spot for trout-fishing we halted here for a couple of hours, and my trout rod was quickly put together, and I set to work. The river is narrow and shallow, but there are plenty of large rocks scattered about its bed, which give snug sheltering places to the trout, which, notwithstanding the coldness of the day, rose pretty well to my flies. It seemed an odd spot to choose for trout fishing, surrounded as we were by vast mountains covered with snow to their summits, the weather being as cold as Christmas time at home, and the stream itself being some 4000 feet above the level of the sea.

There seemed to be some trout of a large size in these waters; especially at a place a little way below the bridge, where it enters a small lake, but the big ones only rose very shyly. My spoils only amounted to ten good trout (many small ones being returned to the water), and six large grayling, but of the latter fish we lost several, owing to not having a landing-net available. I have no doubt that, on a warm day in July or August, very fair sport could be obtained in this stream, and in the numerous mountain lakes that we passed to-day. We eat the eggs and other good things that we found in our carrioles as we sat under shelter of Aufin's Bridge, which we were obliged to leave before we had intended owing to the great cold, and the heavy clouds drifting along the fjeld threatened a snowstorm.

The station at Hjerdkin is a capital one, but situated in one of the wildest spots it is possible to conceive. It is surrounded on every side by the snow-capped mountains, which tower upwards till lost to view in the mass of dark clouds which to-day make the Dovre-fjeld look exceptionally dreary. This is a large station, and offers excellent accommodation to the traveller, and the shooting in its vicinity is some of the best to be had in this part of Norway. Part of the outbuildings of Hjerdkin are very picturesque, the wooden rafters being decorated with reindeer's horns, giving it a wild aspect, the whole place somewhat reminding one of a Swiss hospice. Hjerdkin is stated to have existed since the beginning of the 12th century, and is rent and tax free. We were shown some nicely carved wooden spoons, but the price asked was very high, so that we contented ourselves with a prettily wrought birchen tankard, elaborately carved upon its sides and lid.

It was even colder when we quitted this station than when we had arrived, and we thought the drive to Kongsvold very long indeed, the six miles and a half which the postboy stated to be the distance between the stations appearing to us much more like ten. The country we have traversed to-day looks a first-rate one for ptarmigan, and we saw a good number of wild fowl in the mountain lakes, while the great abundance of the reindeer moss tells the traveller that there is also large game to be found on the Dovre-fjeld. On first leaving Hjerdkin our road ascended a very steep brae, and we soon reached the highest part of the fjeld, which is some 4600 feet above the sea. The road is here marked out by tall poles at certain distances apart, whose use in winter is to guide the traveller over the snow which then entirely hides the highway from his view. It not unfrequently happens in winter that these poles are entirely covered with snow. At this great elevation the cold was severe, and we were glad to find, on consulting my aneroid, that we were gradually descending, and the road improved considerably, although there were some of the steepest hills that can be imagined towards the end of this stage, just before reaching Kongsvold. The highest mountain in this part of Norway has been in view during the whole of our drive to-day, although unfortunately we were unable to see its summit on account of the heavy mists hanging over its topmost ridges, and which did not lift all day. Its name is Sneehætten, and it is covered with perpetual snow, being about 7720 feet in height, and for many years was considered the loftiest hill in the country; latterly, however, it has been ascertained that the mountain of Skagstöltind on the Sognefjeld is nearly 200 feet higher. The country through which we have travelled since leaving Dombaas is wild in the extreme, huge masses of rock of all shapes and sizes being strewn over the surface of the fjeld, while the richness of the countless varieties of mosses, lichens, and wild flowers between Hjerdkin and Kongsvold would make the mouth of the botanist water.

Upon the summit of Sneehætten is a crater, surrounded, we are told, by huge walls of black rock which seem to have been dropped into the snow from the sky, the interior of the crater being also filled with frozen snow. That there must have been great volcanic disturbances in bygone days in this desolate region is apparent to even the ungeological mind; and we especially marvelled at the abundance of excellent sand, which we found at the altitude of over 4000 feet, and the fantastic groupings and varied hues of the rocks were most remarkable. There were rocks of the brightest red, others of dull grey, some almost white, and many with even a bluish tinge upon their surface; while those that were coated with the beautiful lichens before mentioned shone in the frosty air with almost every colour of the rainbow. Before reaching Kongsvold we drove along the eastern bank of the Driv river, which is a rapid stream abounding in capital trout, of the excellent flavour of which we were able to judge soon after our arrival at the station, which we were very glad to have reached after the coldest day's driving we have experienced. The station is most comfortable, and leaving L——— indoors I tried for some trout in the Driv after dinner, but though I saw a peasant sitting upon a huge rock some thirty feet above the stream with his feet dangling over the deep pool below, patiently fishing with a huge rod, and who had caught several large fish with worm, I soon found it was far too cold a night for any chance of success with the fly.

I must not forget to mention that we saw a fine eagle hovering over a lake near the roadside, during the early part of our drive, evidently on the look-out for prey. The snowy owl is seen on the Dovre-fjeld occasionally, and the large eagle owl is often obtained, there being a fine stuffed specimen in our sitting-room in the station.

Sunday, June 18th.

There being no church within many miles, we were unable to go to any place of worship; and as the morning was bitterly cold, and the wind blowing hard from the north-east, we were not sorry to stay indoors during the forenoon. Kongsvold is one of the best posting houses on the route between Throndhjem and Christiania, and the clean tidy look of our rooms was only equalled by the excellency of the reindeer, ptarmigan, and other delicacies set before us, and by the civility of the people.

From Kongsvold, as well as from Hjerdkin, the ascent of the mountain of Sneehætten may be made, but the weather was so cold that we did not think of attempting the expedition, which would be pleasant enough later in the summer. For the botanist I can imagine no more charming quarters than Kongsvold at which to stay, while he searches the Dovre-fjeld for specimens of flowers. Some of the rarest wild flowers in Norway are to be found in the neighbouring mountains, and weeks might be pleasantly and profitably spent in examining the plant-life of this wild region. It is stated that one of the first Norwegian botanists, the late Professor Blytt, discovered in his rambles over the Dovre-fjeld no less than 440 plants and ferns, 200 mosses, 150 lichens, and some fifty species of algæ, which list ought to be a sufficient attraction to the botanist to linger here awhile.

L—— and I took a walk over the hills near the station during the afternoon, and were delighted with the extraordinary variety and beauty of colouring in the flowers which carpetted the fjeld in every direction; but we much regretted having no good book of reference at hand to enable us to identify the countless kinds of lichens and mosses we saw in every direction. Among the scarce flowers which are found here, the Rev. R. Bowden mentions the following: *Triticum violaceum, Stellaria alpestris, Woodsia ilvensis, Woodsia hyperborea,* and *Epilobium origanifolium*. Along the rugged banks of the river Driv wild flowers, many of which were quite new to us, were especially abundant, whilst the pretty grey blue of the masses of reindeer moss, which was growing on both sides of the high road, afforded a charming contrast to the reddish-brown towering rocks which stood here and there like grim sentinels to guard the solitude of the Dovre-fjeld. The only trees we could see were a few stunted osiers and willows, and some very sorry apologies for birches. Had we been able to spend a week at this place, I feel sure we would not have found time hang heavy on our hands, and for an artist a more lovely headquarters for sketching expeditions could not be hit upon.

The reindeer moss, of which we gathered and took away with us a good supply, is remarkably pretty, and it will keep a long time and does not lose its colour.[1] Here and there among the patches of snow, we found large clusters of the heartsease, just coming into flower, while the "stag's-horn moss" (so common on Scottish mountains), the *Ranunculus*

---

[1] The moss we gathered on this day is as fresh-looking now (1878), after being kept nearly two years, as it was when growing on the fjeld.

glacialis, and other wild flowers and mosses too numerous to mention, all helped to increase the beautiful aspect of the district. Birds seemed to be very scarce; nor did we see any reindeer, although we thought that we saw some yesterday, but as the evening was closing in at the time, and they were some distance from the road, we could not be quite certain. Good shooting is to be got on this part of the Dovre-fjeld; and reindeer stalking is also fair, but hard work and only fit for those who can rough it in the true sense of the word, and who, moreover, can walk all day long, and do not object if called upon to sleep upon a rocky couch with only the sky for a curtain.

At about midday it was bitterly cold, and as we were writing letters in the sitting-room at the station, we were not surprised, on looking out of window, to see flakes of snow actually falling. This was news indeed to fill up the gaps in our letters for friends at home, and when they hear we were in a snow-storm on the 18th June, they will believe we are truly making rapid strides towards the Arctic Regions!

The snow, after falling for a short time, changed to sleet, and eventually heavy rain teemed down from the leaden skies, and the temperature became rather warmer, although we were very glad to sit close to the roaring fire of huge pine logs which blazed merrily up the wide chimney of the little stove.

Monday, June 19th.

A gloriously bright sunny morning has succeeded the night, which was very wet; but that there must have been a sharp frost before we were out of our beds was proved by the fresh icicles which hung from the banks above the mountain rill where we saw the "pige," or woman servant, filling the wooden pails with water for our baths, and icy cold that water was! Soon after five o'clock L—— was awakened by the bells of the cattle, which were being driven out by a young girl to pasture on the fjeld; and the little cows, together with a large flock of goats, looked very picturesque as they toiled up the rugged path at a slow pace, the old goats jumping from rock to rock at a great rate, and the cattle carefully picking their

way among the large boulders of stone, the
bells round their necks tinkling merrily on the
frosty air.

After purchasing some specimens of carved
woodwork, which are very reasonable in price
at this station, we left Kongsvold at nine
o'clock, and our carrioles rolled along the
excellently engineered road at a great pace, as
the whole distance to the next posting-house
was all down-hill, and the "fall" was some
850 feet in the eight miles and a half between
Kongsvold and Drivstuen. The road is
quarried in many places out of the face of the
solid rock, and follows all the windings in the
Driv river, which rushes along on the left hand
of the traveller for many miles, making several
pretty waterfalls, whilst other fosses are seen
pouring down into the stream from the
mountains above. The whole of this drive was
beautiful, patches of flowers taking the place
of the reindeer moss, and snow quite disappear-
ing towards the end of the stage; and when
Drivstuen was reached we found, by reference
to my small pocket aneroid, that the tempera-

ture had risen considerably, and instead of the dreary wintry aspect the Dovre-fjeld had presented, all here reminded us of summer.

There is good trout fishing in the river close to Drivstuen, and indeed large fish are to be caught all along the valley. I fished for a short time near the station while our ponies were changed; and another drive of nearly eight miles, still down-hill, brought us to Rise. Between these stations we noticed a curious feature in the river, which from being of a fair breadth suddenly closes itself in between two solid walls of the rock, and is for some distance so narrow that a man can easily leap across the stream which rages in a foaming torrent far below. The peasants have christened this spot the "leap of the stomach." Near Rise and in the vicinity of the next two stations on the road to Throndhjem, good shooting may be obtained, black game being very abundant in some parts of the forests, and various rare birds are also to be collected in the same district.

From Rise we had a charmingly warm drive through the wide valley, here covered with cultivated fields and dotted with farm-houses, but our pleasure was rather marred by the execrably bad quality of our steeds, which were the slowest we ever had while in the country. Most ponies never require the whip, and we seldom have to use it, but we applied it with full force to these animals, but without the least result in an increase of speed. On this stage we were for the first time supplied with a young girl of about ten years old by way of "skydsgut;" and the last we saw of her, as we were leaving Aune, was a glimpse of her little legs stretched on either side of the bare back of one of the ponies, while she lead the other by a rope, on her way home to Rise. At Aune, where is a very good station, we were told good ptarmigan shooting is to be had in the surrounding mountains, and we here saw a fine skin of a brown bear, which the landlord or his son had shot last winter. The price asked for this skin was not high, but I would caution tourists from purchasing skins at the stations without first inspecting them very thoroughly, as frequently the peasants do not take the trouble to clean the skins properly, and a mass of moth is the result.

From the next station, Stuen, our road led through a large forest of dark pines to Austbjerg, and the scenery here was remarkably pretty, and the woods had a charmingly green look about them to our eyes, weary as we were of the desolate fjeld.

Whilst driving through the pine forest near Austbjerg, I noticed a large hawk, as I at first thought, flying slowly along the outskirts of the wood, apparently in search of prey, but on its coming nearer I soon recognized it as the hawk-owl (*Strix funerea*), which, although by no means a rare species in Norway, is not often seen by the traveller, as its natural habitat is in the gloomiest recesses of the forest. Contrary to the custom of owls, this bird hunts during the daytime; but its flight much resembles that of a hawk, having, however, at the same time a quiet steady manner of using its wings in the same way that an owl does. The hawk-owl is a very brave bird, and makes great havoc in the woods with all kinds of small songsters, while its favourite food consists of mice, especially the wood-mouse, various insects, and the lemming. Its nest is placed in a hole in an old fir-tree, at a good height above the ground, and the eggs are laid on the bare chips of wood that are at the bottom of the hole, its nest in fact exactly resembling that of a wood-pecker. It is a very daring bird, and appears to throw off all fear during the nesting season, at which time both the male and the female are said to assist in sitting on the eggs.

The late Mr. Wheelwright, so well known by his books under the *nom de plume* of the "Old Bushman," was well versed in the ornithology of Norway, and from his work on Lapland I have extracted the following note upon the daring of the hawk-owl. "Seated on the top of a dead pine," says Mr. Wheelwright, "close to the nest where his mate is sitting, the old male bird keeps a constant watch, and as soon as any one appears to be approaching the nest, he raises his tail and head, after the manner of the cuckoo, and uttering a shrill cry, not unlike that of the kestrel hawk, down he comes full on the head of the intruder; dashing by with the speed of lightning, he returns to the charge again and again, till he has either cleared the coast, or has paid the penalty of his rashness with his life. My lad," he continues, " was really frightened at this bird, and always hated to go up to a nest: and well he might, for on one occasion, when taking the eggs out of a dead pine, without a branch to help him, holding on, as the sailors say, ' by his eyelids,' forty feet from the ground, the old bird made a swoop down on his head, struck off his cap (through the top of which a large slit was cut), and in a moment returned to the charge, tearing off a very fair sized claw-full of his hair." This shows that taking the eggs of the hawk-owl is by no means an easy feat, and the ease with which this species can swoop and turn quickly again proves it to be closely allied to the hawk tribe.

On leaving Austbjerg, where we lunched, we had a "skydsgut" in the shape of a tall young man who spoke English fluently, and told me that the sport in this neighbourhood is very good, as far as capercailzie, blackcock, and hares, are concerned; but his heavy weight so "ballasted" my carriole that we found it a long stage and slow travelling to Bjerkager. At one point the road led alongside a steep precipice, at the bottom of which the river runs at a depth of about seven hundred feet, and the view here is splendid, a perfect sea of pine-trees appearing to enclose one on every side. We noticed a small cross cut in the rock by the road side, at nearly the highest part of the road, and this our skydsgut told us was to mark the spot where one of the men who was making this road fell over the cliff, and was dashed to fragments at the bottom.

On our way from Garlid to Præsthuus, we fell in with a wedding party, which were driving home from a church some twelve miles distant, and all were in their best clothes, and appeared in the highest spirits. The procession was composed of some dozen vehicles, all of which were carrioles with the exception of the first one, which contained the bride and her happy mate. The newly wedded pair were seated side by side in a double cart, and following them were the carrioles loaded to overflowing, and each containing some three persons holding on behind; there were also several peasants on horseback. The men were all dressed in the deepest black, as if to attend a funeral instead of a wedding, the women on the contrary being attired in shawls, hats, and cloaks of the brightest hues possible.

We added to the imposing appearance of the wedding procession by driving close behind the rearmost carriole, and it was a remarkably pretty sight to see the long line of vehicles slowly climbing up a steep mountain side, or dashing at breakneck pace down some steep brae. At length a large farm-house hove in sight, with flags flying from fir-poles which had been erected near the front doors, and a large crowd of friends and neighbours collected to grace with their presence the festive occasion. As the bride and bridegroom passed the rough kind of triumphal arch that had been erected in their honour, guns and pistols were fired in the farm-yard, and the cheering was enthusiastic as the bride stepped from her cart into the arms of her friends, when all entered the house, and the festal evening was about to commence.

We had no time—much as we should have liked to have seen the festivities—to spare, so we contented ourselves with wishing the happy pair good luck, and then rattled away again, through lovely woods, with many open glades studded with fine birches, with much the appearance of an English park, towards Engen, our final destination, and which we did not reach until nearly nine o'clock. Our drive to-day has been of the most varied as regards the constant changes in the scenery possible to be imagined: this, of course, was consequent on our road descending from the great height of 3063 feet above the sea to Engen, which is scarcely fifty feet, I believe, above the level of the fjord at Throndhjem. L—— was glad to find a nice little hotel here close to the railway-station, for our day has been rather a fatiguing one for a lady, as the distance we have traversed is about sixty-nine miles.

Tuesday, June 20th.

The heat was terrible, and we were much

surprised to find it so after the snow we had seen on Sunday! The people here tell us that the weather in this valley has been excessively warm for the past week, and so hot did we find the rooms in the hotel, that we were obliged to go to the little railway-station, and sit on a seat upon the platform, where there was a certain amount of air, and to have ventured into the sunshine would have been to risk a *coup de soleil*.

The salmon-fishing in the Guul river is very good, and a certain part of it is leased by the landlord of the hotel, and in the afternoon L—— and I took a pleasant stroll by the river banks, and I fished for some time, but with no success, the day being still very hot, and the salmon have not yet in any numbers come up from the sea. L—— amused herself by gathering wild flowers, which carpeted the whole valley in the most profuse luxuriance and in endless variety. In the evening I drove to call on our friend Mr. J——, and he kindly asked us to pay him a visit to-morrow, which we intend to do. At 11 p.m. we again tried

unsuccessfully for a salmon, and fished till past
midnight, it being quite light.

Wednesday, June 21st.

The drive along the valley of the Guul
from Störens to Rogstad, where our friend Mr.
J—— lives in a snug little wooden house on
the river banks, is very picturesque, charmingly
situated homesteads being continually passed
on our way. Several of these farms possessed
pretty gardens, in several of which we were
surprised to see healthy clusters of hops, which
climb up poles exactly as they do in Kent and
Surrey. A hop-garden was certainly the last
thing we expected to find in Norway, but I
was informed that this valley of the Guuldal
is so warm during the summer months, that
these hops readily ripen, and excellent malt is
obtained. We also noticed clustering vines on
the walls of some of the cottages, with a show
of comparatively large grapes, and of these
"wine" is made by the peasants in the autumn.
Guuldal was the scene of some of the bloodiest
battles in the wars between Norway and
Sweden, and we thought it one of the most

interesting and beautiful valleys in the country. The abundance of wild flowers is astonishing, and we found several fresh species that did not exist on the Dovre-fjeld; many of the forests on the banks of the Gaul are now carpeted with lilies of the valley, and this familiar flower we did not meet with in any other part of Norway, although it also grows abundantly near Christiania. As to wild strawberries, one can pick any quantity in July, but they are not quite ripe yet; and the wild cherry (*Prunus avium*), the red currant (*Ribes rubrum*), called "Ribs" by the peasants, the wild raspberry (*Rubus idæus*), and the gooseberry all grow in this district. Apricots, we are told, ripen well as far north as the Throndhjem, as do also walnuts. To the fern collector this valley offers great attractions, while the shooting and salmon fishing are both first rate.

A terribly hot morning almost dissuaded us from our proposed trip to Rogstad, but as we had promised to lunch with Mr. J—— we decided to go. We started in my wife's carriole, she driving and I sitting behind in the post-boy's place and holding with some difficulty a large umbrella over both our heads. The heat of the sun was really awful, and reminded me of Egyptian deserts, the glare from the sand of which could not have been more tiring to one's eyes than was the white dusty road along the Guul-Elv. The road was very stony, as well as dusty, and right glad were we to see Mr. J—— leaning over his wicket-gate when we arrived at Rogstad, nor were we sorry to help him dispose of a capital cold luncheon which he had prepared, and at which the half of a silvery fresh-run salmon of eleven pounds, caught by our friend early this morning, formed the *pièce de resistance*.

Mr. J—— was very anxious for us to remain at Rogstad till the evening shades began to fall on some of the pools higher up the river, when I should have had a good chance of killing a salmon; but as we were not quite certain as to the times of sailing of the steamers from Throndhjem to the Arctic regions we thought it wiser to give up the fish, and push on to Throndhjem by rail at once.

After bidding adieu to our friend, and wishing him good sport for the season just opening, we drove back to the hotel, packed up our baggage, and sending our carrioles and harness to the station to be placed upon trucks, we left Engen i Stören by the evening train, and accomplished the pretty run of forty miles to Throndhjem in somewhat over three hours, the train being dreadfully slow, and as it was timed to do the distance in less than two hours, some idea may be had of the delays, which were endless, and principally consisted of the long stoppages at each station, where the guards and engine-drivers carried on interminable conversations, the train of course being at a standstill until their stock of small talk was exhausted.

It was past 9 p.m. when we reached Throndhjem, and leaving our carrioles at the station, we walked to the Britannia Hotel, which is much frequented by the English, and very comfortable, though decidedly dear.

After supper at 11 p.m., my wife and I took a stroll down the then deserted streets to the edge of the fjord, where we remained until midnight, looking on the bright calm waters of

the fjord. It is "midsummer's night;" all is
peaceful; the city is wrapt in sleep, and no
noise is heard to break the stillness around us.
Yonder we can see the dome of the cathedral
where the sovereigns of Norway have been
crowned from time out of mind. It is nearly
as light as broad day in England, but an indescribably lovely mellow tint rests upon every
object in our view, and the delicate white
plumage of the hosts of seagulls, which are
hovering over the still waters of the fjord, has
a roseate hue which causes them to appear even
more beautiful creatures than ever. As we
stand gazing on the peaceful aspect of the
ancient town, one cannot but think of the
glorious deeds and daring adventures of the
Vikings of old; and one feels almost as enthusiastic for the well-being of Norway as are its
own sons, than whom no people in the world
could be more patriotic; and as we turn our
steps homeward, our thoughts revert to the
stirring lines of Mrs. Hemans' mountain war-
song, which we believe would rouse many a
stout heart to-day, as it did of yore, to do battle
for their beloved "Gamle Norge."

" Arise! old Norway sends the word
    Of battle on the blast;
Her voice the forest pines hath stirr'd,
    As if a storm went past.
Her thousand hills the call have heard,
    And forth their fire-flags cast.

Arm, arm, free hunters! for the chase,
    The kingly chase of foes;
'Tis not the bear or wild wolf's race,
    Whose trampling shakes the snows.
Arm! arm! 'tis on a nobler trace
    The northern spearman goes.

Our hills have dark and strong defiles,
    With many an icy bed;
Heap there the rocks for funeral piles,
    Above the invader's head!
Or let the seas, that guard our Isles,
    Give burial to his dead!"

THE FULMAR PETREL.

CHAPTER VII.

"Come, while in freshness and dew it lies,
To the world that is under the free blue skies.
Leave ye man's home, and forget his care—
There breathes no sigh on the dayspring's air.
Joyous and far shall our wanderings be,
As the flight of birds o'er the wandering sea."

HEMANS.

Thursday, June 22*nd*.

THE heat was very oppressive, so we did not go out early, but found ample occupation in the perusal of our letters and newspapers which we had found awaiting us at Throndhjem. Several people assured us that the weather of the last few days is hotter than has been known in Throndhjem for upwards of twenty years! We were almost roasted indoors, although the hotel was comparatively cool compared with the streets, which were unbearable, the pavement feeling quite hot to the soles of our thickly-soled boots. When it became a little cooler,

L——and I went to inspect the large store of furs and eider-down quilts, belonging to Herr Johan Bruun, in the Strandgaden. Here we spent a long time, and more money than we ought to have done, as we found the articles for sale very tempting. I can testify to all the skins and furs that we purchased from this store being well cured, none of them having shown any symptoms of moth. As to prices, every one of course must make their own bargains. Some of our fellow-countrymen I am aware object to this bargaining, thinking it beneath their dignity: perhaps they are right. But for our part, we always find it very amusing, the great object being to see whether buyer or seller will hold out the longest. The prices asked in many Norwegian fur-stores are sometimes perfectly absurd, and the scenes that follow often brought to my mind many a similar spectacle in the bazaars of Constantinople and Cairo. The Americans, we were again informed, pay any sum asked for a good skin, but their poorer British relatives can ill afford to throw away their money. Among the articles in which we invested was a very large polar bear-skin, mounted upon red cloth, and for which we were at first asked ten pounds; but after ten minutes, on my refusing to buy it at any price, it was given to us "a great bargain," for 4*l*. 19*s*. 0*d*.! One of these skins in London will readily fetch 20*l*. or 30*l*.; whilst those of the white fox, of which we invested in eight skins, at about seven shillings per skin, would be worth in England several sovereigns a piece. Our other purchases consisted of a splendidly marked skin of the glutton (*Gulo borealis*), a curious animal nearly allied to the bear, and which still exists in small numbers in the forests of both Norway and Sweden. Very pretty muffs and ladies' collarettes are made from the ermine in its winter coat of white; and of these we laid in a small stock, as they were remarkably cheap, being indeed some ten times less in price than at a Regent Street furrier's.

Of eider-down, Mr. Bruun showed us an enormous stock, giving us some as a specimen; and hundreds of soft pillows and bolsters, filled with the same material, were piled one above the other in his large warehouses. The prettiest things, however, in the shop were some lovely quilts made of the skins of the eider-fowl and edged with down. We selected a small one, of some eight feet square, and which was composed of about thirty skins of the eider-duck, all stitched neatly together in a square pattern; each of these skins was denuded of the feathers, only the fluffy down being left. Fifteen or sixteen other skins of the male and female birds were arranged alternately round the edge of the quilt, and these had their plumage entire, the whole having a very pretty effect. The price of this quilt was small, being only 3*l*. 15*s*.; but we saw many large ones, composed of from fifty to a hundred skins, whose price ranged from ten pounds to fifty guineas, and even more. These quilts are not made in either Lapland or Norway, but are purchased from the Greenland women by the crews of the whaling-ships which annually go to those seas in pursuit of seals and whales. We found, on inspecting these quilts, that the string with which they were stitched together was formed of the sinews of the reindeer, and very strong thread it is.

Having taken our berths on the steamer, which sails this evening for the north, we had no time to see the Cathedral and other sights of the city and vicinity; and L—— amused herself by letter-writing, whilst I searched through a host of shops before I found what I wanted, which were simply inexpensive articles to give to the Laplanders, when we pay our proposed visit to them. At length I found some little circular looking-glasses, which fold up and go into the pocket; and, as their cost was about one penny each, I invested in enough to supply a small colony. Sham rings, decorated with coloured glass, resembling rubies, emeralds, and diamonds, and some brooches for the women of the like material, made up the rest of my stock. The rings and brooches were of about the same value as the mirrors!

We find that most unfortunately we have missed the steamer for Hammerfest and the North Cape, which sailed yesterday morning, and in which we had meant to have taken our passage; but another steamer leaves to-night for Tromsö, which will answer our purpose very well, as it is only about one hundred miles south of Hammerfest (the most northerly town in the world), and quite far enough north for us to see the midnight sun, and to have a glimpse at the Arctic seas.

We placed our two carrioles under the charge of the landlord of the "Britannia" until our return from the north, and we also left most of our luggage behind us, so as to give ourselves as much space as possible in our little cabin. We find somehow that we have lapsed into the habit of dining at a very late hour; but the evenings being quite as light as at midday, we do not notice the lapse of time, and our dinner was not over to-night until 11.30 p.m., when we walked down to the quay, and, pushing through a large crowd of porters and passengers, went on board the "Nordland," where the captain civilly showed us the cabin, containing four berths, which he had reserved for us, for which we were very grateful, as the ship seems quite full, and there is not a berth to be had in the vessel.

The ship was advertised to sail at midnight, but the delay in getting rid of the large number of non-passengers was so great that the "Nordland" did not actually leave the quay till 1 a.m. on the morning of—

Friday, June 23rd.

The view of the sleeping city, as we steamed slowly down the fjord, whose waters were calm as a pond, and on which the beams of the rising sun were already falling, was very picturesque. The stillness of the town, and of all the surroundings was very marked, and the only noise to be heard was the talking amongst the knots of our passengers, who sat laughing and smoking on the upper deck under an awning. It was broad daylight, and we could hardly realize that it was only one hour after midnight.

In many parts of Norway on the evening before midsummer, which is called St. Han's day, the peasants light bonfires upon the hills, and rejoicings take place often accompanied by dancing and the letting off of fireworks. We saw several rockets sent up from the shore near Throndhjem, but I should imagine the effect of the fireworks on any scale would be marred by the brightness of the nights. It is, however, we are told, the remnant of some ancient festival of the Norsemen, and is kept up on that account.

One of the principal objects of interest that we passed on our way down the Throndhjem fjord was the gloomy-looking rock of Monkholm, on which a strong fortification has been built. It is said that King Canute founded a Benedictine monastery on this island, but nothing is left of the old buildings except a single tower, in which (we were informed by the captain of the "Nordland") there is a small dungeon where Count von Grieffenfeld, a prime minister of Denmark, was imprisoned for eighteen weary years, during which period his footsteps, as he paced his solitary cell, wore away the flooring to such an extent that for many years after his death the traveller was shown the floor of this chamber as one of the "sights" of Throndhjem. Another legend states that Christian V. once took the long journey from Denmark to the island where his late minister was confined, but Grieffenfeld hid himself behind the door, and was not observed by the king, who was much disappointed at the result of his journey.

We quitted the deck at 1.30 a.m., as it was becoming rather chilly, although we could just see the uppermost ridge of the sun rising over the low mountains that lie between us and the sea. The "Nordland" is a fine steamer, and everything is arranged with a view to comfort, the officers being all most civil and kind, especially the captain, who, as well as the two junior officers, holds a commission in the royal navy of Norway. Most of the larger passenger steamers that ply along the coast are commanded by officers of the navy, and in almost all instances they speak English fluently and show special marks of attention to our countrymen.

I did not get up till eight o'clock, and left my wife in her cabin, as she was rather tired, after sitting up so late. At breakfast I only found two passengers out of some forty first-class travellers that were on board, and we afterwards found that very few of them ever turned out for breakfast; most indeed sleeping away the whole of the forenoon, and seldom going to their berths till past midnight. Early this morning the steamer touched at the small ports of Beian and Valdersund, landing passengers at both places, and arrived at Besaker while we were breakfasting. Here one small boat manned by a crew of sturdy young women came off from the shore to take a load of goods from the ship, and they rowed quite as well and with a more even stroke and regular "swing" than the men. The prevailing custom throughout Norway of making the most of the women cannot fail to strike the traveller, who will often notice a boat on the fjords pulled by girls and even by old women, while in the stern sits the father or husband quietly smoking his pipe and enjoying life; and in the farmyard the heaviest share of the work always falls to the lot of the wives and daughters.

This is not as it should be, but the fair ones seem to take it very easily, and doubtless would even be offended by the suggestion that their sons and husbands might work a little harder.

There were immense numbers of jelly-fish (*Medusidæ*) of all sizes in the sea near the village of Besaker, and we watched them from the deck with great interest, and thousands upon thousands, some of far larger size than any I ever saw on British coasts, floated past the steamer, and for at least two hours after leaving this place the ship literally cut her way through floating masses of jelly-fish. Some of these curious creatures were milky-white with a pretty cross upon the centre of their discs, and others appeared to be at least three feet or more in circumference and were furnished with brown-coloured tentacles of about two feet in length, and would be formidable fellows, we thought, to meet with whilst bathing. As the bright rays of the sun shone down upon their milky transparent bodies, they were lighted up as they moved lazily along with the tide by every hue of the rainbow; and their remarkable bell-shaped "organisms," first slowly contracting and then expanding gracefully as they swam close to the surface of the water caused them to appear very beautiful. A passing insight like this of the very simplest and apparently most uninteresting of nature's works cannot fail to make even one who cares not for her treasures, pause for a moment and feel grateful to the hand of that all powerful Being who has indeed made all things well.

L—— came on deck at eleven o'clock and found the sea as calm as a mill-pond, with not a ripple to be seen excepting where the fish were rising to the surface, pursued by a huge porpoise, which kept in view for a long while, and we watched him as he rolled his fat body over and over in the water, turning and twisting after the fish with great rapidity, accompanied by a cloud of small gulls, which as they now and then dashed downwards into the sea were evidently sharing the sport. Here and there a pair of eider-ducks were seen floating lazily close inshore of the numerous rocks and islets which dotted the sea in every direction. Soon, however, we left these clusters of islands, and standing farther out to sea, coasted towards the entrance of the Namsen fjord at a distance of several miles from the land. The view towards the south, looking back in the direction of Throndhjem was novel to us, the countless islands that studded the ocean all having the same remarkable rounded appearance, said to be caused by the action of ice in bygone days; and, as I have before observed, this is a land of great interest for the lover of geology, and also to the mineralogist.

At midday we found the sun, which shone down out of a perfectly cloudless sky, very hot indeed, but it was pleasant enough on the upper deck, sheltered as we were by a thick white awning. The principal object of interest to us during the morning was the sight of a whale not more than a hundred yards from the ship. This was a whale of about twenty feet in length, and I recognized it as belonging to the "bottle-nosed" tribe, through large "schools" of which I have often sailed when boating amongst the Orkney Islands. The bottle-nosed whale (*Delphinus tersio*) is common on the Norwegian coast, and is so called owing to its rounded snout. It often consorts in large numbers, and is sometimes hunted with the harpoon, as its blubber makes good oil, which supplies many a Northern fisherman's home with light during the dark nights of winter.

Soon after noon our course was changed to the westward, and we entered the Namsen fjord; and after a couple of hours steaming up the channel between very rugged cliffs, sometimes of great height, and presenting beautiful views of snow-capped mountains far inland, we reached the little settlement of Namsos, situated at the mouth of the famous salmon river of the Namsen, where fish up to sixty pounds in weight have been killed by the rod. It is needless to say that this river is always in private hands, and the angling lets for a large sum. It is recorded that four Englishmen, in two months' fishing here, in the year 1841, killed each over 1000 pounds weight of fish. Namsos is quite a small place, and, being composed entirely of wooden houses, was burnt to the ground on a fire breaking out four years ago. The town is, however, entirely rebuilt, on the original site, the houses still of wood, and of course as inflammable as ever. Fire is one of the chief scourges of Norwegian towns, but the inhabitants of Throndhjem have, after repeatedly suffering great losses from fire, at length learnt their lesson; and a wise law has there been promulgated, which enforces any one whose house is burnt or pulled down to rebuild it of brick or stone, instead of wood.

We were told that seals are sometimes very numerous at the mouth of the Namsen, and it is remarkable in what a short space of time these creatures will clear the surrounding waters of salmon. We sailed from Namsos after an hour's stay, and made our exit by another arm of the fjord, which afforded even finer scenery than that by which we had entered. We were soon out in the open sea again; but the islands at this point were so numerous that one could scarcely realize that we were truly sailing in salt water. In some parts of the fjords through which we sailed during the day the plantation of fir-trees grew down to the very edge of the water, and we sometimes noticed fishermen angling in the sea while comfortably sitting smoking a pipe under the shade of a tall fir! The water is generally of a great depth close under the cliffs, and our large steamer occasionally passes huge rocks at such close quarters that one could with ease throw a stone against their rugged sides.

There was a vast mass of bird-life to be seen on every islet, and some were perfectly white with seagulls which sat on their nests that covered the rocks in all directions, and did not seem at all alarmed at the passing ship; whilst whole colonies of terns or sea-swallows (*Sterna hirundo*) occupied other small islets, keeping themselves perfectly distinct from their larger friends the gulls, and the constant screaming of the two species filled the air for many a mile with discordant music.

The islands of Apelvær were reached at seven o'clock in the evening, and while our passengers were landing we had time to observe the

extraordinary quantity of cod-fish which were
piled up in immense heaps to dry, all over the
islands. These heaps had a most curious
effect, resembling large haycocks, and some
were covered over with pieces of sail-cloth, each
heap containing many hundreds of fish. The
fish are in this stage known as "klipper" cod,
and after being spread upon the sunny rocks for
some days to dry, are then collected in baskets
by men, women, and even children, and piled
up into the before-mentioned "haycocks." A
large number of women were at work among
the fish whilst we remained at Apelvær, and I
had sufficient time to make a hurried sketch of
the island, the atmosphere surrounding which
was redolent of cod for a great distance.
These cod-fish are caught in the most extraordinary numbers along the whole northern
coast of Norway, but more especially in the
waters surrounding the Loffoden Islands,
where during the winter months the fishery
is carried on, on a very extensive scale. Nearly
3000 boats, having 124 steam tenders, and the
combined crews of which number over 16,000

men, are employed in this fishery. It is stated that one year's produce of the cod-fisheries of the islands alone averages upwards of 16,000,000 of fish, about 21,500 barrels of cod liver oil, and some 6000 barrels of cod's roe!

The fish we saw to-day spread out upon the rocks at Apelvær were in all probability caught in or near the Loffodens, as in those isles the climate is usually far too humid to dry the cod quickly; and for this reason great quantities are bought by the traders from the islands, where they are merely salted, and then finally distributed along the coast at various stations, where the climate is dryer, and where there are abundance of flat rocks on which to spread the fish. On some of the dreary rugged islands along this wild west coast hundreds of acres of rocks are covered with split fish lying in long rows to dry, and very curious and white they appear shining in the hot rays of the sun.

We sat on deck till the sun set, which it did not do until 11.15 p.m., when we saw it sink into the western sea in a glow of light, and I watched the spot where it had last been seen until 12.45 a.m., at which time the golden rim again appeared rising out of the water, and throwing a beautiful tint upon the snow-crowned hills under which we were steaming. At what hour the birds sleep in these northern seas I am at a loss to imagine, as we see long lines of various birds, such as oyster-catchers, eider fowl, cormorants, and the like winging their way over the sea at all hours of the night; and as for the divers and the gulls and terns, they are as noisy at midnight as at any other time. Just before turning into my berth I saw a huge white cliff, which looked at a distance as if snow-covered, but on our approaching closer to it I noticed a large array of gaunt-looking cormorants perched on every ledge and in every crevice, the whiteness of the cliff being due to the accumulation of their droppings during a period, doubtless, of many years.

Saturday, June 24th.

At an early hour the "Nordland" passed Torghatten, a very remarkable rock of some 1000 feet in height. It is a huge granite rock upon the island of Torget, and has a large aperture apparently knocked through its centre, through which one can see the sky, and the hole is large enough it is said to contain a church or other building of a like size. When seen from the southward the form of this rock is rather like a "sou'-wester" hat, and for this reason it has been christened by the sailors "Torget's hat."

During the night we passed the towns of Bronö and Thjotto, neither of which were of the least interest. At breakfast-time the character of the scenery entirely changed, the cliffs being far higher, and the mountains of much grander outline, and with far more snow upon them, than those we saw yesterday. The sunset last night was beautiful beyond description, and I fear the reader will weary of our eulogies, but I truly believe no effect of light and shade can be more splendid than may be seen on the wild western coast of Norway at this time of the year. There is ever a wonderful and new diversity in the outlines of mountain, cliff, and rocky isle, as we travel northward; and these, together with innumerable islands, teeming with noisy seafowl, complete a picture which at sunrise and sunset is lighted up in such a fantastic manner that, as we watch the changing hues of sky, earth, and sea, we almost forget we are still on board a steamer, our fancy having set before our mind's-eye a *beau-ideal* of the fairyland we pictured in our youth.

Whilst breakfasting, the ship touched at Vefsen, at the mouth of a celebrated salmon river of the same name, and after a very short stay we proceeded on our way, passing to our right a curious pile of mountains, seven in number, which are about 4000 feet in height and appear to rise almost out of the ocean. These quaintly shaped hills go by the name of "the Seven Sisters," on account of the separate peaks of that number which stand out conspicuously against the blue sky. At mid-day we found ourselves still quite landlocked by the myriads of islands of all sizes, which shut out from our view the open sea. At the port of Sannossoen, near the mouth of the Vefsen fjord, the scenery was extremely wild and fine, and so indeed it

continued throughout the day. Although the
mountains near the seaboard are, at this point,
often from 2000 to 3000 feet in height, they are
very seldom at all rugged, nor have they even
pointed ridges or summits, which are almost
invariably rounded. This effect is said by
geologists to have taken place during the
"glacier period" by the action of the ice.

At 7 p.m. the dinner in the saloon was just
finished, when the captain came to tell me that
in less than an hour's time we should cross the
Arctic Circle; so we hastened on deck, and
settled ourselves comfortably in our armchairs
in a snug corner of the deck, whence we could
enjoy to the best advantage the splendid scenery
through which we were now passing.

The surface of the sea was placid enough
amongst the shelter of the islands, but a chilly
breeze sprang up directly we stood more out
for the open ocean. Exactly at eight o'clock
we crossed the "line," and found ourselves at
length truly in the Arctic seas! It seemed very
odd to us to see such a bright sun overhead,
and to feel its genial heat, while the mountains

around in every direction were now quite white
with the snow which glistened brightly in the
rays of the northern sun, which never sets here
at this season. We passed more than one fine
glacier, on the blue expanse of which the lights
were remarkably beautiful, and we could see the
ice very distinctly, without the aid of a glass.
One of these glaciers, we were told, is the most
extensive in Norway, with one exception.
Under some of the mountains near this part of
the province of Nordland, there are subterranean passages, through which flow rivers for,
it is believed, several miles in some instances,
finally falling into the sea, and indicating the
probable volcanic disturbances that must have
visited this district.

As we crossed the famed Arctic Circle, we
saw, far away to the westward, the four isolated
peaks of the islands of Threnen, which stand up
erect as towers in the ocean, as if placed there
as sentinels, to keep watch and ward over the
entrance to the Polar seas. Nearer to our ship's
course, we passed the curious isle of Hesta-
mando, or Horseman's Island, so called by the

sailors of these seas from the likeness which it is supposed to bear to a huge cavalry soldier riding through the waves. The fishermen always take off their caps, and make an obeisance to the "horseman," as their boats float past him.

L—— and I remained on deck to watch for the "midnight sun," the mountains to the northward of the polar circle being nearly all snow-covered, with many a large glacier topping the highest hills, or appearing between their ridges.

The lights at 11.45 p.m., when the sun appeared as if about to set, although it of course did not do so, were splendid, and the white-capped mountains were covered with a panoply of every hue of the rainbow, while the sea around was one golden-purple blaze of tiny wavelets.

The scene presented to us at twelve o'clock (midnight) altogether baffles description; and a far abler pen than mine would be required to do a tithe of justice to such a glorious panorama.

There, some distance above the horizon, we saw the blood-red ball of the sun, and so bright

was the round mass of flame that our eyes could
scarce bare to look at it. Its warm rays could
still be felt, although the wind now met us, and
a very cold north-easterly breeze it was, straight
from the frozen shores of Spitzbergen; this
alone was sufficient to remind us that we were
in a far northern land. No one on deck spoke,
and the extreme stillness and solitude was very
striking, and the effect solemn. The colour of
the sun was even redder than it is in full daylight, but the spectacle cannot be described
properly by a writer, and can hardly be imagined
by any one who has not been in these northern
latitudes.

The way in which the hundreds of huge snow-
capped mountain peaks, and their rugged sides,
were lighted up by the bright rays was almost
magical; and the varied colours, which danced
in constant motion upon the snow, and on the
surface of the sea, were worth coming all the
way from England to gaze upon.

The sun appeared, as nearly as we could judge,
to remain quite stationary from a quarter to
twelve o'clock till about 12.30 a.m., when the orb

began to rise again slowly; and by one o'clock the heavy mists, which had been resting for the last two hours on the summits of some of the highest mountains, gradually merged into the skies, and as we went down to our berths all nature was fully as bright as at midday.

Truly it was a sight not to be forgotten as long as memory lasts.

SEALS "AT HOME."

CHAPTER VIII.

"Traveller, whence comest thou?
From icy oceans, where the whale
Tosses in foam his lashing tail;
Where the snorting sea-horse shows
His ivory teeth in grinning rows;
Where, tumbling in their seal-skin boat,
Fearless the hungry fishers float,
And from teeming seas supply
The food their niggard plains deny."

AIKIN.

Sunday, June 25th.

DURING the night the "Nordland" anchored off the little town of Bodö, in the province of Nordland, after which our steamer takes her name. It is a very dreary place, without any attractions saving being the best spot from which to pay a visit to the upper end of the Salten fjord, where a dangerous whirlpool known as the Saltenström is to be seen; and some wandering families of Laplanders may generally be met with near Saltnæs, if the traveller cares to go in search of them among the mountains, as they seldom remain long stationary in any one spot. Bodö is the most southerly town where the midnight sun can be seen, but as most of the steamers proceed farther north nothing is gained by staying here, unless it is in the autumn, when very good snipe-shooting can be got not far from the town, and great quantities of duck are always to be met with on the fjord. If the tourist has two or three days at his disposal, however, he might find instruction and amusement by going on board some of the fishing-boats or "jagts" which carry the cod-fish from the Loffoden Islands to other parts of the coast. The fishermen are always glad, on receiving a present of tobacco or spirits,—of which latter they are, I fear, too fond,—to give information about the various modes of catching the fish, the manner of curing them, and other matters of interest.

We only remained at Bodö a few hours, in order to take coal on board, and then put out into the great Vest fjord, a broad expanse

of open sea, some forty miles across, between
the mainland and the Loffoden Islands. The
Vest fjord is often very stormy, and Captain
Beck assures me that he considers it by far the
most tempestuous part of the Norwegian coast
during the winter months, and he adds that
nothing more dreary can be imagined than the
appearance of this fjord at that time of year,
when there is little light beyond that supplied
by the *aurora borealis* to help the mariner on his
way; while in stormy weather it is pitch dark
both night and day, and as the vessel, compelled to lie-to all night, tosses on the waves
in the inky darkness nothing can be heard by
the half-frozen sailors on deck but the weird
screams of the sea-fowl sounding loudly above
the wailing of the wintry wind.

To-day, however, luckily for us the scene is
vastly different. It is the merry month of
June, and the sun pours down upon the deck
with almost tropical warmth as the " Nordland" steams across the calm waters of the
fjord, on whose surface the largest flocks of
sea-birds I ever saw in any part of the world

were swimming and diving; whilst now and
then vast swarms of ducks and gulls, alarmed
by the noise of our engines, would dash upwards into the blue sky, and after taking a
short flight they drop into the sea, the noise
of their countless wings resembling the distant
rattle of musketry, while their hoarse cries add
to the wildness of the scene.

I think that we enjoyed the view from the
middle of the Vest fjord as much as any in
Norway. Its wildness and sublime grandeur
is indescribable. The distant mountains along
the mainland near Bodö are very rugged, and
formed as picturesque a distance to our view as
could be wished for; while innumerable snow-
capped summits more inland pierced the sky
line; for many a mile to the southward the eye
rested on the still blue expanse of open sea;
and before us, to the north-west, lay the
splendid panorama of the islands of Loffoden,
which we thought very beautiful at the distance
of twenty miles or thereabouts, but when the
separate islets gradually opened out to our
view as the steamer drew nearer to their shores,

each precipice and mountain unfolded itself by degrees, combining to form a scene to which no pen could do justice.

We passed the world-famed Mäelström at the distance of about eight miles, and indeed ships generally give it a wide berth, and besides to have visited it would have taken us out of our course. There is not much to be seen, even if the traveller makes a point of going there—merely a rough stretch of water between two islands, and which at certain states of the tide is dangerous enough. Those who expect anything resembling Edgar Allen Poe's description of this whirlpool will be woefully disappointed, the old traditions of whales and ships being sucked into its lowest depths never to be seen again by mortal eye being simply fabulous. There is, however, no doubt that wrecks have many a time taken place in the immediate neighbourhood of the Mäelström, and a terribly strong current flows at racing pace between the two islands of Verōe and Moskenæs when winds and tides meet. But at other times, when the tide is slack or nearly so, the hardy fishermen of the Loffodens pass and repass the whirlpool often (excepting of course in rough weather) in their little undecked open boats, as it has long been known to them that some of the best and largest cod-fish are to be found in the very centre of this much-dreaded Mäelström. It is well known to any one who has amused himself with the sport of sea-fishing that the best fun may always be expected at a spot where two tides meet, as the fish are certain to congregate in large numbers at such a place, on the look-out doubtless for the food which is found in the disturbed water. This is probably the reason why so many fine fish are caught by the fishermen of Loffoden in the turbid waves of the famous whirlpool.

The following excellent description of the Mäelström is from Mr. Everest's "Norway." "The agitation of the current," he says, "arises from an immense body of water being forced by the flowing tide into the narrow passage between the isles. In addition to this the depth decreases most suddenly as the stream enters the straits. Outside, on the west of the Loffodens, the soundings show a depth of 100 to 200 fathoms, while in the straits, and in the West Fjord, it suddenly shoals from sixteen to thirty fathoms, and the *whole weight of water* from the *North Sea* is suddenly compressed between the cliffs of Moskenæs and Værœ." This will give some idea of the disturbance created at certain times by the pressure of such a vast volume of water.

Towards midday we passed to our left hand a small wild-looking islet, which Captain Beck informed us was the Flakstad, where it is said that a large number of whales have, during the present century, "grounded" their huge bodies in a certain narrow inlet, where, finding themselves in a perfect natural trap, they became the prey of the farmer to whom the island belonged. This inlet is extremely narrow and very deep at the spot where the whales entered with the tide, but suddenly the water shoals, and the fish were at once stranded, the passage being too narrow to enable them to turn round their long bodies in order to beat a retreat. These large whales were of the species which is from sixty to seventy feet in length, and were a very valuable godsend to the poor farmer. The stranded monsters are stated in more than one case to have lived as long a time as eight days in their prison, the fishermen witnessing their attempts to escape, which they say are incessant during the whole time of their captivity, and their blowings and bellowings were horrible to listen to until death at length relieved their sufferings, and gave up the monster's carcase to the farmer of Flakstad.

We coasted up various narrow inlets and winding fjords during the whole of the afternoon, now and then stopping for an hour or more at the small fishing-villages, which at frequent intervals line the shores of the barren Loffodens. At each town we stop at, L—— and I amuse ourselves by fishing from the deck with a strong hand-line which the captain very kindly lent to us; and we found it very good fun, pulling up fish after fish, as they generally bit very freely, and almost as soon as the line was over the side of the ship a series of sharp tugs would tell us a fish was on the hook, and the captive was duly handed up struggling on to the deck, where he was soon despatched with a smart blow on the head with a thick stick. It was astonishing to us to find such quantities of fish everywhere in these northern seas; and it either proved that they were very fearless of the appearance of the ship and the commotion made by her engines, or that they were very hungry, for no sooner was the vessel steady or only moving slowly through the water than the fish seemed to be there in swarms. Those we caught to-day were principally coal-fish (*Gadus carbonarius*), or "lythe," as it is usually called on most of our Scotch and Irish coasts, and small cod, which were capital eating, and we were so successful that a large dish was sent to the saloon for dinner this evening. We also secured several other species of fish, but none of them were so good for the table as the codlings and the lythe, so they were cut up for baits wherewith to captivate their neighbours.

A most picturesque scene was presented as we approached the town of Stockmarknoes, where we remained nearly three hours, as there happens to have been a large "fair" held there during the past three days, and a large number of passengers and baggage consequently had to be taken on board, which was by no means a pleasant occurrence for us, as the new-comers were mostly of the lower class of merchants, whose habits were far from cleanly, and the nicely-washed, smart-looking deck was quickly converted into a large "spitoon" by these gentry. It is certainly one of the greatest drawbacks to ladies who travel by steamers in Norway that the natives smoke from morning till night, and the disgusting habit above named makes the deck of a ship perfectly abominable. The people seemed too lazy to walk from their seats to the side of the vessel, and I fear that this universal custom will never be stamped out by any orders of the authorities on board, however stringent. Stockmarknœs is situated upon a low-lying promontory, and its houses had a very curious effect, being painted blue, bright green, chrome-yellow, and red, while those of them which were built

nearest to the sea were supported by long stout
poles which were embedded in the water that
in some cases flowed under the very floors of
the dwellings. The harbour swarmed with
eider fowl; and flocks of male and female birds,
carefully separate the one from the other, were
floating in all directions on the sea, whilst by
the help of our opera-glasses we could see on
many of the rocky islets the old birds sitting
quietly upon their nests. Gulls and terns of
various kinds were fishing in myriads in the
little harbour, and the air was filled with their
loud cries. The great northern diver seemed
very numerous near this place, and seals were
common; while the bottle-nosed whales, porpoises and other *cetacea* are often met with
in considerable numbers off these islands. The
fair, we were told, which had just concluded
when we reached Stockmarknes, was held every
summer, and a large number of merchants are
always present to buy up the articles which are
exposed for sale, and the demand as a rule is so
great that the whole supply is generally bought
up. Eider-down, from the islands in the neigh-

bourhood, formed the principal article of barter; and immense numbers of cod-fish, salted and ready for drying, were disposed of; while walrus-tusks, brought from Spitzbergen by whalers, and reindeer skins and horns purchased from the Laplanders, were among the merchandise. The amount of eider-down sold during the last three days, we are told, must have been enormous, and judging from the prices said to be paid for this valuable commodity by the local merchants, the poor fishermen must be great losers, but of course, poor fellows, no other market is get-at-able to them, and they must fain content themselves with the utterly inadequate payment which these merchants offer them. In some of the more out of the way islands, the villagers prefer payment in kind, and in this case they receive tea, coffee, grain, woollen clothes, and what they prize most, execrably bad spirits, in exchange for their eider-down and fish. We were glad to find that there are churches and resident clergymen on several of the Loffodens, and the simple folks will go any distance to their places of worship, rowing often many weary miles against wind and tide to pay their devotions in their little wooden "Kirke."

It was a most gloriously bright warm day until towards six o'clock, when the wind suddenly blew strongly from the north and the evening was remarkably cold. We continued our way among the winding passages which separate the various islets, so that being well under lee of the land we were not troubled with a boisterous sea. It became very cloudy as we proceeded northwards, and eventually a cold rain began to fall. We continued on deck, however, as the wildness of the ever-varying scenery was sufficient attraction to us to do so, the vast black and white mountains towering to the skies on every side of the ship, making one feel almost fearful that the purply black masses of rock were about to fall upon and crush to atoms the ship which steamed along beneath their frowning precipices. Few of these cliffs, I especially noticed, were exactly perpendicular, but gradually sloped downwards to the water's edge, as if to allow the continually falling *débris* from above to have an easy descent into the ocean. Quite Arctic was this fantastic scene at midnight. A mass of heavy white cloud lined every mountain, by many of which we were entirely surrounded, at the height of about 2000 feet; while at from 3500 to 4000 feet above the sea-level we saw innumerable jagged summits piercing the vapoury mass which rested on their rugged sides, and upstanding gaunt and grand in the solemn silence which reigned around, their topmost ridges being lighted up by the lovely and ever-varying hues of the midnight sun, which was of course quite invisible to us. Most of these grim-looking mountains are vast masses of black rock, and the great abundance of unmelted snow made the picture quite one fit for the " black and white exhibition " at home. Almost every fissure and cranny in the sides of these cliffs was filled with glistening snow, which here and there touched the sea itself. This effect of sameness in colouring was greatly reduced by the little patches of bright green grass which now and then met the eye beneath some frowning rock, and where perhaps one would see a small cluster of fishermen's houses, painted in gay red or blue colours; but pleasant as such a home appeared to the passer by to-night, we could not help pitying the poor toilers of the sea in such a dreary spot during the long northern winter.

L—— was especially pleased with the innumerable cascades which we saw during to-day's voyage, falling from the snow-capped mountains and glaciers into the fjords, often from a height of over 3000 feet. The summits of most of the loftiest hills were very rugged, having the appearance of the craters of extinct volcanoes. No pen *can* describe such wonderfully grand scenery, and any one who has seen the Loffoden Isles will agree with me that, as far as coast scenery is concerned, nothing approaching to it is to be met with in Europe. Beautiful alpine flowers can be seen with the naked eye upon the lower slopes of the mountains in many parts of these wild islands; and there is a great variety of seaweeds, which I do not suppose have ever been properly investigated.

Monday, June 26th.

The morning was bitterly cold, and when I went on deck I could quite realize the fact that we were truly in the Arctic Ocean. We had quitted the islands of Loffoden, and the tall hills on every side were now covered to the water's edge with deep snow; the air felt like winter, and many a large glacier could be seen between the sloping mountains; and having touched at Sandtorv, and one or two other places of no importance to any one besides the fish-merchants, we coasted up a very narrow channel of some thirty miles in length, until we once more entered more open water, and arrived at the port of Harstædhavn, after leaving which an arm of the And fjord was crossed, and here we saw such a vast mass of birds that one could scarcely have believed it possible for the ship to have passed through them without steaming literally over them.

There was a strong head-wind blowing at the time, and the progress of the steamer was necessarily slow, and had it not been so, some of the countless young of the gull and duck tribe, that darkened the water on all sides, must have been destroyed by the ship. The quantity of gulls was simply astonishing, and of five or six different sorts, including the large black-backed gull (*Larus marinus*), and that fine bird, the Iceland gull (*L. Islandicus*), of which several were to be seen.

Eider ducks, in vast numbers, were to be observed on all sides, and flocks of little ducks and gulls just out of the shell, were following their parents among the tumbling waves. Skua gulls were there, too, in considerable abundance; and robbers as they are, these birds made a capital thing of it as they pursued the other species of gulls after their successful fishing, and, dashing at them with loud cries, caused them to disgorge whatever they had caught at once, which the Skua picked up before it even reached the water. Large shoals of mackerel were sporting on our starboard bow; and the fat bodies of their pursuing enemies, the porpoises, were now and then seen rolling over and over in the surf. More than one sea-eagle (*Haliætus albicilla*) was soaring far up in the dusky sky, and golden-eye ducks, great northern divers, terns, mergansers, guillemots, cormorants, razor-bills, and hosts of other species too numerous to name, made the sea and air dark with their ever-moving forms. Such an ornithological treat is not often to be obtained, and we stood on deck for a long time watching, with the greatest interest, the varied forms of life around the ship, which often has to be put at reduced speed in the narrow fjords to give the birds time to hurry their young broods out of danger of being run down.

As we progressed northward the vast flocks of eider ducks seemed ever to increase, and so great were the crowds of the female birds upon some of the numerous islets, that their brown forms perfectly covered the rocks, and they themselves were hardly distinguishable from the tangled masses of dark seaweed.

It was nearly seven o'clock in the evening when the "Nordland" steamed up the Tromsö fjord, and nothing more truly Arctic could be imagined than the scene before us. The town, with its wooden houses and large warehouses, lay to the westward, sheltered by sloping hills, but of no great height, terribly barren looking and uninviting. Towering mountains shut out any distant view towards the east, and snow, in great white masses, covered their precipitous sides down to the edge of the fjord, whose grey waters looked very cold and cheerless; and the few ships at anchor were rocking from side to side against the dismal background of snow and ice, which lay to our north, the bitter east wind howling loudly through the rigging.

There was no confusion at all at the little quay, where a boat from the steamer landed us, and though there were plenty of idle sailors and women congregated to stare at us, no porter of any kind was available. L—— and I therefore carried our bundles of rugs and other small things, while a couple of diminutive boys were engaged, after great trouble, to drag our portmanteau as best they could to the hotel. A lad also took charge of my small hand-bag, but being very small he fell headlong over it before he had gone many steps, and I eventually was obliged to carry it myself.

The little inn at which we took up our quarters was kept by one Schmidt, and called itself an "hotel." It was a small wooden building, and we were made very comfortable by the landlady, who could speak a few words of English, and who much wished my wife to take her back to England with us in the capacity of cook. We dined in company with a Norwegian infantry officer, who civilly gave me some useful information about Lapland, and the sport to be obtained in the neighbourhood of Tromsö; and on leaving the hotel I was agreeably surprised at meeting my old friend W——, of the Grenadier Guards, whose yacht was in Tromsö harbour, for a couple of days, previously to continuing her voyage round the North Cape to the Pasvik river, for salmon fishing. The yacht had been fortunate in having a fair, though strong wind during her voyage to Tromsö from the west coast of Scotland, making the passage in a very few days' time.

At 11 p.m. L—— and I walked down the winding streets to the quay, where, after a little bargaining, we engaged a boat and man to row us out into the middle of the fjord for an hour's fishing. We were soon at anchor, and working away with two deep-lines apiece; but the evening was terribly cold, and our fingers became very numbed after a short time. We caught, however, a good many fish, about three dozen in all, but none of any size, as they ranged from half a pound to two pounds each in weight, and were principally codlings with half a dozen "lythe" or coal-fish. The heavy clouds which had been hanging over the fjord all the afternoon at length came down in a regular heavy shower of sleet, and it was so bitterly cold, and the everlasting glittering of the white snow on all sides so trying to one's eyes, that at 12.30 a.m. we returned to the shore.

Whilst fishing, an immense porpoise came up unexpectedly quite close to our boat, but there was a marked absence of bird life. My wife was delighted, just before the hour of midnight struck from the clocks of the old town, to hear in the distance a well-known note borne towards us upon the breeze, and as it approached nearer to the western bank of the fjord, the familiar "cuck-oo," "cuck-oo," echoed again and again on our ears, reminding us of very different scenes in quiet English woods, and the shady recesses of the forests of Scotland.

The tall hills on every side returned the cry of the bird, which, multiplied a thousand-fold, made the whole air seem full of cuckoos. Wordsworth should have been with us to-night, when he wrote the following lines, which were singularly appropriate on the present occasion :

> "It was the mountain echo,
> Solitary, clear, profound,
> Answering to the shouting cuckoo,
> Giving to her sound for sound.
> Unsolicited reply
> To a babbling wanderer sent ;
> Like her ordinary cry,
> Like ——, but oh, how different !"

There is a curious custom prevalent in Tromsö, as well as in several other of the larger towns in Norway, of a paid watchman being stationed all day and night in the highest part of the tower of the loftiest church in the city. His duty consists of extreme vigilance in case of fire; as, on account of the inflammability of the wooden buildings, the danger from an unchecked conflagration is very great if timely warning be not given.

In order to prove to the public that he is wide awake, this watchman puts his head out of a small window in the tower of the church, and shouts in a loud voice some verses, generally selected from the Bible, and of which the most common form seems to be the couplet—

"Unless the Lord the city keep,
The watchman wakes in vain."

These words are sometimes called out by the watchman four times, he turning, as he delivers them in a sing-song voice, to north, south, east, and west.

The midnight sun was quite "put out" to-night by the rain and heavy wintry-looking clouds which still lined the sky as we reached the hotel, only too glad to warm ourselves, and especially our half-frozen hands, at a good fire, before retiring to rest.

A HUNGRY ARCTIC FOX AT A TRAP.

CHAPTER IX.

"'With blue cold nose and wrinkled brow,
Traveller, whence comest thou?'
'From Lapland woods and hills of frost
By the rapid reindeer crost;
Where tap'ring grows the gloomy fir
And the stunted juniper;
Where the wild hare and the crow
Whiten in surrounding snow;
Where the wolf and Arctic fox
Prowl among the lonely rocks;
And tardy suns to deserts drear
Give days and nights of half a year.'"

AIKIN.

Tuesday, June 27*th.*

WE were up by eight o'clock, and although the sun was shining feebly from a grey, but not a cloudy sky, his warmth was not to be felt; and the mountains on all sides, with their mantles of white snow and ice, make us feel much as a dull winter's day at home would do.

After breakfast L—— and I walked down to the little harbour where we found a small open boat, manned by two hardy Norsemen, which I had ordered last night, all ready for us. Having stowed plenty of eatables and Norsk ale under the thwarts, and wrapped ourselves well up in "Ulsters" and warm rugs, the word was given to start for a visit to the Laps.

These little folks are to be found rather later on in the summer, in a narrow valley called the Tromsdal, upon the opposite side of the Tromsö fjord, and only about two English miles distant from the town; but this family we heard had not yet come down from the mountains. The next nearest spot where these wanderers were likely to be found was upon the large island of Kvaloe, so I directed our "crew" to proceed thither, with all possible despatch.

I hope for the credit of tradition that the hardy Norsemen of story were made of somewhat different material to the pair of bearded scamps to whose tender mercies we had consigned ourselves; for a lazier brace of rowers never were seen. The distance from Tromsö to that part of Kvaloe island where we expected to find the Laplanders, was only ten miles; which distance, with the tide in our favour most of the way, and a perfectly calm sea, our crew took exactly three hours and a half to accomplish.

The scenery that we passed during this trip need only be described as wintry in the extreme, the usual gloomy cliffs and towering white mountains being seen in every direction; and right glad were we that we had our rugs and cloaks in the boat, for as we were sitting still we felt the cold very much.

Some parts of the lower slopes of the hills were here and there covered with fir-trees, but they were sorry specimens and only added to the weird aspect of all around us. On our way across the fjord we passed a great many small islets and detached rocks, most of which were literally covered with eider ducks.

The female birds seemed remarkably tame and sat upon the rocks quite quietly as the boat passed within twenty yards of them, apparently as much at their ease as if they had not even noticed the presence of man. Many of them were sitting on their nests among the shingle, while now and then we noticed an old hen followed by her troop of five or six young ones taking their first lessons in the art of swimming, or scrambling over the rocks, as they dashed after their mother with frantic haste. Very few of the old cocks were upon the rocks, but large flocks of male birds were disporting themselves in the water at some distance from the land; and very beautiful they appeared when an alarm was given by one of their number, on which the whole mass of from fifty to a couple of hundred birds would rise from the surface with a loud noise of wings, their lovely white plumage, with its markings of black and green, having a very pretty effect, especially if the sun was shining on them at the moment.

We landed upon one island, some six hundred yards or so in length, but very narrow, and a cloud of birds rose into the air, shrieking round our heads, with angry voices at our uninvited intrusion of their rocky home.

A great percentage of these fowl were gulls, of both the lesser black-backed and the common (*Larus canus*) species; there were besides a large number of terns, who flew noisily overhead as long as we remained on the island; and many pairs of oyster-catchers, with their prettily pied plumage, were running about among the rocks.

The main objects of interest, however, to us, were the eider ducks, of which there were plenty to be seen in all directions, both on land and in the water.

After searching for nests for a short time we came upon several eggs of both gulls and oyster-catchers, principally broken pieces of shells, and proving that the young had been hatched out already. At first we were unable to find any of the eider's nests; but as we were almost despairing, we suddenly almost trod upon one, and were soon busy examining it with great interest. It was placed in a slight depression, hardly to be called a hole, amongst the shingle, and was beautifully lined with the softest of dark-brown down, plucked from the breast of the poor mother, who had kept out of the way until she saw that we had actually discovered her nest, when she at once came up on the rocks out of the water, and commenced waddling round us in wide circles, at the distance of only a few yards, and looking so beseechingly into our faces that it would have been cruel indeed to have robbed the nest of its four dark-green eggs, which reposed so snugly upon their bed of down.

We did not disturb this nest, but were glad to find immediately afterwards a second nest close to the first one, and from which the young had apparently been hatched, as the down was covered with broken fragments of shell. It was full of down, all of which we appropriated, and just as we had finished stuffing it into our pockets our boatmen hailed us, and we saw to our horror a man tearing along in our direction at a great pace, so as we had no right in the world to take the down or to trespass on these islands, we made for the boat as fast as we could, and started once more, much to the relief of the birds, who at once returned to see what havoc had been made, and we hoped they were agreeably disappointed.

The man, whose sudden appearance had caused our undignified stampede, turned out, as he came nearer, to be only a small boy, but it served us right and proves what it is to be troubled with a guilty conscience. All the islands, with hardly an exception, belong to private individuals, and are very strictly preserved; the eider ducks themselves being also accounted the private property of the persons on whose lands they have made their nests.

Eider down is of considerable value, and indeed, may be said to form one of the staple commodities of Norway, of which the three principal are timber, dried fish, and the spoils from the nests of these birds. The annual production is stated, in an average year, to be as much as six thousand pounds' weight of down, which would be worth about five thousand pounds in British money. The marketable value of uncleaned down, exactly in the state in which it is taken from the nests, is about eight shillings or rather more *per* pound; while the cleaned down fetches nineteen shillings for each pound.

The habits of these birds are very curious and the female is wonderfully devoted to her nest and young. The eider duck is common throughout Norway, but rarer in the south than it is in Lapland, where we have already seen many thousands; and indeed their number may be truly termed "legion." They pair in April in these northern regions, and breeding commences towards the end of May or early in the month of June. When the females commence to sit upon their eggs, the males leave their consorts, and assemble in flocks, spending most of their time floating lazily in the water. They make their nest in any hollow or crevice of a rock, or among the loose stones upon the islands, and not very far as a rule, from the water's edge. The term "nest" must be used here merely as a figure of speech, for it only consists of a slight depression in the sand or among stones; or (as the one from which we to-day took the down) amongst little shells and corals, and lined with a few small pieces of dried sea-weed. Both the male and female birds help to make the nest.

The nest is then filled by the softest of soft down plucked from the breast of the hen by the bird herself, and she is by no means selfish in denuding her own bosom, giving a very liberal supply for the nest. Two hens occasionally use the same nest, and live together in a very friendly way, each one contributing her own share of the eggs. Rather less than half a pound of down is the general average quantity placed in a single nest; and this is reduced by one half by the process of cleansing, which consists of extracting carefully all the tiny particles of sea-weed, coral, sand, small shells and such things as will be found mixed with the down.

It is a curious fact that the down taken either from birds found dead, or from those that have been shot, is said to entirely lose its elasticity; that only which comes from the living birds' bosom having that wonderful elastic property which fetches so high a price in the markets.

When the old hen wishes to go in search of her food whilst sitting, she carefully turns over with her bill the soft down upon the eggs, so as to entirely cover them; and no mother could be more anxious for the welfare of her youthful family than the eider duck is when the young are hatched out of the eggs. The down is generally plundered from the nests three separate times in the course of the summer; but if the fourth and last nest be disturbed, the birds will forsake the spot never to return. When the eider is robbed of all its eggs, it frequently steals those of other birds from neighbouring nests, and sometimes it even appropriates the young which belong to other parents. After the hen has plucked off all the down she can spare to replenish her unfortunate nest when robbed, the male bird comes to her assistance with his share, but seldom does he do so until it has been plundered at least twice; and this, I fear, only proves that the cock is more selfish than his mate, which is popularly said to be also the case with the human species!

In many parts of Iceland, where the eider duck is found in considerable numbers, the owners of the breeding-grounds on the coast actually take the trouble to make small islands for the use of the birds, which always choose an islet for nesting purposes in preference to the main land. The Icelanders are also said to cause holes to be dug in regular rows in the smooth, steep banks on the islands where the birds would not build of their own accord did they not find these artificially-constructed receptacles for their eggs ready for them. The rules laid down by law are very strict for the protection of these valuable birds, and no guns are permitted to be fired near the breeding-grounds during the summer months; and it is even asserted that no ship is allowed to fire a salute within a certain specified distance of the eider's islands. Quaint old Bishop Pontoppidan, in his work on the natural history of Norway, in speaking of the habits of this species, gives the following curious account of the bird:—

"If the first five eggs," he observes, "are stolen away, then the bird lays again, but only three eggs, and in another nest; if these are lost, then she lays one more. Four weeks the mother sits alone on the eggs, and the cock stands watching underneath in the water, so that if any human creature, or beast of prey, approaches, he gives her notice by crying *hu, hu;* and then she covers her eggs with moss and down, which he keeps ready prepared, and comes down to her mate in the water. But he does not receive her very kindly; and if her eggs are lost by any accident, he gives her many blows with his wings, which she must take patiently; and after this he entirely deserts her, and she is obliged to join the flock of her kind under the same disgrace."

There are many odd sayings in Scandinavia concerning this bird; and Lloyd, in his "Game Birds and Wild Fowl of Sweden and Norway," states that he was once assured by a respectable man at the Winga lighthouse, that when the nest of the eider duck is built at any considerable elevation above the water, and the mother experiences any difficulty in bringing her youthful brood down to the sea, owing to inequalities in the ground, she merely throws the chicks over her shoulder, as a fox does a goose, and thus speedily conveys them to their proper element. This requires confirmation, however, to my mind; but there is of course no reason why the statement should not be true, for many will recollect the amount of ridicule which was at first launched against those who asserted that they had seen the woodcock carrying its young by clutching them in its feet, but which now has long been admitted as a true statement both by naturalists and sportsmen.

The tameness of the female eiders during the breeding-season is remarkable, and they will often remain within a few yards of a person who is intruding on their domains, whilst the fishermen tell us that these birds become so tame as to permit themselves to be taken up in the hand while sitting, and that they sometimes even nest in the huts of the fishermen, so accustomed do they become to the presence of man.

After this lengthy digression I must return to the journal of our proceedings. On quitting the islands we rowed leisurely along the barren coast of this bleak-looking Lapland, until the shores of Kvaloe island hove in sight, and after rowing across the open strip of water which separates Kvaloe from the island on which the town of Tromsö is built, we entered a narrow bay, where the water shoaled so rapidly that our little boat grounded a great many times, and we had some difficulty in reaching the head of the inlet. This, however, was at length accomplished; and on rounding a little headland the tents of the Laplanders were seen for the first time.

The prospect was wintry in the extreme, and very dismal. The sky was now of a dull, leaden colour; the sea of a dirty green hue; and tall mountains on all sides, covered almost to the edge of the water with unmelted snow, shut out any distant view. The air was extremely cold, and our feet so benumbed from our cramped position in the boat, that when we landed we found that to stand upright and walk about was by no means easy. The little bay was lined by a shingly shore, to the very edge of which extended a thick carpet of beautiful little flowers, which had a black centre and snow-white petals, but with the name of which we were unacquainted.

At the distance of a couple of hundred yards from the beach a thick "scrub" of juniper, considerably stunted by cold winds, was doing its best to flourish and look green, but failed signally in having a picturesque effect; immediately in the rear of this brushwood towered the white peaks of a steep snow-mantled mountain, between which and the junipers the little huts of the Laps were pitched.

Huts, indeed, they could not be called, as they bore more resemblance to tents, but with a large orifice at the top to let out the smoke, which curled upwards in thick clouds from each domicile. As soon as we landed we were saluted with a rough welcome by several very noisy and remarkably mangy dogs, somewhat like our Scotch collies, but with rougher and longer hair than the shepherd's dog, and altogether wild-looking brutes, and decidedly "unco uncanny." These dogs are very useful in assisting their masters to drive the herds of tame reindeer from place to place; and we were informed that the deer know the dogs so well, that they will at once obey the bark of the latter. The animals accompanied us up the hill, until we arrived at the tents, when several of the smallest and ugliest human beings appeared upon the scene, having apparently just been waked up from sleep by the noise of the dogs, if one could judge by the extremely "touzled" look their dresses, and especially their heads presented.

It was at first very hard to tell which were men and which women, as they all wore the same short coatee, called a "paesk," made of the skins of their reindeer; but we soon found that their head-gear differed according to sex. The caps of the men were square at the top, while those of the women were somewhat rounded in shape, with a sort of peak surmounting them. Most of the women also wore coloured girdles of yellow, green, and red worsted round their waists.

The little people were not in the least put out of their usual routine by our unexpected visit, and although we were their earliest visitors this season, they evidently had entertained English travellers before. Our boatmen explained to the head Lap, (an old wrinkled patriarch who could scarcely walk at all, so stiff were his ancient limbs,) the object of our visit, which, we told them, was merely to say " how do you do " and buy some reindeer horns from them. In this, however, we were doomed to disappointment, as they said that they had bartered all their deer's horns already in Tromsö. They were very civil and friendly, and after we had examined the outside of their " wigwams," the head of the family kindly asked us to come in and sit down by their fire to warm ourselves.

The tents, if I may so term them, belonging to this colony of Laplanders, were only four in number, and accommodated about forty-five individuals, including babies, of which there were a large number in proportion to that of " mammas." The men are taller and more strongly built than the women; but it is rather remarkable that one never, or at all events very seldom, sees a Lap with any hair on his face. For this reason it is by no means easy to guess the ages of the men, and they are all more or less marked by deep wrinkles, both old and young alike, showing how severe the weather of an Arctic winter must be. I certainly subsequently saw more than one so-called Lap, with an apology for a beard, but we were told that these were not the true Laplander, but a half-breed between Norwegians and the *bonâ-fide* Lap. This, I believe, is the true state of the case; but one cannot help wondering why nature did not decorate the poor little Lap with hirsute adornments to assist him to keep his face warm! The Laps are often also termed Finns, but are more commonly called by the former name. The men we saw to-day were one and all decidedly ugly, and the same may be said for the women, we being quite unprejudiced judges, as my wife took stock of the gentlemen, while I did the same of the fair ones. We both agreed that "very ugly" was too mild a term to be applied to our entertainers, and so dubbed them once for all perfectly hideous.

Their homes were curiously constructed, being made of several stout but pliant branches of the birch of considerable length, which were stuck in the ground so as to form a circle of about eight or nine feet in diameter, the tops of the branches being joined together by strong thread made of the sinews of the reindeer. A quantity of rough half-worn-out mats had then been laid upon the branches, the whole being covered over with a large number of pieces of brown sail-cloth and old reindeer skins, which kept out the rain and cold winds, but smelt most abominably, and kept in the smoke from the large wood-fires that blazed in every tent, notwithstanding the large aperture at the top of the edifice.

So great was the volume of smoke, and so dense was the atmosphere when we entered one of the dwellings, that we were nearly choked; and after recovering from the coughing caused by the smoke, we had the doubtful advantage of the combined aroma of some sixteen Laps, who crowded in to inspect us, and who were all indulging in execrably bad tobacco, some chewing it, and others smoking pipes. As soon as we entered, the deer-skin which formed the "door" was pulled down and made fast, thus shutting out all the air of the outer world. And the atmosphere within, who shall now describe it? First, "a maun premese," as the Scotchman is reported to have said, that the statement is true that the Laps are guiltless of washing from year's end to year's end, guiltless not only of soap (which of course they could not be expected to procure), but of cold water also. Secondly, be it known that these good people never change their garments, excepting when literally worn out, and when they begin to crumble to pieces upon their backs; this is the case at least, so we are informed on the best authority, with respect to the clothes worn next the skin, for they occasionally don a gay woollen frock termed a "gappe," which is reserved for Sundays and other festivals, and which is handed down sometimes from father to son.

In the third place, the tents, the skins of the deer which were given to us for seats, the dogs, of which there were four or five curled around the fire, and the Laps themselves were pretty freely furnished with their share of minute vermin of several species! Add all these interesting facts to the presence of the thick clouds of smoke, the awful smell of a combination of horrors, and the continuous noisy chattering of all the inmates of the dwelling, and the reader will have a fair idea of the spot where L—— and I spent half an hour in company of our strange-looking little hosts.

The women evinced considerable curiosity as to my wife's dress, her locket, earrings, and other ornaments; and they were very pleased with some brooches and rings (value about one penny each), which we had bought at Throndhjem, furnished with coloured glass to represent rubies, emeralds, and diamonds, and which we gave to each of them. This was rather curious, as we thought they would have at once found out that the rings were of no value, especially as many Laps wear good silver ornaments upon their dresses. The men, however, to whom we presented little mirrors, fitted for carrying in the pocket, were not so civil, and did not seem to feel the smallest degree of pleasure, having evidently expected some more valuable gifts, and they were very greedy, asking us over and over again for money. The women showed my wife some of their babies, and these little creatures were not quite so repulsive in features as their mothers were; and I was subsequently told by more than one Norwegian friend that occasionally the children were even considered pretty, but indeed this is hard to credit if one ever saw the happy parents.

The babies were each provided with a snug cradle, which in itself was a most remarkable piece of workmanship, but had withal a comfortable look about it. The cradle is made of tanned reindeer-skin, and seems to me to be constructed so as to be sufficiently long for a baby until the occupant is about one year of age; its shape is oblong, somewhat like a goose's egg, and it literally has no bottom, being almost round, except at the top, where the infant is

inserted upon its bed of dried moss, or (much
more frequently) of the hard dung of the reindeer! The child is wrapped in a tiny deer-skin
blanket, with a small pillow for its head to rest
upon; and then sown up, with its little arms
close to its sides, by string made of the tough
sinews of the invaluable reindeer. In this
rough leathern case the child is perfectly safe,
as only its head is to be seen, and as far as
we were enabled to judge, their babies are not
addicted to crying, those we saw in these tents
being very quiet in behaviour, and grave in
countenance.

The child, when in its curious cradle, requires
no further looking after, until it is in want of
food, and when not engaged in taking its
refreshment, the cradle with its tiny occupant
is hung up by a leathern strap upon the branches
of any convenient tree, where it remains until
its mother thinks fit to " take it down." The
Laps are said to sing nursery ditties to their
progeny, and the most approriate one certainly
would be "Hush-a-bye, baby, upon the tree
top"!

The wind, when blowing freshly, literally executes in first-rate style the office of nurse, by swinging the cradle backwards and forwards, but with oftentimes a rather more rough style than English "mammas" would sanction. When not hanging on the branch of a birch-tree, the cradle and its inmate is thrown aside into a corner of the tent until wanted, or laid upon the beds which we saw in all these dwellings, and which are constructed of birch twigs, where the entire family repose at night, huddled together, and covered only by skins of the reindeer. The Laps always sleep in their clothes; and such articles of domestic luxury as blankets, sheets, and pillows are quite unknown to these hardy folk.

The fire, which is kept constantly alight both night and day, is in the centre of the hut, and is arranged upon a circular layer of large flat stones, over which are suspended from the roof, immense iron pots in which the food of the family is cooked.

A meal was just about to be commenced when we entered the first of the four tents, the repast being "served" in one of the afore-mentioned iron cauldrons, and was said to consist of soup with large lumps of reindeer venison, though it was hard to see what its nature really was, so terribly thick was the smoke and steam which filled the crowded apartment that we were nearly blinded. Each member of the family was armed with a large bone spoon, manufactured by the Laps out of that part of the reindeer's horn which is strongest and thickest, being just at the place where it joins the skull.

At a given signal every one stood up round the steaming cauldron, and at once thrust the pieces of meat, which must have been absolutely at boiling heat, into their mouths with their spoons. Men, women, children, and servants all attend these "feeds" at one and the same time; and there appears to be no distinction drawn between masters and servants, excepting that we were told when it happens that a Lap serving in the capacity of a domestic extracts an especially fat and savoury piece of venison from the public "pot," the custom is for him at once to hand the tit-bit to his superior, who seldom is sufficiently bashful to decline it.

The life of these primitive people is said to be remarkably happy, and free from care; and Linnæus, in his " Flora Lapponica," has described the felicity of their simple habits in the following words :—

" O favour'd race ; whom partial Heaven design'd
To free from all the cares that vex mankind:
In life's mad scenes while wayward nations join,
One silent corner of the world is thine;
From busy toil, from raging passions free,
And war, dire stain of lapsed humanity !
Far from thy plains the hideous monster roves,
Nor dares pollute thy consecrated groves.
Indulgent Nature yields her free supplies,
And bids thy simple food around thee rise.
Along thy shores the scaly myriads play,
And gathering birds pursue their airy way.
Gurgles to quench thy thirst the crystal spring,
And ranging herds their milky tribute bring.
No fell disease attacks thy hardy frame,
Or damps with sullen cloud the vital flame ;
But flies to plague amid their tainted sky,
The sick'ning sons of full-fed luxury.
Thy aged sires can boast a cent'ry past,
And life's clear lamp burns briskly to the last.
In woods and groves beneath the trembling spray,
Glides on, in sweet content, thy peaceful day :

Gay exercise, with ruddy health combined,
And, far beyond the rest, the freedom of the mind.
Here stands secure, beneath the northern zone,
O sacred Innocence, thy turf-built throne:
'Tis here thou wav'st aloft thy snowy wings,
Far from the pride of Courts and pomp of Kings."

Among the large flocks of eider fowl that we saw to-day, more than one pair of the beautiful King Duck (*Anas spectabilis*), or " King Eider," more properly speaking, was noticed. This splendidly-plumaged bird is by no means numerous in Lapland, though fairly common in Spitzbergen and Novaya Zemlya. Its down is as much esteemed by the Greenlanders as that of the common eider.

PAIR OF KING EIDER DUCKS.

CHAPTER X.

> "Reindeer, not in fields like ours,
> Full of grass and bright with flowers;
> Not on hills where verdure bright
> Clothes them to the topmost height,
> Is thy dwelling; nor dost thou
> Feed beneath the orange-bough;
> Thou wast made to fend and fare
> In a region bleak and bare,
> In a dreary land of snow,
> Where green weeds can scarcely grow!
> Where the skies are grey and drear;
> Where 'tis night for half the year;
> Reindeer, where, unless for thee,
> Human dweller could not be."—HOWITT.

To the scene of felicity pictured in the poem at the close of the last chapter, there are, however, in reality serious drawbacks. The weather is bitterly cold in the dreary winter season in this bleak Lapland, and the rays of the sun are never seen for several months; but a provident nature gives the Lap, in its place, the aurora borealis.

In the summer months also the climate is by no means an enviable one, as when that season is at its full height, the heat is often almost unbearable, and the brightly blazing sun throughout the night as well as all day, must be very wearying after the charm of novelty has worn off. In hot weather the legions of mosquitoes are perfectly marvellous, and there is hardly any escape from their assaults, unless the plan adopted by the natives be followed, which consists in anointing the face with a composition of tar and milk, and which is said to be an excellent, though slightly odoriferous safeguard.

During this present season, as far as our experience goes up to this date, there has been no hot weather here, and we would gladly feel a little warmer; and as for the mosquito veils which we brought from England, they have never yet been unpacked. The Laps tell us that it has been a very long winter, and consequently a backward summer. To the Laps themselves this change of season does not much matter, as they have no crops, buying what flour they require for food from the nearest town.

The life of the farmer in these northern regions must be a very anxious one, as it not unfrequently happens that his crops do not ripen at all. Sometimes, however, a good harvest is secured, and so rapidly does barley grow that it is stated it will sprout a length of more than two and a quarter inches in twenty-four hours, and this for several consecutive days. At the latitude of 65°, peas have been found to grow three inches in a like period. The shortness of the nights, and the continual presence of the sun, is of course the cause of this rapid progress of vegetation; and the grass even grows and flourishes beneath its warm covering of snow. The extraordinary growth of barley may be better understood when it is stated that the annual harvest in Finmark is sown, grows, and is reaped and gathered into the garner, in the incredibly short space of about three months! Thus we were informed, that the crop of barley is sown in the neighbourhood of Tromsö at the beginning of June, or at the end of May; it attains its full growth by July, or early in August, and the "harvest-home" is all over before the 1st of September.

For these remarkable effects of the warmth of the short Lapland summer, the Gulf Stream has to answer to a considerable degree, as its waters touch Norway somewhere near the 62° of latitude, whence it continues in a northerly direction round the entire line of coast, to the borders of Russia. The climate on these parts of the coast of Norway and Lapland is consequently wonderfully mild, when one takes into consideration that latitude 70°, a little to the south of which Tromsö is situated, is the same parallel of latitude under which are the cold, bleak, and ice-bound regions of Baffin Land, Victoria Land, Disco, and King William Island, near the northern extremity of which the "Erebus" and "Terror" were abandoned!

The great discrepancy in temperature in various parts of western Scandinavia is well set forth in "Sport in Norway," where the author, in speaking of the Gulf Stream, remarks that it is owing to its influence that the "mean temperature at the North Cape and at Christiania, during the winter months, though these places are separated from each other by 12° of latitude, is the same."

"But," he continues, "on penetrating for a few miles into the interior, out of the influence of the sea air, the cold in winter is intense to a degree, while the heat in summer is equally oppressive. Thus, at Valle, in Sætersdal, lat. 59°, lying at an altitude of 1000 feet above the sea, the thermometer in summer may stand at $+42°$ Cent., and in winter fall to $-35°$!"

Before bidding adieu to our friends the Laps, they offered to us for sale some curiously wrought spoons, made from the reindeer's horns. These spoons were from seven to eight inches in length, the bowls being the broadest part and some three inches in diameter; the handles were carved in a very rough but fantastic manner, the fancy designs being carved with a very sharp knife. We invested in four of these spoons, and also in one of the woollen girdles of brightly coloured materials worn by the Lap women. The price of the horn spoons was about one shilling apiece, and the girdle was double that price. The women also offered to our notice some of their boots, called "komager," made of the skin of reindeer with the fur outside; but they asked such high prices that we declined to buy any, and I afterwards got a pair at Tromsö from a Norwegian merchant at a far lower sum. These "komager" are picturesque boots enough, and are generally adorned with yellow or red braid, being stitched with thread made out of the sinews of the tame deer. The boots ordinarily used by the Laps reach to the ankle, and are turned up at the toe, and have the long fur on the inside, being far warmer and more durable than if it were on the outside, where it would speedily be worn out.

Some of the girls were engaged in making these boots, ready to be offered no doubt to the coming tourists; and others were hard at work, engaged in the manufacture of long lines for deep-sea fishing. These lines are like their thread, made out of the strongest sinews of the reindeer. Their mode of "spinning" this thread is curious. The woman takes three or four pieces of the tendon, places them alongside each other, and by a somewhat lengthy process of rubbing, and a constant application of saliva from the mouth, she at last weaves the fibres together, in such an extraordinary manner that it will be found very hard indeed for a man to break one of these rudely-made fishing-lines.

I have already said that the Laps as a rule are remarkably dirty, and that they invariably exhibit great greediness in their dealings with travellers; but I feel bound to state that it is universally admitted that they are a strictly honest people, and this I firmly believe. They try to get the utmost they can out of you; but, having once concluded a bargain, they never wish to back out of it.

These little folks are very attentive to their religious duties, whenever a place of worship happens to be within a reasonable distance of their encampment; and they will even sometimes travel a long way in order to go to church. If they are far from a church, as is often the case in summer when up on the fjelds, the member of the family who has had the best education reads the service to the rest. They form a quiet and attentive congregation so long as the clergyman happens to please them; but should his ideas, or his mode of expounding religious truths, not quite fall in with their own views on the subject, the Laps manifest their disapprobation by loudly shuffling their feet upon the floor, and actually by groaning aloud in concert!

The healthiness of these diminutive folk is marvellous, considering that the vice of drunkenness prevails to a great extent among them, their favourite beverage being a very strong spirit, called "finkel," distilled from corn and potatoes. They are so hardy, however, that it is said they will often fall into a ditch dead-drunk, and remain there until perhaps half covered with snow, and becoming sober again, go on their way as if nothing had happened. The women are as bad as their lords and masters for their addictiveness to strong liquors. If the traveller desires to win the heart of these people, he need only give them a present of a bottle of brandy or a little tobacco. The Laps are great smokers also, their pipes being always in their mouths; their pipes are objects of the greatest care, and the men carefully clean them with the bill of a curlew or other long-billed bird, which is kept carefully in a case made out of the leg of the wild swan. The women are as much addicted to smoking as are their husbands.

The Lap seldom requires the services of a doctor, and if he did it would be useless, as these luxuries are few and very far between in Finmark. When the poor Laplander is brought to the bed of sickness, it is probably his last illness, as these hardy people will struggle on to the last, and are so unacquainted with disease that they are seldom attacked with any serious ailment until their last hour draws nigh. They are an extremely superstitious people, and put great faith in the signs of the stars, the sun, moon, aurora borealis, and the like natural phenomena; and like the augurs of old they direct their attention to the flight of birds, which they regard as omens for good or evil.

The food of the Lap is simple in the extreme, "fläd-bröd," and fish, and what game they can shoot, forming the only additions to the flesh of their tame reindeer, which of course forms the principal article of diet. This useful creature gives its owner meat, soup, milk, and excellent butter; cheese and hams; coats, cloaks, caps, boots, blankets and bedding, thread and fishing-lines; harness for the deer to be driven with; besides a variety of other useful articles, such as forks and spoons from its horns, and others too numerous to mention.

The reindeer is to the Laplander the truest source of riches. Money, in their uninhabited land, is of little service to the Laps, but their deer supply every want, given as they are to those poor "dwellers in tents" by a watchful Providence. Those Laps are accounted richest, and are most looked up to by their fellows, who possess the most reindeer; the family which we visited to-day have about four hundred deer, but they were all away on the fjeld, and not nearer than twenty miles from the encampment, so that we had not sufficient time to spare to await their arrival, which our hosts were anxious for us to do.

The most opulent Lap in the neighbourhood of Kvalöe Island is said to possess as many as ten thousand deer, but this sounds very like an exaggerated statement. He has, at all events, an immense large herd of these useful animals; and although so wealthy, differs in behaviour and in his manner of life in no degree from his inferiors, but sleeps in the same tent with them and eats out of the public "pot." The reindeer gives so little milk that it is said, at least three hundred of these animals are required to form the support of a family of half-a-dozen persons. The Laps make a large sum of money annually by bartering the skins of those deer which have died or have been slaughtered for food, and large prices are obtained by them for the horns and tanned hides, which are resold at a considerable profit by the merchants in the villages and at those ports where the steamers call; and by the time the skins reach Throndhjem they are generally quadrupled in price.

The horns are sometimes of great size, in the tame as well as in the wild species; I have seen pairs which branch as much as four and a half feet in the widest part. And so tall does the animal appear, when lying down, that its horns even when in that position will reach as high as an ordinary man's shoulder. During the summer months the herds of tame reindeer are kept in the fjelds, on the snowy wastes of which they can only exist in very warm weather, as their food, the moss (*Cenomyce rangiferina*) called after their own name, only grows in luxuriance at a considerable altitude, where also the animals are not so annoyed by the continuous attacks of the innumerable mosquitoes which swarm in the valleys and by the sea-coast. Without the moss the Lap would be a pauper, as without it his deer would die, but luckily for both master and beast it flourishes in ample abundance. While in search of this food the deer often wander great distances, and are accompanied by men or boys to watch that they do not stray too far, and dogs are used to collect the herd when scattered. When food grows scarce in one spot, deer and owners must perforce move on to the next district where it is to be obtained.

The whole life of the Laplanders is, in short, made up of wandering from place to place in order to obtain food for their deer, and thus for themselves. A good fat reindeer weighs about one hundred and thirty or one hundred and forty pounds, or even more, so that a large supply of fresh meat is obtained when one of the creatures is killed. The skins sell, on an average, for about four shillings or four and sixpence apiece; and the horns of a single deer fetch from three to five shillings a pair, the price depending on the size and quality. Besides being useful for the manufacture of forks, spoons, and knife-handles, the horns when boiled down make very good glue. The rough coats with which the deer are furnished during the winter months fall off in summer time, and the hair is sold for stuffing pillows and mattresses, but I should think such a bed would have a very " high " scent !

When the Lap wishes to kill a deer, he does so by thrusting a very sharp knife into the back of the creature's head, which separates the brain from the spinal marrow, causing instantaneous death. The knife is then at once imbedded in the heart, when all the blood will be found in the stomach. The whole of the animal, with hardly any exception, is good for human food; the saddle being thought the choicest part, and this the Lap generally reserves for his own eating, as it is the fattest flesh on the deer. I can testify to the steaks cut from a freshly-killed animal being most excellent, and quite as good as the best English or Scotch venison. The hams, which the Lap smokes and dries, are very good eating, as are also the reindeer tongues, many of which are exported from Tromsö, Hammerfest, and other places, and eventually find their way to Fortnum and Mason's.

In one important respect the Laps differ from the Norwegians, who are always glad to get as much work out of their women as possible, while the little Lap treats the female portion of his family with far more consideration. The Lap women of course take care of the household and of their children, and also make the principal portion of the stock of clothes, fishing-lines, and the like, for the men, but they are never called upon to carry heavy burdens, nor do they as a rule assist in collecting the deer for the purpose of milking; but that operation is generally, though not invariably, done by the women, after the animals have been captured by the men, and brought to a standstill. This is, however, by no means a very easy operation, as the deer occasionally object to being caught, which is effected by means of a long lasso cast around the horns of the does, which are then easily approached and the milking begins.

Each female reindeer does not produce much more than sufficient milk to fill an ordinary tea-cup, so that it can easily be believed that a great many does have to be relieved of their milk before enough for the Lap family is obtained. But it ought to be remembered that this milk, though deficient in quantity, is remarkably rich in quality; and it is thick in substance, very nourishing, and so rich that it tastes much more like cream than milk.

The Laps with whom we conversed to-day, though living so near to the sea, where fish could easily be obtained in abundance, did not seem to trouble themselves with anything but the care of their deer, nor did we see any dried cod among their little stock of provisions. Their food is generally kept in a sort of "larder" at a little distance from their tents; and this storehouse merely consists of a raised platform of birch branches, at a height of five or six feet from the ground to be out of reach of dogs and children. When travelling during the winter from place to place in the mountains, the Laps sometimes leave a small supply of food in a rough kind of box, which is placed on the top of a long pole and stuck into the ground, so as to be ready for them if they return that way. And it not unfrequently happens that before the owner revisits his larder, the contents have all been removed by some animal or bird, the glutton (*Gulo borealis*) especially being a frequent thief, as he is an excellent climber.

Besides those Laplanders who are fortunate enough to possess a herd of deer, there are some born under a far less lucky star, and these drag out a very different existence to that of their richer relatives, having to subsist almost entirely on fish. These people are termed "Fisk Lappar," and generally dwell near the sea-shore, not as a rule in the tents which I have already described, but in miserable hovels constructed of turf and stones, which are even more unbearably hot and stuffy, and indescribably more dirty, than the tents of the "Fjeld Laps."

The one great use of the reindeer to its owner in winter is that it makes the most excellent beast of burden that could be found, few other animals having the same special formation of foot which enables the reindeer to travel over the wastes of snow at a great pace.

The foot of the great moose of the Canadian forests is remarkably ill adapted for travelling over the snow, in which his sharp and pointed hoof sinks deep at every step; but that of the reindeer, being hollow and light, and furnished with rounded edges, enables its fortunate possessor to be a proficient in the art of " making tracks," as our American cousins would express it.

The reindeer is all in all to the Lap; and is even more valuable to him than is the camel, the "ship of the desert," to the Bedawy Arab. Graphically and truly has Mary Howitt, in one of her pretty poems, described this animal:—

> " When thou wast at first design'd
> By the great Creative Mind—
> With thy patience and thy speed;
> With thy aid for human need;
> With thy foot so framed to go
> Over frozen wastes of snow;
> Thou for frozen lands wast meant,
> Ere the winter's frost was sent;
> And in love God sped thee forth
> To thy home, the barren North,
> Where He bade the rocks produce
> Bitter lichens for thy use.
> What the camel is, thou art—
> Strong of frame, and strong in heart!
> Serving man with right goodwill;
> Asking but a scant reward;

> Of the snow a short repast,
> Or the mosses cropt in haste:
> Then away! with all thy strength,
> Speeding him the country's length."

The sledge, which is termed "pulk," in which the Laplanders travel from spot to spot in winter, is an oddly-shaped conveyance. It is just large enough to hold a man seated comfortably in the bottom with his back resting against the rear-board of the sledge. The curious appearance of the "vehicle" is added to by its depth being much greater than its total length, and it looks somewhat like a tiny, half-decked fishing-boat, as it is furnished with a seal-skin covering over the fore part, which prevents its being filled with snow. The bottom is, as a rule, covered with the skin of a deer, care being taken to turn the hair so as to glide with ease over the ground. It is furnished with a broad keel, on which it runs with great ease, but it is a difficult task for a novice to keep his balance, as the reader will find out for himself if he tries. Unless the inmate keeps his body exactly in the centre of the sledge, it at once capsizes, but as the ground on which a fall occurs is nearly always soft, no harm ensues from an overthrow beyond the inconvenience and the filling of one's gloves with snow, and getting oftentimes a good supply down one's neck.

One of the most amusing sights to be met with in Lapland is when a family is moving from one camp to another during winter, and the herd of reindeer, the Lap household packed tightly in their sledges, the deer-steeds, which are often very refractory, the barking of the dogs, the shouts of the drivers, and the picturesque costume of the women, and lastly, the grandeur of the scenery, lighted up perhaps by the aurora, combine to make the wildest picture imaginable.

Whilst the Lap sits in his sledge, which speeds through the cold wintry air at a great rate, he would run a considerable risk of being frozen, did he not take the precaution of wearing a very loose dress of deer-skin, filled with soft grass (*Carex sylvatica*), which is very warm and promotes free circulation.

The reindeer is " broken in " to sledge work when quite young; and although it is popularly believed that they are very docile creatures, the Laps frequently experience much difficulty before they are safe to drive. The harness is very primitive, and consists of a strong reindeer hide collar round the animal's neck; and from the bottom of this collar stretches a long trace between the creature's legs, and attached to a ring in the front of the sledge, while round the middle of his body is bound a broad cloth band, through the lower part of which the before-mentioned trace passes. A bell round the neck, a head-stall made of a strip of seal-skin which is fastened under the ear, and a single long rein of the same material attached to the head-stall under the *left* ear, completes the list. The driver holds this rein in the *right* hand, which at first appears to the observer rather remarkable, but this is necessary in order that the deer may be brought quickly to a standstill, which is effected by swinging the rein very suddenly round to the left side. The rein is also useful in place of a whip, when it has of course to be held in the right hand, though it naturally continually keeps getting over to the left side.

These so-called "tame" reindeer are by no means always docile to drive; and it not unfrequently happens that the animal, from sudden caprice, will turn suddenly round and attack its master in a very savage manner. Under these circumstances, the master has need of the utmost dexterity in jumping out of his sledge, which he at once turns upside down, and covering himself with his "carriage" remains *caché* until the deer has tired itself in butting the sledge with its horns, which have the points taken off, so that little harm ensues. The attack over, out creeps the little Laplander, rights his conveyance, and proceeds once more merrily on his journey.

These tame deer are decidedly on the whole far smaller animals than the truly wild species, from which they were originally descended, but some of them have very fine heads; though I fancy that the in-and-in breeding, which has gone on for so many years amongst the domesticated herds, must have helped to a very great degree to cause them to deteriorate both in size and strength.

Many of the deer, however, seem to be really much attached to their masters, and will readily follow the women about the camp, and take food from the hands of the children. Their legs and hoofs make a very odd crackling sound as they walk along; and when I have heard a large herd of the wild species going over the fjelds in winter, the noise they make when trotting resembled a constant succession of crackers exploding.

The deer have a wonderful instinct given them for finding out the whereabouts of the moss on which they feed, when the country is snow-covered, and they will dig with their feet to a great depth in their search for this food. They almost invariably sleep upon the snow, and even bury themselves under its warm surface; some travellers who have seen a herd thus concealed say that nothing is to be seen of them but the very tips of the horns! By this means, they certainly would defeat their persistent foes, the flies and mosquitoes.

A reindeer drawing its sledge can cover a long distance in a day; twenty or thirty miles without halting being, I believe, an average journey. It is possible, however, for the reindeer to travel as long a distance as even sixty miles, for this animal is very strong and "plucky," and never gives in till the last. If it arrives at its journey's end very much fatigued, it generally dies within a few days; but the Laps are always most considerate and kind to their patient steeds, as indeed they ought to be.

But I fear my readers must have tired by this time of this somewhat lengthy description of the Laps and their habits, and of the life-history of their faithful allies, the reindeer.

So, I will only add, that after bidding adieu to the Laps at the encampment, we took to our boat once more, and made an expedition, which took us some miles out of our way, in search of a second family of the little folks, who were said to possess a very large herd of reindeer;

but after a long and very cold row in the cutting northerly wind, which had risen considerably since the morning, we arrived at the mouth of a little river, at the head of a bay some way to the south of the first encampment, and our boat here thinking fit to stick in the mud, we sent one of our crew ashore, to find out if the deer were at hand.

He then waded to the land, and held a noisy conversation with a solitary Lap, who stated that the herd (as usual) were up on the fjeld, but that they would be down in two hours' time at the tents. It would have been beyond a joke, however, to have had to sit still in the boat for that period; so we were obliged to decide, though with great regret, to return to Tromsö without delay. The cold was increasing every moment, and we had a very rough row homewards, the water splashing into the tiny boat considerably more than was pleasant.

When about half-way to Tromsö, we passed a large rudely-built boat, containing some seven or eight Laps, both men and women, some of the latter of whom were rowing away sturdily.

The men were dressed in their best suits, red tunics trimmed with yellow braid, and some of the women had a great deal of green and blue in their no less gaudy costumes.

The only other object of interest to us on our homeward passage was a fine golden eagle, which we watched for a long time as he soared, on apparently motionless wings, high up in the grey sky. I had a line overboard, with a "spinning" minnow attached, during most of the day, but no fish were captured, owing, I think, to the fact that our men rowed so slowly, that the proper motion was not given to the bait, and it continually got foul of the bottom, so shallow and rocky was the water.

Many of the islands near Tromsö swarm with wild fowl, and there are a fair number of ptarmigan on some of the larger islands; but in most cases leave will have to be obtained before the traveller can shoot the latter, but a duck-punt in the shallow fjord in fine weather would afford grand sport, but of course such a craft would be very unsafe in the open sea.

By the time our boat landed us at the little

pier in Tromsö, it was nearly six o'clock, our
expedition having taken us about eight hours.
The evening turned out bitterly cold, and we
were glad to be once more on dry land, where
we soon warmed ourselves by running at a good
pace up to the hotel, where a good dinner
awaited us. I afterwards went to some of the
"shops" in the principal street of Tromsö, but
the largest of them were merely large storehouses, and the miscellaneous collection of wares,
which were hung up upon huge nails on all sides
to tempt the purchaser, was most remarkable to
behold. The windows of the store which I
visited first were completely filled with tar-
paulin coats, caps, and "sou'-westers," of all
the hues of the rainbow, green and yellow being
the most favourite colours. Thick woollen gloves
of huge size, and ornamented with the brightest
colours, were displayed in bundles upon the
counter, and were exactly similar to those I
have bought from the Shetlanders, and which
are principally made by the poor natives of the
"Fair Isle." Over the entrance sample pairs
of mackintosh "trouserings" flapped to and

fro in the breeze, side by side with strings of reindeer's tongues; and bales of rope and string nearly filled up the approach to the "magasin," whilst the contents of innumerable barrels of tar filled the air with an unsavoury odour. Brightly burnished guns from Birmingham, of great length of barrel, and with a very light weight of metal, were for sale here; as well as shot of all sizes, and plenty of coarse-grained gunpowder.

Some Laps were haggling over the price of a box of enormous hooks for fishing when I entered, in exchange for which they were bartering pairs of "komager," the boots made of reindeer skin previously described. Worsted nightcaps of two feet in length, thousands of sea-fishing lines and hooks of various sizes, bone-handled knives and forks, long boots of brown leather, to reach above the knee, and the usual amount of groceries (in which rum, brandy, and gin greatly predominated), made up the stock-in-trade of the merchant.

These articles, at least, were all that were to be seen in the shop proper, but on my inquiring if any walrus tusks were for sale, Herr Ebeltoft (for such was the merchant's name) asked me to look "upstairs." In order to get there, however, one had to climb after the fashion of a monkey, up a perfectly perpendicular ladder of some twenty feet in height; having done which with some difficulty, as many of the steps were broken away through age, I was shown into a large low room, some thirty feet square, completely filled with thousands of pairs of reindeers' horns, piled in masses one on top of the other till they touched the ceiling.

Some of these horns were remarkably fine ones, and having obtained candles, as the room was in perfect darkness, I selected after some trouble ten of the largest pairs, for which I was of course asked to pay exactly double the price eventually agreed upon, which certainly was very reasonable, being about four shillings and sixpence per pair. The sum asked in Bergen and other towns in the south of Norway is about three times this amount, and often more.

Herr Ebeltoft had also a large supply of tusks of the walrus (*Trichechus rosmarus*), called by the Laps "Morsk," which were tightly packed in boxes in one corner of the loft. The price of the finest pair I could select from amongst many hundreds of tusks, was six shillings the pair; and they were exceedingly long tusks, and nearly three inches in circumference at the place where they were sawn off from the creature's skull. When I returned to England I had this pair of tusks cut in half, when the thinner portion made a capital pair of handles for carvers for a round of beef, and the slightly-curved part of the tusk fits one's hand very nicely when using them.

The tusks of the walrus fetch a fair price in the Continental market, though not nearly so valuable as elephant ivory is. Dentists purchase walrus tusks to a certain extent for the manufacture of artificial teeth, but an eminent London dentist told me a short time ago that the "best teeth" are never made from the walrus, which would be far too brittle when cut into the small portions necessary for making artificial "grinders," and would be besides too white in colour.

The tusks of the walrus are of great weight, and its blubber is of considerable value. The oil obtained from a full-grown walrus is stated to be as much as half a ton, and I believe fetches a higher price than does that of the whale. In parts of Arctic America, such as Greenland, the natives make various tools for domestic purposes, and weapons for hunting, out of its ivory. In many parts of the Arctic regions it is becoming year by year less common, and if walrus-hunting is carried on to the extent it is at the present day in Spitzbergen, Novaya Zemlya, and other northern lands, the time cannot be far distant when it will cease to exist.

HEAD OF THE REINDEER.

CHAPTER XI.

"Up, up! let us a voyage take;
　Why sit we here at ease?
Find us a vessel tight and snug,
　Bound for the Northern Seas.
I long to see the northern lights,
　With their rushing splendours, fly,
Like living things, with flaming wings,
　Wide o'er the wondrous sky.
There shall we see the fierce white bear;
　The sleepy seals aground;
And the spouting whales, that to and fro
　Sail with a dreary sound.
And whilst the unsetting sun shines on
　Through the still heaven's deep blue,
We'll traverse the azure waves, the herds
　Of the dread sea-horse to view."
　　　　　　　　　WILLIAM HOWITT.

THE excellent description given above of the sights to be seen in Arctic seas is very true and vivid; but the traveller would be obliged to leave the coast of Lapland far behind, and to steer his bark due north if he wished to fall in with the sea-horse and the grim Polar bear. Whales in some numbers, and of several species, are to be found upon the Norwegian coast, and we often pass the choicest haunts of the seal as we steam amongst the rocky, uninhabited islands of both Lapland and Norway.

The white bear (*Ursus maritimus*) is but very rarely seen in Lapland; any individual that may have occurred has been probably brought upon a drifting iceberg from the inhospitable shores of Spitzbergen or Cherry Island. The habits of this ferocious creature have been so well described in Lamont's "Yachting in the Arctic Seas," that it would be superfluous to repeat the observations of others here. I believe that most of the skins of the white bear which come to Tromsö and Hammerfest are brought by Russian whalers from Novaya Zemlya, and by the Norwegian walrus sloops from Spitzbergen; but the sailors, as a rule, skin the few bears that they may be lucky enough to shoot so badly, that all the skins I saw for sale in Tromsö were not worth buying at any price.

There seems, from what the traders told me, to be no doubt that the polar bear is becoming scarcer every year, owing to the ever-increasing number of hunters that pursue the exciting trade of walrus and seal shooting, and harpooning in these northern waters. The principal food of this bear appears to be the seal, and as his whereabouts depends on the movements of the *cetacea*, he is generally to be met with in places where they are most abundant.

The digestive powers of the bear must be enormous, as he can eat an entire seal at one meal, but he sometimes pays forfeit with his life for his greediness, as the following anecdote from Mr. Lamont's work will show. When near the entrance to the Kara Sea, in 1868, after a heavy fog, which had prevailed on the previous day, had cleared off, Mr. Lamont's yacht was passing through a small stream of ice, when a round, yellowish mass was observed lying upon a slab of ice. "With the glass," says Mr. Lamont, "I made it out to be a bear fast asleep beside the krang of a seal; the engine was stopped, and I went at him in the small boat. He had evidently gorged himself with seal, and was so sound asleep, we might have rowed up to his very nose. At fifty yards, however, I fired, and gave him my favourite shot in the shoulder. He sprang to his feet with a terrific roar, but instantly fell over on his back, and lay roaring and kicking all fours in the air. Another bullet in the chest seemed to revive him, for he took to the sea and swam, but was evidently dying.

"A third shot in the neck now finished him, and we towed him behind the boat to the yacht. The foreyard and the very mast shook and trembled with his weight as we hove him on board. This bear was so old that his canine teeth were broken and carious. Still he was very fat; the blubber weighed two hundred pounds, in addition to which we got a large bucket of internal fat, the veritable bear's-grease, which 'it was a pity,' as my valet once remarked, 'was not worth three-and-sixpence a pot, as in the Burlington Arcade.' In the stomach were the remains of the seal banquet in the shape of three buckets-full of muddy oil. Ye powers! what a digestion!"

The same author, than whom could be no better or keener sportsman, or more plucky sailor, goes on to say that he killed in Spitzbergen, in 1859, the biggest white bear he ever met with, which, being shot whilst swimming, had to be hauled up out of the water on to the ice by means of a noose round the neck, and with the additional help of an ice-anchor and a block and tackle. Its weight was very large, the skin alone being upwards of 100 pounds in weight; he produced nearly 400 pounds of fat, and his entire carcase could not have been less than 1600 pounds. His length was more than eight feet; his body was almost as much in circumference; he stood four and a half feet high to the shoulder, and his fore-paws were thirty-four inches in circumference. This, however, is certainly a very unusual size, but what a perfect Hercules such an animal must be! With such a description before us, we can easily understand the tales related by Arctic sailors of bears slaying walruses of three times their own weight, by suddenly attacking them from the rear, and battering in the skull with blows of their immense paws.

I must not weary the reader with more descriptions from Lamont's most interesting book, but if any one wants to have sport with walrus, bear, reindeer, or seal, he cannot do better than study the "Seasons with the Sea-horses," and the "Yachting in the Arctic Seas;" as both these volumes contain a vast mass of most valuable and *authentic* information.

We noticed in Tromsö harbour several Russian whaling ships, and their crews appeared to be a set of half-tipsy and very savage-looking fellows, if it was fair to judge by their countenances, which were indeed as repulsive as need be. The season of 1875, we were told, had been fairly good for whaling and also for walrus, but the Norwegian walrus sloops are all absent at the present time on their annual hunting expedition.

The chase of this creature is by no means

child's play, and is attended with great risk to both the lives and the limbs of those who engage in it. When the ships approach the ice in the neighbourhood where the walrus is expected to be met with, the long boats, all ready and equipped for the purpose, are kept hanging on the davits, so as to be lowered in a few seconds when the game is sighted. The crew of these boats, which are built of the strongest materials especially for the purpose, as a rule consists of five sailors, one of whom has sole charge of the harpoons. These weapons are very sharp, and have strong shafts; and each harpoon-head has a stout line of fourteen or fifteen fathoms in length, very firmly attached to it. These lines are kept neatly coiled up in small boxes. The un-initiated sportsman would naturally think that a line of this comparatively short length would not be long enough when a walrus is struck; but as we are informed by Lamont that this animal is hardly ever found in water more than fifteen fathoms in depth, the length of line is amply sufficient.

The sport of walrus hunting must be very exciting, and but few *amateurs* have ever engaged in it. The walrus is, if possible, first shot with a large-bored rifle, carrying about nine drams of powder and a heavy bullet, or, better still, by one which carries an explosive shell. After the shot has taken effect, the boat rows up with all possible despatch, and a harpoon is thrust into the wounded beast in order to prevent its sinking, or to frustrate it from its attempts to reach the water, supposing it was upon the ice when shot at. When once the harpoon has fairly entered the flesh, and keeps its hold, the game may be generally accounted as already bagged. The danger and excitement, however, are by no means over, as the animal will exert his utmost power in order to escape, and sometimes will drag the bows of the boat under water, and even occasionally charges it furiously, endeavouring to rend holes in it with his long tusks. Numerous are the accounts I have heard of accidents at the walrus hunting, the boats being often capsized and their inmates drowned; and there is also a danger of the ropes, which are tied to the harpoon, getting entangled around the legs of the men when a walrus is "on," if the greatest care is not exercised.

The walrus is sometimes approached from land, and harpooned when lying asleep on the ice, but it is always safest to give the animal a bullet first if it can be possibly done. The mother-walrus is extremely devoted to her cub, and will defend it to the last if attacked either by man or by the white bear; and in the account given by Captain Cook, when his vessels the "Discovery" and the "Resolution" were returning from Behring's Straits, it is observed that on the approach of one of his boats to the ice on which several walruses were lying with their young ones, all the mothers at once took their cubs under their fins, and endeavoured to escape with them into the open water. "Several," it is added, "whose young were killed and wounded, and were left floating on the surface, rose again and carried them down, sometimes just as our people were going to take them into the boat; and they might be traced bearing them to a great

distance in the water, which was coloured with
their blood. We afterwards observed them
bringing them up at times above the surface, as
if for air, and again diving under it with a
dreadful bellowing. The female, in particular,
whose young had been destroyed and taken into
the boat, became so enraged that she attacked
the cutter, and struck her tusks through the
bottom of it."

On my return from the merchant's storehouse, I found, on reaching the little hotel, that
a number of Laps had arrived from Kvalöe
during my absence, together with six of their
tame reindeer. They demanded a large sum of
money for their trouble in bringing the animals
such a long way, as it seems that somebody (who
it was, never transpired) had ordered them to
come to the hotel to-day. As no one acknowledged having sent the message, a great amount
of wrangling and noisy discussion followed, and
it was eventually settled that Herr Schmidt, the
proprietor of the "hostelrie" was the most
responsible person on the spot, so he was
deputed to arrange matters, and they went

away quite satisfied with what was given them.

These Laps were, if possible, even more hideous in features than those we had seen in the morning, and as we went down to the steamboat-pier at eleven o'clock, they were evidently enjoying themselves vastly, and more than one of the little folk looked decidedly "groggy" on his legs, and we feared they had been spending at least a certain portion of their gains in the purchase of that execrable spirit "finkel," to which they are so sadly addicted.

I should mention that all sorts of land-birds were notably scarce in the neighbourhood of Tromsö, with the one exception of our familiar English summer-friend the cuckoo (*Cuculus canorus*), whose well-known voice we heard throughout the whole of the Arctic night, as well as at all times of the day, while we remained in these northern latitudes. Indeed, the cuckoo would not find it an easy task to mark any difference betwixt day and night, so exactly do they resemble one another as to lead to sad confusion, not only among the birds as to their roosting-time, but also to the human species!

We have decided that one of the greatest drawbacks to our personal comfort north of the Arctic Circle, was the difficulty of obtaining a truly refreshing sleep. It was of course easy enough to get into bed and shut one's eyes, but as there are not such things as blinds or shutters to the Tromsö windows, it was excessively hard to go to sleep with the strong beams of a bright midnight sun streaming in one's face. It was certainly novel just at first, but that sensation speedily wore off, and we found the everlasting sunshine rather monotonous, and were not altogether sorry when the time came when it was necessary for us to bid adieu to Tromsö, and again return on board the "Nordland" for our southward voyage.

Before quitting this primitive northern town, perhaps never to return to it, I must not omit to notice a custom which prevails here, and which will not fail to attract the attention of the traveller. Great precautions against the outbreak of fire have to be taken, as I have previously mentioned, in all the larger cities of

Norway, on account of all the buildings being made of wood; and it is to ensure the safeguard of the city that a watchman is stationed in the tower of the loftiest church in Tromsö, and the visitor will hear his sing-song voice, every quarter of an hour throughout the night, proceeding from the steeple overhead. This quaint but useful custom is of very ancient date; and it is curious to listen to the lugubrious tone of the watchman's voice, as he shows the public his vigilance by chanting some doggerel lines, having reference to the weather and the time of the night or day, the whole oddly mixed up with a verse from the Bible, or a species of "summons to prayer," which vividly recalled to my mind the banks of the far-away Nile, where we used to lie lazily on the deck of our *dahabieh* in the calm evenings, listening to the voice from the minarets of the village mosques echoing over the shining bosom of the historic river.

The watchman in the tower of Tromsö church appears to be most partial to the following words, which he repeats in a loud voice:—

> "Unless the Lord our city keep,
> The watcher wakes in vain."

A favourite rhyme in the south of Norway, which the sentinel shouts from his point of vantage commences "Ho, vægter, i ho!" &c., which is translated literally by Mr. Shepard[1] thus,—

> "Ho, the watchman, ho!
> The clock has struck ten,
> Praised be God our Lord!
> Now has the time come,
> In bed to lay us down,
> The housewife and her maid,
> The master and his lad.
> The wind is south-east,
> Hallelujah! praised be
> God our Lord."

Before going on board our steamer, we purchased at a store two capitally made dolls, representing most truly the costume of a Laplander and his wife, and I beg to recommend to any future visitor to Tromsö these dolls as excellent gifts for small folk in England, their gaudy dresses and quaintly shaped headgear ensuring their being highly appreciated.

[1] "Over the Dovrefjelds," page 142.

The owner of this "house of merchandise," for a more heterogeneous collection of goods for sale could hardly have been brought together in one place, kindly gave me a sample of the thread made out of the tendons of the reindeer by the Laps; and he also presented me with a small packet of grass of a dull green colour, and neatly tied up with the afore-mentioned deer-thread. We were quite at a loss at first to imagine any use to which this little bundle of grass could possibly be put; but the merchant at once explained that it was "rein" grass. It seems that at certain times of the year the Laps are accustomed to tether their tame deer to a stick fixed in the earth in the vicinity of their camp; and the cord being quite short, the animal can only wander over a space of a few yards distant from his tethering-post. The ground is generally nearly destitute of any herbage in the spots where the Laps encamp, and the animals are supplied with cut grass and moss brought down from the mountains; but in a very short time the manure deposited by the deer causes a long grass, of a dull greenish colour, to spring up around the post, which is then removed to a fresh spot at a short distance. The reindeer appears to thrive upon this grass, of which it is said to be very fond, and this plan certainly must, in a great degree, recommend itself to economical farmers, but I fear no one besides the Laps are likely to breed reindeer for profit!

The particular use of the little bundle of this "rein" grass which was given me was next explained, and we were told that it would act in the same manner as a weather-glass, becoming dried up and brittle, and assuming a very dull colour during, or immediately before, hot weather, and turning green and very limp previously to a heavy rainfall. Of its supposed merits I must admit I was very sceptical, but subsequent experience proved that this curious grass did in reality act as a very fairly accurate barometer, and it certainly is a very curious and inexpensive one.

A small and very leaky boat took us, our reindeer horns, and the little baggage we had, on board the "Nordland" at eleven o'clock p.m.; and having some time to spare before the ship was ready for departure, the captain produced some fishing-lines, with which we amused ourselves for an hour fishing over the stern of the vessel, and finding plenty of cod and haddock (which the Laps call "husse"), of which we hauled up forty-five victims kicking and struggling on to the deck. The lines were each furnished with two large-sized hooks, and were baited with limpets, of which I had taken care to obtain a good supply from the rocks just to the southward of the town.

The sun, although of course we knew it was above the horizon, was not visible to us on board the steamer at midnight, as it was hidden by the snow mountains; but its beams were to be seen lighting up the distant white peaks of the dreary-looking hills, and as the whistle gave the signal to the engineers to start, it was just breaking through the heavy banks of rolling clouds which lined the sky in every direction.

Wednesday, June 28th.

There were but very few passengers from Tromsö on board the "Nordland," and as there was nothing to be seen of any special interest after we had left the town behind, and got clear of the Tromsö-fjord, and as it was dreadfully cold, and the scenery indescribably bleak and dreary, we soon turned in, very well satisfied with what we had seen during our short stay in the Arctic regions, but by no means sorry to have turned our backs for some time, possibly for ever, upon wintry Lapland. In a fortnight's time, probably, the climate will be much more enjoyable, this season being, as I have before stated, a very late one.

As we had enjoyed so little sleep during the last few days, we thought it no disgrace to "take it out" in an extra supply this morning, and consequently did not awake till nearly midday.

The prosperity of Tromsö depends mainly on the trade it carries on in connexion with the cod-fisheries, and the little town swarms with merchants and sailors, and has to a stranger a very animated appearance, though the lower orders are terribly fond of spirits, and drunken-

ness is said to be very bad here, especially
during the long winter, when no work can be
carried on to any extent, owing to the very
short time the sun is above the horizon. At
that season of the year there are only about
four hours of daylight, that is to say, from 10
a.m. until nearly 2 p.m., whereas in the summer time their sun never " sets " for the space
of ten weeks.

Tromsö may be considered decidedly the
"fastest" town north of the Polar circle, and
it has made very rapid strides in the world of
commerce since 1816, when I believe it only
possessed about 300 inhabitants, whereas in
1876 the number has risen to more than 5000.

In order to assist any one who proposes to
make a trip to these northern latitudes, to be
able to see to the best advantage the midnight
sunshine, I have taken the following very
useful table from Mr. Bennett's handbook, by
referring to which the traveller can regulate the
more conveniently the day on which he wishes
to arrive at Hammerfest, Bodö, Tromsö, or
any other special destination.

THE MIDNIGHT SUNSHINE.

Localities for observation.	Bodö 67° 17'.	Tromsö 69° 39'.	Vardö 70° 22'.	Hammerfest 70° 40'.	The North Cape 71° 18'.	To be seen for the first time
The upper rim of the sun	31 May	18 May	14 May	13 May	11 May	
The centre part	2 June	19 "	16 "	14 "	12 "	
The whole sun	4 "	20 "	17 "	15 "	13 "	
The whole sun	8 July	22 July	26 July	27 July	30 July	To be seen for the last time
The centre	10 "	24 "	27 "	28 "	31 "	
The upper rim	12 "	25 "	28 "	29 "	1 August	

And it is worth remembering that if one can ascend a hill 200 or 300 feet in height, with a free horizon, a whole day may be thus gained.

We have already found a remarkable and pleasant alteration in the climate since leaving Tromsö, and although we were still in Lapland proper most of the day, the sun is far warmer than was the case yesterday, and the bitter easterly wind has died away, the water being quite calm, and hosts of eider fowl, gulls, sea-swallows, guillemots, razorbills, and queer little puffins dot its surface on all sides of the ship; and now and then a vast flock of birds suddenly rises into the air with a deafening roar, and we call to mind the lines, beginning,—

> " We'll pass the shores of solemn pine,
>   Where wolves and black bears prowl ;
> And away to the rocky isles of mist,
>   To rouse the northern fowl.
> Up there shall start ten thousand wings,
>   With a rushing, whistling din ;
> Up shall the auk and fulmar start —"

The immense quantity of sea birds in the seas around the Loffoden Islands and off the coast of Finmark is truly marvellous; and if the steam-whistle of the ship is suddenly sounded when passing one of their breeding-cliffs, where they stand sedately in long rows, like a well-behaved white-waistcoated audience at a theatre,—the din caused by the fowl, as they leave the ledges and dash into the air in one darkening cloud, jostling each other roughly in their ludicrous fright, as they tumble off the rocks, is almost deafening, reminding the traveller of the ceaseless roar of a vast city.

The puffin (*Fratercula arctica*) is one of the most odd-looking of all curious sea-fowl, its thick coat of white and black feathers, and its remarkably-shaped bill of orange and blue, together with its "squat" form and bright red legs, all combining to render it a most conspicuous, though scarcely handsome bird. The thousands of puffins that breed year after year in undisturbed security on the rocky islands in the Loffodens is past belief; and their great abundance is, in my opinion, due to a considerable extent to their habit of breeding in cavities among the rocks, or in deserted rabbit-burrows, where they lay their single dull-white egg, which is quite safe from the attacks of hawks, skua-gulls, and other enemies, which wage a never-ending war against the eggs of the other small sea-fowl.

The abundance of the puffins, razorbills, and gulls of all kinds among the Loffodens is also doubtless owing to the large numbers of the fry of the coal-fish (*Gadus carbonarius*) which is very common in the Arctic seas, and indeed on all parts of the coast of Southern Norway.

By midday we were once more in the very heart of the gloriously savage scenery of the Loffodens, whose rugged mountains often seemed to enclose completely the narrow channels through which the "Nordland" steamed, causing them to appear much more like wild inland lakes than arms of the open ocean. We only touched at the small ports of Haerstadt, Sandtorv, Lodingen and Svolvaer, during the day, at all of which places we spent the time pleasantly by letting down our hand-lines over the side of the vessel, and generally catching half a dozen cod or haddock at each stopping point. These fish were small, only scaling some two pounds apiece, but they were always welcomed by the cook, and made a change in the *menu* of the breakfast-table in the saloon.

Considerable excitement was caused on deck, when during the afternoon the sailors had occasion to uncoil a large hawser, and a large weasel, disturbed by the operation from his nap, suddenly dashed out of the coil of rope, and at once put to flight the whole of the ship's company who were standing near. Every one seemed to be much afraid of the unfortunate little creature, and a great hunt was immediately organized by the officers, in which all present joined ; but, after great excitement and a very ludicrous scene on the usually quiet decks, the poor animal finally made good its escape by hiding itself amongst the coal, whence it was impossible to dislodge it. The only remarkable thing about this incident was that it was not easy to account for the weasel's presence in the ship, and the captain supposed that it had come on board to hunt the rats,

which sometimes are very numerous on board
these coasting steamers. The weasel is by no
means common in Lapland, whereas the stoat
(*Mustela erminea*) is very numerous in Finmark,
but is principally confined to the high mountains
inland.

My readers may, I fear, be tired of these
constantly-recurring allusions to the natural
history of the countries through which we are
passing; but I shall make no further excuse for
devoting a few lines to the description of the
habits of that truly northern creature, the Arctic
fox.

This handsome animal (*Canis lagopus*) is fairly
numerous throughout the entire district north of
the Arctic circle, and it is also found on many of
the fjelds of Southern Norway, where it dwells
among the large boulders of rock upon the
mountains. These foxes live in holes, whence
on the approach of any enemy they emerge for
a moment and bark angrily, immediately dis-
appearing if the intruder approaches their hiding-
place; but if not molested their curiosity prompts
them to peep out again, when they are often

shot by the natives, who are aware of this habit of the white fox.

These foxes have handsome coats of long white hair, and are much sought after by furriers. They are very hardy little creatures, being found on many of the almost barren islands in the more northern part of the Arctic seas, to which they must have been brought upon pieces of floating ice.

This is notably the case upon Cherry Island, which is about half-way between Spitzbergen and Finmark, being three degrees south of the former, and about four degrees north of the Finnish mainland.

It is certainly very extraordinary how they can support life in these almost barren wastes, and they are often put to great straits to find sustenance.

In Greenland, for instance, they are said to live principally upon what berries, small shell-fish, and other miscellaneous food, they can discover thrown upon the beach by the sea. These little foxes can run at a great pace; they also can swim well, and the Laplanders say that they often swim from one islet to another, and across rivers, especially when following the migrations of the lemming.

Pennant, in his "Arctic Zoology," mentions that the Greenlanders are accustomed to catch them by means of pit-falls dug in the snow, and carefully concealed, and baited with fish, of which the fox is very fond. Another method of taking them is by means of "springs" constructed roughly of whalebone laid over a hole made in the snow, strewed at the bottom with the Capelin fish,[2] which is a small species of the salmon tribe, exceedingly abundant on the Newfoundland coasts, and much used by the fishermen there as a bait for cod-fishing.

Yet another mode adopted by the Greenlanders for the capture of the Arctic fox consists of traps made like little huts of large flat stones, with a broad one by way of a door, which, when the fox enters the trap and pulls at the piece of meat that hangs upon a string, at once falls and squashes the unlucky animal. The Laplanders, however, seldom I believe kill these

[2] Its specific name is *Mallotus Groenlandicus*.

foxes; but the natives of Greenland turn them to a good use by trading with the skins, and sometimes even eating the flesh; they also make buttons for their coats out of part of the hide, and split the tendons in order to manufacture thread.

The black fox, sometimes called also by the name of silver fox, is a scarce animal, being, I am told, more common on the borders of Northern Russia, than anywhere else in Europe. Its fur is finer and far thicker than that of the white fox, and its dark coat is furnished with long hairs tipped with silver-white, whence it takes its name. The fur of this fox is very valuable, and so much was it esteemed at the beginning of the present century that it was said to be worth its weight in gold. That it is still much appreciated, is proved by our being asked *ten guineas* for a single skin at a furrier's store at Throndhjem, while the white fox was offered for sale at *eight shillings* per skin!

By tea-time, which meal takes place at 5 p.m., we were leaving the Loffodens, and steering south-east for Bodö.

Before I take final leave of Lapland, I may mention that these simple folk are very fond of various childish games and sports. Ordinary gaming-cards are unknown to them, but the Laps are much addicted to the amusement of "fox and geese," which is played with wooden pegs and a large square board. The men are capital hands at wrestling, "which kind of exercises" (to quote the words of Joseph Acerbi, whose "Travels in Sweden, Finland, and Lapland," were undertaken in 1798 and 1799) "are found necessary to keep their bodies warm, as well as to fill up the intervals of leisure, when they are upon a journey, during the stoppages requisite to be made to give their reindeer an opportunity of baiting, for which purpose those animals must dig up the snow in quest of moss, as it is not possible to carry forage with them in their sledges."

Towards the end of the last century, the Laps were very fond of practising throwing the javelin at a mark, a prize, generally consisting of spirits or tobacco, being contended for. "Besides this diversion," says Acerbi, "they have another with a leathern ball stuffed hard, which is struck in the air and caught before it falls to the ground." Another favourite amusement is that of "pull devil, pull baker," the only difference from the English game of the same name being that, instead of a rope, the contending parties hold on to a stout young fir-tree!

Music and dancing are, I believe, quite unknown among the fjeld Laps, nor are they ever heard to sing. The only vocal accomplishment the Lap possesses is the ability to groan in a most dismal manner; and when a Lap congregation in church does not approve of the sermon delivered by the pastor, they at once manifest their disapprobation by shouting and groaning loudly, and continue to shuffle their feet until the clergyman concludes the service abruptly.

I have before stated that doctors are very few and far between in Lapland, and some of the receipts of the natives for curing the sick are most remarkable. Toothache is cured by drinking the warm blood of the seal. This, however, is a comparatively modern remedy, the old cure being to take a splinter from a tree which had been struck by lightning and apply the same to the tooth! Chilblains are treated with an ointment made from reindeer-milk cheese. Ordinary flesh-wounds are healed by the resin of the fir-tree; and before treating a fractured bone the Lap drinks a small piece of brass or silver beaten up into a paste, as this is believed to hasten the cure. Sprained ankles are bound round with the sinews of the fore-leg of the tame reindeer, and they are very careful to observe this particular restriction, namely, that the sinews of the buck only are to be applied to the legs of a female patient, while those of a doe are used exclusively for curing the male Lap.

Quaint old Acerbi tells us that the Laplanders make it a rule, " on the birth of a child to assign a female reindeer, with all her future offspring, as a provision when the boy or girl shall be grown up, which he or she becomes entitled to, however the estate may be disposed of, at the decease of the parents. By this provision, the child sometimes becomes the owner of a considerable herd."

Their funerals, according to the same author, were, at the time he wrote, conducted with but scant ceremony. The body, only slightly wrapped up in a coarse cloth, was borne to the place of burial, attended by a few friends, for whose entertainment a repast of reindeer venison, soup, and some spirits was prepared. " It was an ancient custom with the Laplanders to bury those who excelled in shooting with the bow, or with fire-arms, in the ground consecrated to the rites performed in honour of their deities. The sepulchre is no other than an old sledge, which is turned bottom upwards over the spot where the body lies buried. Another circumstance prevailed amongst the Laplanders before their entire conversion to Christianity; namely, that they place an axe with a tinder-box, by the side of the corpse, if that of a man, and if a woman's, her scissors and needle, supposing these implements might be of use to them in the other world.

" For the first three years after the decease

of a friend or relation, they were accustomed, from time to time, to dig holes by the side of the grave, therein to deposit either a small quantity of tobacco, or something that the deceased was fondest of whilst living." They also believed their reindeer would partake in the bliss of heaven.

BOAT APPROACHING A WALRUS.

CHAPTER XII.

> "Day rose on Norway's woody shore,
> And dark blue hills and forests hoar.
> Upon the grass the rain-drops bright
> Blink'd in the sun like gems of light:
> And the soft wave that kiss'd the strand
> Scarce raised the limpet on the sand.
> Around upon the waters blue
> Skimm'd the grey tern and white sea-mew;
> The flies danced idly in the air,
> And o'er the headland's forehead bare
> The dun sea-rook and clamouring daw
> Mix'd in the sun their busy caw."
> Lays of the Deer Forest.

L—— and I remained on deck during the whole evening, as the weather had become very pleasant and warm, and the magnificent scenery between the Loffoden Islands and the mainland of Norway was most beautiful, and could be thoroughly appreciated by all the passengers, as the captain had put up a large awning to keep off both the hot rays of the sun and also the continuous clouds of black smuts which fell on deck from the funnel.

The crossing of the open stretch of sea, which goes by the name of the Vest fjord, occupied no less than nine hours, although at no time were we out of sight of land; and the view at midnight, at which hour the vessel had got half way across the fjord, was far beyond all my powers of description to depict with a tithe of justice. The effects of the "sunset" at this point were glorious, although, in truth, of course the orb did not actually set, as we are still many miles to the north of the Arctic circle. And as we gazed on the brightly-beaming rays of the midnight sun for the last time (as we shall have crossed the "line" by this time to-morrow), we agreed it was well worth all the trouble of the long journey we had undertaken, to be able to look upon the thousands of jagged peaks of the desolate Loffodens—now lying in one blaze of mellowed ruby light behind us, and, at the same time, to see the snowy summits of many a lofty mountain on the mainland to the eastward, where great glaciers lay stretched out, one behind the other, in a misty haze of blue light, piled as it were in picturesque confusion upon the top of the smaller hills and black-fronted cliffs which lined the rock-bound coast both to the north and south of Bodö.

Thursday, June 29th.

The " Nordland " remained at the little port of Bodö for three hours, and the noisy process of coaling went on during the whole of that period, not conducing in a very great measure to the quiet enjoyment of that sleep in which we only wished we had been wrapped.

There is a certain hill, about a mile to the northward of the town, whence a good view of the midnight sun is always obtainable in clear weather, between the 1st of June and the 10th of July; and from this point of vantage the far-away peaks of the Loffodens can be seen to the westward; and their aspect has been truly described by a certain traveller who compared their sharp, angular outlines and crystal-like spikes to a row of shark's teeth, and I think this resemblance cannot fail to strike any one. The ridge or hill to which I have alluded has an uninterrupted view to the north, with the huge cliffs of the mainland on one's right hand (the westward); "and," to quote "G. B. A." in "Murray's Guide," "a huge mountain, island, or island-mountain to the left, and the northern peaks of Loffoden, about seventy miles distant, in front."

This writer's description is so simple, and yet so graphically true, that I cannot resist repeating his words here. "I have seldom seen," he says, "a more majestic sight than that of the midnight sun gliding horizontally over these peaks. Everything seems as light as at midday, but with an air of great beauty and softness. But when the sun has sensibly risen, as by one o'clock, the splendour is inexpressible. It seemed culpable to go to bed."

One of the most striking features, geologically speaking, upon this part of the Norwegian coast is, the remarkable absence of "sands," by which I mean the ordinary stretches of sand with which we are so familiar in England, Scotland, and Ireland; but we vainly looked for the sand that we expected to see sooner or later on the Norwegian seaboard, and have never yet met with anything like it excepting a species of sticky clay, or masses of broken shells and tiny white corals, which are especially numerous on the Bodö shore. Being, unluckily, but a poor geologist, I cannot venture to expound any theory to account for this phenomenon, which to my mind is very interesting.

We certainly cannot complain to-day that we are not fortunate in our weather, which is all that mortal could desire, and it was to-day even warmer than yesterday, excepting when, shortly after leaving Bodö, we passed close to the shore in the immediate neighbourhood of some extensive glaciers, the chill air from which was borne down to us in icy gusts by the light north-east breeze.

Many of the mountains that were passed during the day were very remarkable in outline, and we constantly found ourselves wondering whether volcanic action had to answer for the fantastic shapes which the summits of some of the highest of these hills assumed. Most of their topmost ridges were pointed, exactly after the manner of the teeth of a huge saw; and so sharp were the summits of several of the loftiest amongst them, that the observer would scarcely believe the mountain-goats could obtain standing room, which we are told they manage to do. I must request the reader to imagine these peaks to be about 2000 feet in actual height, according to the calculations of my friend the captain of the "Nordland," and in some cases very precipitous.

Our attention was especially attracted to a "pair" of hills, each of some 1900 feet in altitude, which faced each other, a narrow inlet of perhaps half a mile in breadth only separating them from each other. The formation of outline of these mountains, which I should add were covered with a considerable quantity of snow wherever the slope was not too steep for it to lie, differed so much that the several separate summits of one hill were almost rounded, whilst those of the other were very sharp, and even pointed, which, considering their proximity, was curious.

The coast of Lapland and parts of Norway, and especially that of the Loffoden islands, would, I should imagine, be a perfect paradise for the lover of geology, and it is a great pity that so little comparatively is written in any of the existing guide-books upon this absorbingly interesting subject.

Just before we crossed the Arctic Circle, my wife and I were sitting on deck and examining the varied features of the coast with the aid of the captain's telescope, when our attention was suddenly directed to a considerable number of small black specks upon a large island, which the vessel was approaching. For a long time it was not easy to determine what these were, but when we were abreast of the island, it became apparent that the objects which had attracted our attention were cattle, but of a very small size indeed. There were some forty or fifty of them in all, and I subsequently ascertained that these little animals were veritable Kerry cows, imported from Ireland by an enterprising Norsk farmer, who has successfully fostered the breed on this island for some years. They are said to thrive very well in this far northern land, although their offspring have slightly deteriorated in size since their arrival from Kerry, and I fear that they can scarcely find as much pasturage amongst the barren, rocky islands of the Arctic seas, as the bogs of their native wilds near Killarney afforded them.

Our time in Arctic seas was rapidly drawing to a close, when at two o'clock the luncheon bell summoned us below; but we were soon again on deck to see the last of the sights of the Polar ocean! There was, in truth, nothing more to be seen than when we crossed the "circle" during our northward voyage, but we now recognized as old friends the famous Hestemando, but the rider, as seen from the north, does not bear the same resemblance to a cavalry soldier as he is stated to do when one is approaching the island from the opposite direction.

Away, far out in the western sea, the four

rugged isles of Threnen stand clearly defined against the blue sky; and as the ship crosses the imaginary line, we feel that we are once more in southern seas. We left the Arctic ocean proper at 3 p.m., and soon after two neat-looking yachts flying the familiar British union jack passed us in the opposite direction, and as it was almost dead calm they were not making much progress, though a tiny tug was doing her best for them.

Whilst crossing the Polar Circle Captain Beck told us the story (with which, no doubt, many of my readers are acquainted), of a youthful passenger on board his vessel, who had never travelled before, and who, when given by the captain a telescope wherewith to inspect the "Arctic line," declared that he could see it very distinctly, which was not at all surprising as the glass had been carefully furnished with a piece of black thread stretched across one of the lenses.

Sitting on deck was very pleasant, and no incident worthy of notice occurred until the evening, when a large whale was sighted at the

distance of about a mile from the ship. Of
course every one at once rushed to the side to
have a view of the monster, which was, as far
as we could judge, some seventy feet in length,
and great excitement among the ladies took
place when the big fish spouted a large cloud
of water high up into the blue sky, and its
effect as it fell once more into its own element
in misty spray was very pretty to witness.

This whale was called by the Norsk sailors
on board, the "Rorq-val," which is the commonest large whale found in the Arctic waters
of Norway and Finmark; but it is generally
called the "Finner," or razor-backed whale, by
the natives of Orkney and Shetland, its
scientific designation being *Balænoptera musculus*. A still larger species is Sibbald's
rorqual (*B. Sibbaldii*), and possibly the whale we
saw to-day was one of this kind, as it is a
bigger whale than the "finner."

Shortly after this whale had disappeared
from view, we were amused by the playful
gambols indulged in by five or six fat porpoises,
which were accompanied by a small "school"

of bottle-noses (*Delphinus tursio*), which latter are about twelve feet in length, and are generally termed by sailors bottle-nosed whales, (though in truth belonging to the dolphin tribe) on account of the curious formation of their skulls.

During our voyage up to Tromsö I had authentic information concerning a certain private whaling expedition, of which I was very desirous of obtaining further particulars; but unfortunately we failed to ascertain where the permanent headquarters of the individual under whose management the concern was conducted, were to be found. It appeared, by the account which Captain Dominicus Beek, of the "Nordland," gave me, that a certain Norwegian, possessing a small private fortune of his own, and who moreover had gained in his youth considerable experience when on numerous whaling expeditions in the Greenland seas, had returned to his native shores so imbued with the spirit of adventure, and so filled with love for whale hunting, that he determined to turn the knowledge which he had gained to some account.

He therefore purchased a small steam launch, in which, with his small crew of half a dozen men, he could cruise about the mouths of the larger fjords, and in fine weather even venture some miles out to sea, in search of the whale, the grampus, the porpoise, and other *cetacea*, all of which numerous tribe were welcome fish to his "net." The little vessel was armed with harpoons and guns, and was well supplied, of course on a small scale, with all the necessary implements for successfully following up this exciting sport.

It is easy to imagine with what comparative facility the steam launch could follow the movements of the prey when harpooned; and we were greatly disappointed at not being able to hear of this enterprising whaler, who would no doubt have been glad, in return for a small sum, to have taken my wife and self in his vessel for a cruise. He often, we were informed, remains out at sea for several consecutive days, but is never very far from shore, and in rough weather he finds a safe shelter in the innumerable fjords which stud the coast between Tromsö and

Bergen, betwixt which places his operations are carried on. He has made a very large sum of money, as he generally "bags" from one hundred to one hundred and fifty "head" of animals during the summer months, and the blubber obtained from which brings him in a considerable annual income. Captain Beck told us that his principal captures consisted of the grampus (*Orca gladiator*), which is some twenty feet in length, the bottle-nosed dolphin, previously alluded to, and the common porpoise; whilst a right whale of fifty to sixty feet long only falls to his lot perhaps three or four times a year. It would have been a charming and luxurious way for L—— to have been witness of a whale hunt; and we had fully made up our minds to have taken part in one of this *amateur* whaler's exciting forays.

That we were indeed south of the Arctic Circle was proved this evening, for as we sat on the upper deck watching one of the most lovely sunsets imaginable, we saw the glowing ball of fire first touch the water, then dip below the horizon, and finally disappear from our view at exactly a quarter to twelve o'clock; but that we had but just left Polar seas was quickly demonstrated by the sun only remaining hidden for the short space of twenty-five minutes, as he was up again from his watery couch by 12.10 a.m. on

Friday, June 30th,
and one glorious blaze of changing colour rested upon the hundreds of little islands with which the ocean was studded; and the rosy hues of the distant glaciers were reflected on the blue waters, which danced up and down in the light west wind, and sent into the air little showers of shining spray tinged with all the rainbow-colours; while the black, beetling cliffs upon the mainland assumed an indescribable softness of outline as the warm beams of the rising luminary fell upon their hoary and precipitous sides.

We had not been more than an hour in our berths, when the captain sent the mate below to tell me that we were passing the curious island of Torghatten, and that he was going to stop the ship for five minutes, to enable my wife to come on deck and see the large aperture through the upper part of the rock. L—— came on deck just as the vessel passed abreast of "Torget's hat," as the Norsk seamen term the island; and Captain Beck kindly fulfilling his promise, the engines were stopped, and we had a capital view of the cavity which pierces entirely through this mountain-rock, as it may fairly so be termed, its summit being more than a thousand feet in height, and the hole itself is some seven hundred and fifty feet above the sea.

It was a curious sight from the deck of the steamer, looking up to the towering rock high above us, and to see the blue sky literally *through* the hill itself. This perforation extends for many yards completely through the rock, and is stated to be eighty feet high, and forty feet in width; while the aperture is said to be quite large enough to contain a large building, such as a church. The rock itself is of granite, and the aperture is supposed to have been caused by the falling away of a large quantity of mica. At the time we saw through this opening, the vessel was nearly three miles distant from the island of Torget, and even then the hole appeared to be of considerable size, but had we been nearer the land, we should not have seen through it at all, the aperture being invisible excepting from ships passing at a certain distance.

The scenery in every direction around Torget island is very wild, and it looked especially so at this early hour; and the only sign of life that we noticed on the broad expanse of calm ocean was a single small boat, whose occupants were fishing with great energy three or four handlines apiece for codling. Having spent so much of our night upon deck, we were not very early risers to-day, and towards the luncheon hour we found that the sun was extremely powerful, and the heat made itself felt so suddenly that it had great effect upon us, coming, as we were, from the north. This sudden heat quickly brought a strong wind with it, and the "Nordland" made everybody on board aware that the weather had changed by rolling considerably; and before we had time to shut the ports in our tiny cabin, more than one wave had paid us a flying visit, and the state of the berths and luggage was far from satisfactory.

Had not the vessel been in comparatively calm water, sheltered as we were by numerous islands from the strong west wind, we should have experienced a very nasty rough sea during the afternoon; but as it was, the only sufferers were a few of the lady passengers, who beat a hasty retreat below, and a little black pony which had come on board as we were passing through the Loffodens. A large number of ponies are purchased in Lapland, and the northern parts of Norway, at a comparatively cheap price, by regular horse-dealers from the south, and are fatted up, and then resold at Bergen or Christiania for a sum about four times larger than their original cost.

We had hoped to have reached Throndhjem by midnight, but were unable to do so, as the ship remained for more than three hours at the pretty little port of Besaker, where a large "jagt," or fishing craft, was awaiting our arrival, and we were laden with its entire cargo of fresh herrings in barrels, which numbered many hundreds, and quite filled the lower deck of the steamer. During our detention at this

place we had grand sport, fishing with hand-
lines in the harbour, catching several fine fish
of several kinds, especially a large coal-fish, and
an immense cod of more than four feet in length,
and which gave me great trouble before it was
finally hauled on board, and not being in good
condition did not weigh so much as I had
expected. Had it been in good order, it would
not have scaled less than thirty pounds. It is
very rare to find such large cod in the shallow
water in the smaller harbours, such as Besaker,
as big fish generally keep well out in the deep
sea.

I must not omit to mention that we saw
during our voyage northward more than one
pair of that odd-looking bird, the little auk
(*Mergulus alle*), one of the smallest of sea-fowl,
and a ridiculous picture in miniature of his larger
and noble relative, the great auk (*Alca impennis*),
now it is to be feared quite extinct, the continued
persecution of man having swept this interesting
species, as well as many others, off the surface
of the globe. What these individuals could
have been doing so far south as the Arctic Circle

at so late a period of the year as the latter end of the month of June, I do not know; for, although common enough during winter and late into the spring, both on the Lapland coasts, and also at the mouths of the large fjords in the southern part of Norway, the little auk has never been known to have bred in either country, where it must be very rare to meet with this species in summer.

Its nesting-places are in the far north; and it is found breeding in large colonies on the shores of Spitzbergen, Novaya Zemlya, Greenland, on Grimsey island to the north of Iceland, and other distant lands. It is essentially an Arctic bird, and very quaint do the little auks appear as they dive straight through the advancing breakers, or sail at ease upon the crests of the largest waves. They are familiar to every navigator of the Polar ocean, and are called by the sailors "rotchies," and sometimes "dovekies," by which name the small black guillemot is also known.

We are told, in a work on ornithology which I have lately read, that the crews of the walrus-sloops and whalers that visit Spitzbergen consider the greatest delicacies to be obtained there are roasted reindeer and little auks cooked in the same manner! But, although I have more than once shot this bird in the Orkneys, I cannot say that the thought ever entered my mind of eating it; and most decidedly, to say the least of it, there would be a very fishy flavour about such a tit-bit.

Whilst writing of this bird, it will not be out of place to mention that Lamont states that the remarkable appearance termed "red snow," which is so often described in works treating of Arctic travel, is in his opinion merely the result of the mass of droppings from millions of little auks; and which *excreta* being of a pinkish colour, owing to the favourite food of this species being the shrimps, of which they consume immense numbers, causes this curious "red" snow that we so often hear about. Many travellers affirm that a minute reddish fungus grows upon the surface of the snow in parts of Greenland and Spitzbergen, but the author before alluded to says with great truth, that if there is such a fungus, it probably is formed by, and grows upon, the droppings of the birds.

I had some good fishing during the evening at several places at which we stopped for a short time, and owing to the herrings which we had taken aboard at Besaker, we had far better sport with the cod, as they seemed to be particularly fond of pieces of fresh herring.

Saturday, July 1st.

When we were awakened by the noisy stewards ringing the breakfast-bell with more than usual violence, we discovered that the "Nordland" was at anchor, and that we had arrived once more at our old quarters in Throndhjem harbour. Most of the passengers had gone ashore, and as we had not quite settled what our future movements were to be, we talked over our plans whilst breakfasting in the cabin, after which we went ashore and walked up the hot streets (for the sun was literally broiling in the unclouded sky above our heads), to the hotel.

At the "Britannia" we found our rooms had in our absence been occupied by salmon-fishers from England, but they had just left for the interior, so that we were soon once again in the familiar little wooden rooms, which, with their large open windows and uncarpeted floors, were delightfully cool and pleasant. A visit to the post-office was of course the first thing to be done, and after reading our letters, by which we found England was getting on very well without us, we took a pleasant stroll along the shadiest part of the town; but the heat was even there so oppressive that we were compelled to take shelter and rest in a quaint and very ancient church, not far from the cathedral.

This place of worship was curious in the extreme, having such an old-world look about it that we were about to examine it carefully, when we found that we had arrived just in time to witness the conclusion of a marriage in low life, which had just been celebrated. There were some fifteen persons in all composing the bridal party; and as the bride and groom, followed by several young ladies and groomsmen, passed us on their way to a curriage which was waiting at the porch, we could not help noticing in what a very doleful garb the whole of the festive party were arrayed. Every one was dressed in the blackest of black clothes, women and men alike, the effect being indescribably more like a funeral than a wedding, with the only redeeming point that they each wore a brand new pair of milk-white gloves, and looked exceedingly jolly and well pleased with themselves and the world in general.

After the bridal party had driven off, we walked round the church accompanied by a little Laplander, bent on sightseeing like ourselves, and he seemed equally interested with us in looking about him. He wore a high, square, blue and red cap, with a tunic of the brightest blue with red facings, and long boots reaching to the knee, and had besides a girdle of many-coloured worsteds round his waist. He came from near Vadsö, I believe; and he was dressed in far gayer clothes than any of his fellow-countrymen we saw near Tromsö.

The church was evidently very old; the

walls being quite invisible, completely covered
as they were with ancient and much worm-
eaten carvings in oak; and the pews arranged
in tiers, piled one above the other, reached
almost to the roof of the building, giving one
the impression of a house made of cards. On
our way to the cathedral, which is *par excellence* the sight of Throndhjem, we walked
through the large churchyard adjoining, and
could not help being much struck with the neat
and pretty appearance of the place, so utterly
different from the smoke-begrimed burial-
grounds that we have in our large English
cities, where tombstones stand crowded back to
back in countless numbers, their once white
faces blackened with the dirt of ages, with not
a tree, excepting, may be, a few dreary-looking
yews, to add a slight colouring of brightness to
the dismal necropolis.

How different from such a picture is the
picturesque churchyard of Throndhjem cathedral. Graves, and plenty of them, are seen on
every side, but the greater part of them are
merely apparently the slightly-raised mound of

the greenest of green grass, upon which parties of little children, accompanied by their elder sisters or nurses, are seen busily strewing bright nosegays of flowers, and lovely bouquets of garden-roses were hanging upon the iron railings round many a tiny grave, while hardly a tombstone did we notice that had not a wreath of wild violets, primroses, or bluebells. None of those hideously ugly wreaths of withered things called at home "immortelles" were to be found in this pretty spot, and numerous merry parties of little ones were playing happily under the purple lilacs and weeping laburnums, which formed shady avenues in various directions. It was not only upon the freshly made graves that clusters of wild flowers were to be seen; but tombstones, the date engraved on which showed that they had stood there many a year, were in numerous instances supplied with wreaths of lilies of the valley or pink rosebuds by some loving hand.

There is nothing specially striking inside the cathedral, excepting a fine cast of a large statue of our Saviour by Thorvaldsen, and some inferior statues of the twelve apostles. The western end of the building, however, is worthy of attention, there being some highly-decorated carvings in stone, especially over one of the entrances. Its style of architecture is Norman as far as regards the most ancient portions of the edifice, but it has so frequently during its long existence suffered from the ravages of fire, that it is not easy, at the present time, to say what other styles of architecture may have been adopted since it was commenced, about the year 1030. The stone of which the interior of the building is constructed is principally of a dull blue colour, easily moulded, and said to harden quickly on exposure to the air. We observed above the rood-screen some projecting pedestals, where we were told the Archbishop of Throndhjem used, in the days of old, to read to the populace those interdicts which the popes were very fond of placing Norway under at short intervals.

Throndhjem was the old seat of the Norwegian Government, and remained the actual capital of the country until the union with

Denmark; and its cathedral is famous, among other reasons, because the kings of Norway are accustomed to be crowned there. The celebrated saint, Olaf, who was slain in the year 1030, built a church on the spot where the cathedral at present stands, and it is stated that he was interred where the high altar now is, and Harold Hardraade, Magnus the Good, and other great men subsequently added to the commencement of Olaf, and eventually a large edifice was constructed out of the result of their combined labours. The history of St. Olaf cannot be here detailed at length; but from what has been written of him we learn that he was a tyrannical, though a just monarch, and was especially noted for his strict observance of all religious ceremonies and ordinances.

Maclear,[1] speaking of this king, says that "the impartial severity with which he administered the laws, punishing equally both small and great, was one of the chief causes of rebellion against his rule. St. Olaf was eventually compelled to fly the kingdom, but was

[1] "Apostles of Mediæval Europe."

recalled three years later by the party favourable to his interests. He had no sooner appeared than multitudes flocked to his standard, but he rejected all who did not comply with the one condition of service—the reception of baptism. The helmets and shields of all who fought on his side were distinguished by a white cross; and on the eve of the combats Olaf directed many marks of silver to be given for the souls of his enemies who should fall in battle, esteeming the salvation of his own men already secured. He also directed that the war-shout should be, 'Forward, Christ's men! Cross-men! King's men!' The battle was hot and bloody, and Olaf was defeated and slain."

His life, nevertheless, was by no means spent in vain; for not many years after his death Christianity took a deep root in Norway, whence it was never again eradicated. The principal sight in Throndhjem in days of yore was the shrine of St. Olaf, which was so magnificent that pilgrims, even in those times of difficulty in means of communication, would come from all parts of Europe to pay their devotions to the famous monarch. His body, it is said, was inclosed in three separate coffins, the innermost one being of pure silver of vast weight, and the outer covering of wood studded with gems of priceless value and golden ornaments. The shrine was plundered of its valuable contents in 1541 by the Lutherans, who, however, did not gain much by the robbery, as the vessel employed to carry the principal part of the booty to Denmark foundered in the North Sea, the remainder being again stolen by highway robbers during its overland transit.

Relating to St. Olaf there are, of course, innumerable legends, one of which is related by Mr. Shepard[2] in the following words:—" One legend recounts how St. Olaf, by the promise of a great reward, persuaded a good-natured wizard to build for him the spire of Throndhjem Cathedral; and it must be owned that for so holy a man St. Olaf treated the poor wizard rather scurvily, after he had faithfully performed his share of the contract. As it may be new to our readers, we give a translation of it:—

[1] "Over the Dovrefjelds," by J. S. Shepard, p. 136.

"'Throndhjem Cathedral is known far and wide as one of Christendom's most remarkable churches, but still more striking was it in the olden time, with its graceful spire towering to the sky. St. Olaf found it easy enough to build a church, but the spire was beyond his skill. In his perplexity he promised the sun to whoever would accomplish the task of raising it. When no one else came forward, a wizard, who lived in a neighbouring village, offered to do it for the stipulated reward, affixing the condition that St. Olaf must never address him by his name, even should he chance to discover it. As the spire rose rapidly towards completion, St. Olaf was soon in a fix as to the payment, and tried his utmost to get upon the track of the wizard's name. Sailing about midnight along the coast, he came to a place called Kjærringen, where he heard a child crying in a field, when the mother, to pacify it, promised it the sun when its father, Tvester, came home.

"'Joyfully Olaf hurried back to the town, and came in the nick of time, for the spire was just completed, and the wizard was on the point of putting the last gilded knob on the weathercock. "Thou art setting the weathercock too far to the west, Tvester!" shouted St. Olaf. The moment the wizard heard his name, he fell down dead.' "

CARVED STONEWORK IN THRONDHJEM CATHEDRAL.

CHAPTER XIII.

"To the west of me was the ocean,
To the right the desolate shore,
But I did not slacken sail
For the walrus or the whale,
Till after three days more.
The sea was rough and stormy,
The tempest howl'd and wail'd,
And the sea-fog, like a ghost,
Haunted that dreary coast,
But onward still I sail'd."

LONGFELLOW.

Sunday, July 2nd.

It was so oppressively hot during the night that even in the comparatively cool, wooden-floored bedchambers we found the heat perfectly stifling, and the sudden change of climate from the ice and snow of Lapland to this broiling city makes one feel the hot weather severely. The forenoon of this day was so roasting that we did not venture out until after two o'clock in the afternoon, when L—— and I walked to the cathedral, where the service was just about to commence.

The building was crammed with people in every corner; but by far the largest portion of the congregation were women and young girls, all neatly dressed, for the most part wearing clean white caps and coloured aprons; and we were much struck by observing with what zest all present joined in the service, and more particularly in the singing, which was very good, and the organ decidedly above the average of those in our churches at home.

The pews are of a considerable height, and when sitting down only the tops of the heads of the rest of the congregation are visible to the occupants of seats. We listened to a sermon—of which I fear we understood but little—lasting rather over an hour, delivered by a clergyman attired in a long black robe ornamented with clean white ruffled cuffs, and a huge Elizabethan ruff around the neck. The priest who was officiating at the altar was dressed much more effectively, being enveloped by a gorgeous robe of scarlet, on the back of which a large

golden cross was conspicuously worked. The
congregation never kneel, but sit or stand
throughout the service, and are particularly
quiet and attentive.

In the evening we made an expedition to a
pretty little tea-garden, at a short distance from
the city, and overlooking the fjord. Here a
military band was playing, and ices, beer, and
cakes seemed to be the principal luxuries to be
obtained. The gardens were crowded with the
citizens of Throndhjem, who are a very well-
behaved, decent set of people, excepting the
lowest classes, who are terribly addicted to
drink; and no wonder it is so, when a man can
buy sufficient corn-brandy for six skillings
(equal in English money to threepence) to make
him utterly oblivious to all around! We saw
nothing of this kind, however, at these tea-
gardens, and we were sorry to be obliged to
leave, when a heavy and sudden shower of rain
came on, but which had the desirable effect of
cooling the heated atmosphere.

Monday, July 3rd.

During the morning we amused ourselves by

visiting some of the most tempting shops, notably Bruun's fur stores and a cutler's, where we obtained some beautifully carved "toll-knives," of walrus-tusk ivory. The price of a large knife of this kind, made of the best walrus ivory, is in Throndhjem rather over one sovereign, while in London I venture to say it would not be bought for five.

Herr Bruun's fur stores are really worth visiting, but as we had spent a small fortune there on our way northward, he could only tempt us to-day with some ermine cuffs and boas for friends at home, which were very reasonable in price. Some idea of the variety of articles on sale at this shop, may be gained by reading the following list, which appears on the cards which Bruun takes care to stick up in a conspicuous place in the hall of each hotel in Throndhjem.

"Johan N. Bruun, Lager af Huer Hatte og Pelsvarer," commences this advertisement, "To touristes; the undersigned begs respectfully to call attention to his furs and peltry, consisting of travelling cloaks, ladies' pelisses, muffs, boas, fur-gloves, fur-collars, wrist-muffs, fur-socks, and foot-bags, fur-linings, &c., Lapland mocassins, all kinds of Norwegian peltry, whitebear, brown-bear, reindeer, lynx and wolf skins; sable, ermine, otter, red, white, blue, and silver fox, &c.

"Also a large assortment of hats and caps, straw hats, fancy rugs, eiders' down, stuffed birds, reindeer horns, Norwegian packing-cases, and others too numerous to mention, the whole at moderate prices!"

It is only fair to Herr Brunn to state that the above list only comprises about a fourth part of the contents of his vast store.

There is not much to be seen in Throndhjem besides the cathedral, but the small collection of northern antiquities in the museum is deserving of a passing call; and a very pretty expedition may be made, by driving a few miles to the south of the town, to the Lierfossen, which consists of two very pretty waterfalls, one about a hundred feet and the other eighty feet in height. The angler may find it quite worth while to ask leave to try for a salmon just beneath the lower fall, where there are always plenty of fish, and permission will be cheerfully given by the manager of the smelting-works close by. The Lierfossen is a waterfall of rather an unusual character, as the whole breadth of the river hurls itself, in an almost unbroken stream, over a perpendicular face of cliff; and this cascade has a wonderfully smooth appearance, which forms such a marked contrast to the broken, dashing downpour of water with which one is always accustomed to associate a Norwegian "foss."

The extensive smelting-works above alluded to, are situated on the right bank of the river, and a great deal of copper ore is annually smelted in the large furnaces. This ore is brought from the mines of Roraas, a distance of at least one hundred miles, and Mr. Shepard states that it is carried from that place in carts to the nearest railway in the Guul valley, whence a train conveys it to Throndhjem. "It is," continues this author, "first crushed to powder in the water-mill. It is then placed in huge iron cauldrons, and cooked for several days, the refuse that rises to the surface being continually skimmed off. When thoroughly purified, it is run into tanks of boiling water, in which it is allowed gradually to cool down. As the temperature begins to lower, a number of sticks are suspended in the water, on which the copper speedily collects, covering them with a mass of bright red crystals, which are withdrawn at the end of the fortnight, perfectly cool and brittle. They are then detached from the sticks, spread out in trays to dry, and afterwards packed in barrels for home use and exportation.

"They told us that the greater part of what they make here goes to Hamburg, where we believe it is used in the colouring of stained glass, imparting to it a rich ruby tint."

The weather was again dreadfully oppressive all day, and the sun so powerful, that the pleasantest place we could find was the shady walk in the churchyard of the cathedral; and L—— discovered a pretty avenue, alongside the river Nid, bordered by lilacs and laburnums in full flower; and in more than one of the numerous gardens near the river bank, the air was filled by sweetly scented flowers, and we saw large clusters of ruddy cherries, almost ready for picking, hanging in the little orchards. It is noteworthy that the cherry ripens almost everywhere on the west coast of Norway, up to a high latitude; the natives, being very partial to cherry brandy, which is called *Kirsebær brændeviin*, cultivate this fruit with great care.

Apricots ripen as far northward as Throndhjem, and so do several kinds of pears and plums; and, improbable as it may appear to the passing traveller, apples ripen almost to the limits of the Arctic Circle.

Towards evening we packed up our goods and chattels, and prepared everything for our departure; as we have settled, after some deliberation, to go to Bergen by sea; and with this purpose in view I superintended the packing of our harness in the carrioles, which were then taken down to the harbour, where I saw them hoisted, by means of a huge crane, on board our old acquaintance the "Nordland," where they were suspended in the lower rigging, high out of the way of the heads of passers-by on the deck beneath.

The steamer was advertised to sail for Molde at midnight, and we bid adieu to our comfortable quarters at the hotel "Britannia" just before that hour; and on walking down to the harbour found that the "Nordland" had left the quay, owing to the falling tide, and was lying-to at a few hundred yards from the shore. By means of a small boat we were quickly put on board, where we again took possession of our old cabins, which had been kindly reserved for us by the captain, the ship being very full of passengers. Among these were several emigrants on their way to America; and I was surprised to learn that the number of Norwegians who leave the country for New York and Canada, amounts annually to nearly forty thousand, a vast quantity for such a sparsely populated land.

As usual in this northern clime, a very beautiful sunset spread its splendours over the sleeping city and its surrounding hills, and ere their topmost ridges were tinged with the ruddier hue which told of the returning orb, the cathedral clock chimed the midnight-hour, the crowd of little boats left for the shore, the whistle sounded, and it was already

Tuesday, July 4th,

when the powerful screw stirred up the deep blue waters of the fjord into a sea of white foam, and the peaceful town was soon left far behind, and was a mere speck in the hazy distance when we retired below.

As we take our last view of the ancient city of Throndhjem, so full of associations of the times of the Vikings, we cannot fail to return in thought to those olden days, when this glorious country was a heathen land, until King Olaf rescued the people, but by no gentle means, from their original faith, and introduced Christianity into Norway. Longfellow has well described, in " King Olaf's Saga," the challenge given out by the God Thor, who is made to say,—

> " Here in my Northland,
> My fastness and fortress,
> Reign I for ever !

> Here amid icebergs
> Rule I the nations!
> The light thou beholdest[1]
> Stream through the heavens,
> In flashes of crimson,
> Is but my red beard
> Blown by the night wind.
> Thou art a God, too,
> And thus single-handed
> Unto the combat,
> Gauntlet or gospel,
> Here I defy thee!"

Upon which Olaf takes up the challenge, and

> "King Olaf heard the cry,
> Saw the red light in the sky,
> And his ships went sailing, sailing
> Northward into Throndhjem fjord."

and the monarch,

> "One summer morn,
> Blew a blast on his bugle-horn,
> Sending his signal through the land of Throndhjem.
> *   *   *   'I command
> This land to be a Christian land;
> Here is my Bishop who the folk baptizes!'
> Then to their temple strode he in,
> 'Choose ye between two things, my folk,
> To be baptized, or given up to slaughter!'

---

[1] The aurora borealis is here alluded to.

> And, seeing their leader [2] stark and dead,
> The people with a murmur said,
> 'Oh, king, baptize us with thy holy water.'
> So all the Throndhjem land became
> A Christian land in name and fame,
> In the old gods no more believing."

On awaking in the morning we found we were in the open ocean, and, though the wind was not very strong, the vessel pitched considerably, owing to being lightly laden, and to the big waves which came rolling in from the westward; and we found that a heavy gale had visited this part of the coast only two days ago, and had put the North Sea in a commotion from which it has not yet recovered.

During the night we passed the large island of Hitteren, on which there is very good shooting, black game and capercailzie being especially abundant.

There are a goodly number of red deer on this island, and it is the only part of Norway in which they are to be met with; and I believe they were originally introduced from abroad.

At noon we arrived at the picturesquely

[1] The farmer Iron-beard.

situated town of Christiansund, where the steamer remained for about three hours, whilst a large quantity of barrels of herrings were hoisted on board from numerous small craft in the harbour. There being nothing of much interest to be seen on shore, we did not land here, but L—— and I amused ourselves by passing the time in fishing over the side of the ship, and succeeded in catching several nice codling and haddocks, which afterwards appeared at supper in the saloon, capitally fried by the captain's *chef*.

The harbour of Christiansund is almost entirely land-locked, being built upon no less than three separate islands, and it would be hard to imagine a town in a more wildly romantic situation. L—— and I were standing together upon deck when our steamer thrust itself between two narrow rocky islets, and on emerging from this contracted channel, the town, which we had then no idea we were approaching, burst in an instant of time upon our view. The aspect of the place, especially if seen for the first time, cannot fail to strike the traveller on account of the odd manner in which the dwellings of the inhabitants are scattered about, with apparently no idea whatever of regularity or plan, there being no such thing as a fairly straight street in the town. The houses seemed to be all upon different levels, and many were built upon ledges of rock, one above the other, the lowermost ones, in some cases, actually projecting beyond the land and overhanging the sea, only prevented from falling into the water by long wooden props, which had a most picturesque aspect as seen from on board the ship. Christiansund is noted for the abundance of flowers which are to be seen in all parts of the little town, and it is especially rich in creepers, such as the honeysuckle, which, in many of the streets, covers the walls of whole rows of wooden houses, perfuming the summer air with a delicious fragrance. Most of the buildings in this quaint old town were painted red, but there were many yellow ones, and one or two green or bright blue.

The great prosperity of Christiansund is entirely owing to the trade carried on in dried cod-fish, the majority of which are brought from the Loffodens by small vessels termed "jagts," which convey great quantities of "klipper" (as the fish, when dried, are called) to the merchants living at this port.

These dealers repack the fish carefully, and despatch vessels of large size, laden with this odoriferous cargo, to distant countries; the principal demand being in France, Italy, and Spain, where the Roman Catholic portion of the population consume an immense quantity of "klipper" on fast-days. It even repays these adventurous Norsemen to send cod-fish all the way to Rio Janeiro and the other countries in South America where the Roman Catholic faith is prevalent.

The abundance of fish in the neighbourhood of Christiansund probably accounts for the presence of the sea-eagle (*Haliaetus albicilla*) which is particularly common on this coast, where it breeds; and it is often to be seen sailing over one's head at a great height in the skies. The Rev. R. Bowden, late English chaplain at Christiania, is responsible for the statement that this bird occasionally, when pouncing upon a large fish, such as a porpoise or large cod, entangles its talons in the flesh of the fish, which, if sufficiently strong, will drag the bird beneath the surface and drown its would-be captor. He also mentions that the skeleton of a sea-eagle was once found in the body of a monster cod, which was supposed to have been drowned in this manner. More than one well authenticated instance has also been recorded of this eagle being pulled under water by a young seal, which the bird will sometimes attack when the seal is lying asleep upon a rock or sandbank. Turbot and overgrown halibut have likewise been recorded to have conquered the eagle! and Lloyd[3] speaks of large pike and other fish being captured with the skeletons of eagles on their backs, and quotes Bishop Pontoppidan, who, writing nearly two hundred years ago, remarks that he had been told that the Sundmoerske fishermen occasionally catch the halibut "with eagle's talons in the backs of them, and covered over

[3] "Scandinavian Adventures," vol. ii. p. 231.

with flesh and fat; this is a mark of the fish's conquering as aforesaid."

This worthy prelate also relates the following curious anecdote of a misfortune which befell one of the "royal" birds in these words:—"I have," writes the Bishop, "been told by several creditable people, from their own knowledge, of another unfortunate expedition of the eagle, which shows that this mighty king of birds is often in the wrong, and extends his attempts beyond his power among the fish. An incident of this kind happened not far from Bergen, where an eagle stood on the bank of a river and saw a salmon, as it were, just under him; he instantly struck one of his talons into the root of an elm close by, and partly hanging over the river; the other he struck into the salmon, which was very large, and in his proper element, which doubled his strength, so that he swam away, and split the eagle to his neck, making literally a spread eagle of him—a creature otherwise known only in heraldry!"

Leaving Christiansund soon after three o'clock in the afternoon, we steamed away to the southward; and, shortly after quitting the friendly shelter of the clusters of islets, amongst which we had passed the earlier part of the day, we found a very heavy sea running in the open ocean, which obliged the "Nordland" to give a wide berth to the precipitous headland to the north of the entrance to the Molde fjord. The vessel rolled very much, sending the greater part of the passengers speedily to their cabins; and L——, on reaching hers, found that everything was wet through, from the waves coming in at the ports. We saw large shoals of porpoises in this rough water, evidently enjoying themselves vastly, if one might judge by their gambollings among the heaving rollers, which were of a greater height than any I ever remember to have seen, excepting in very bad weather in the Bay of Biscay.

On quitting the open ocean, however, which we did on our entrance to the fjord, we were soon in more sheltered waters, although a bitterly cold wind was blowing, and a thick mist came on just before reaching Molde, which was unfortunate, as the panorama of distant hills on

approaching the town is rather fine. L——
was much amused in watching an old eider
duck, which our steamer, upon rounding a point
of rocks on the northern shore of the fjord, had
suddenly disturbed. The mother was swimming close to the beach when we first alarmed
her, followed by her family of several youthful
eider fowl, who, as soon as their parent gave
them a danger-signal by means of a low
"quack," climbed upon her back and seated
themselves there securely and comfortably,
whilst the old bird swam leisurely out into the
open water.

The little town of Molde, at which all
steamers touch, whether proceeding northward
or in the contrary direction, is prettily situated
on a small island, or rather promontory, on the
north side of the fjord, and backed by a sloping
hill, on which a few stunted trees are seen
growing. The view of the splendid range of
the Romsdal mountains is seen to great advantage from the anchorage at Molde; but, as
before mentioned, the mist was so heavy that
only their highest summits were visible during

the short time we remained off the town. As soon as we anchored near the little quay, a perfect cloud of tiny boats came out to meet us, the crews for the most part composed of small boys in red caps and scarlet coats, which gave them a very picturesque appearance. We landed but few passengers here, and only embarked some half-dozen new-comers, so that the fleet of boats did not find much employment.

There is nothing specially to be seen at Molde to tempt the visitor to land; but it is a pretty little town, with wide streets and a thriving population, whose chief occupation is fishing, and the place has altogether a neat and comfortable look about it. There is one peculiar feature about Molde which I think would strike any traveller seeing it for the first time; this is the remarkable abundance of fruit-trees to be seen on all sides, gooseberry-bushes and raspberries growing in many of the streets, while roses scent the air in every direction, and ruddy clusters of apples and cherries hang in profusion in many of the neat little gardens, with which a great number of the best houses are surrounded.

From Molde most travellers take the small local steamer for Veblungsnæset and Næs, the latter being the most convenient place at which to disembark, if it is intended to visit the beautiful scenery of the Romsdal valley. It is generally admitted that this is one of the most lovely districts in all Norway, and so much has been said and written in its praise, that the annual rush of tourists is so great as to cause it of late years to be quite overrun; and the consequence is that the accommodation to be obtained at the Aak hotel and other favourite spots, although greatly improved from what it was a few summers ago, is not always sufficiently extensive to enable the landlords to put up all comers; and many who visit this charming valley in July and August will do well to engage rooms beforehand, or they may be woefully disappointed on their arrival.

The sport to be met with in Romsdalen is very fair, there being a certain amount of game in the neighbouring mountains, and the Rauma river affords very fair salmon-fishing, and holds plenty of trout of a large size. The greater part of this stream is, however, preserved; but by staying at one or other of the stations on its banks, leave to fish may be generally obtained. For those fond of sketching, a finer field for operations than this valley affords could hardly be found ; for every combination of wild and rugged grandeur is to be met with in its varied scenery. To the botanist, also, it possesses great attractions, and a pleasant route will be found by pushing up the valley of the Romsdal as far as Dombaas, whence the tourist can either proceed over the Dovre-fjeld northward to Throndhjem, or return to Christiania *viâ* Gudbransdalen and the Mjösen lake. We were sorry to be unable to visit the Romsdal, but we were informed at Molde that we could obtain no steamer for Naes for two days, and as our time is valuable, we were compelled to give up the idea.

As the "Nordland" steamed slowly away from Molde, the rain ceased, and the heavy mists which had enveloped the mountains encircling the Romsdalsfjord on our arrival gradually rolled downwards, not upwards, thereby producing a remarkable and uncommon effect. The entire line of jagged mountains were exposed to view, but only their topmost ridges and snow-capped summits were visible, the sun shining brightly upon them, and the whole of the lower parts of the hills being covered with a thick cloud-vapour. Standing up alone, conspicuous among the quantities of rugged peaks, we saw the famous Romsdalshorn, a curiously shaped hill about 2190 feet in height, and some 5000 feet above the actual sea-level, and which takes its name from its supposed resemblance to a hunter's horn. It is so steep that for a great many years the peasants considered it to be inaccessible; but one day a blacksmith attempted to reach its summit, and it is said he was successful; and, in order to commemorate his enterprise, he built a large cairn of stones upon the very highest point of the mountain, and which, it is said, can be seen from a great distance. At the foot of this hill may be seen a rent in the solid rock, called by the Bonder the "sword of St. Olaf," for the legend relates that when his army were dying of thirst in this valley, Olaf struck the rock with his weapon, like Moses at Sinai, when an abundance of the purest water at once appeared!

On leaving Molde our course lay due south, and, the rain having ceased, the sun broke forth from the lowering heavens with a pleasant warmth, and L—— and I sat for some hours upon the deck, to enjoy the beauties of the scenery. The fjord to the southward of the town is termed Molde fjord, and at this season of the year it is perfectly alive with herrings, which were on all sides of the ship in countless thousands, their presence being indicated by the quantity of porpoises and other large "monsters" of the deep, which were having a merry time of it as they nimbly pursued their slippery prey.

Whales, of various species, are abundant in this fjord, and L—— was delighted to see a large creature of fully thirty feet in length close to our vessel. We saw this huge fellow jump clean out of the water several times, and when he executed this manoeuvre his size appeared monstrous, and far larger than was really the case. I cannot determine to what species this fish belonged, as it appeared in shape more like a large shark than a whale. His back was of a dark black hue and his belly silvery white, and, as he was pursuing the same direction as the porpoises, we concluded that he was also in quest of the herrings. The officers and sailors called this *cetacea* the "spring val," on account of the high jumps he took at intervals out of the water. This creature was no doubt an unusually large one of his kind, as Captain Beck informed us that it is by no means common in these seas, and added that he never remembered seeing such a big one before. The water being perfectly calm, we were able to see this monster to great advantage, the ship passing him at about fifty yards distance at the instant that he leaped clear into the air, and so gracefully executed was the jump, that his pointed snout seemed to cut through the clear waters of the fjord, as if to force an entrance for the huge body of its owner, which immediately disappeared beneath the surface, without any apparent ripple or splash. We watched him, as he now and again appeared to view, for a long time after we had left him far astern, and he was still visible, with the aid of a glass, at some two miles distance.

Curious as it may appear to many who may be unacquainted with the fish which inhabit these northern seas, there are a very considerable quantity of sharks upon the coasts of both Norway and Lapland; and for some of these a regular fishery is annually carried on by the hardy Norsk fishers. Among the sharks proper that are met with are the Greenland shark (*Squalus borealis*), which is not very uncommon near Hammerfest, Tromsö, and the Loffodens, and which attains a length of from twelve to sixteen feet; the large basking shark (*S. maximus*), also not very rare, and from twenty to forty feet long; and the picked dog-fish (*S. acanthias*), a small species of about two and a half feet in length, but very voracious and a great enemy of the herrings, following the latter fish in large shoals along the coast, and even into the fjords; and so savage are these small sharks, that the Norsk fishermen declare that, if unable to capture their victim whole, and dispose of it at one mouthful, the picked dog-fish will bite it in two pieces, swallowing the tail half only! The Norwegians call this hated fish the "pighaa," on account of the spine ("pigg," or "pig") it possesses in front of each of the two dorsal fins; and it is held in great detestation on account of the trouble it causes the fishermen, by becoming entangled in their nets, and by continually robbing the baited lines.

Lloyd, in his work on the Game Birds of Norway and Sweden, to which I have previously alluded, while speaking of this shark, remarks as follows:—"In Bohus-Län, during the fifteenth century, a regular fishery was carried on for the capture of these fish, which, owing to the diminution in their number, at length ceased. Peder Clausen, who flourished soon after the period in question, when speaking of this matter, says, 'As this fish was known to be very fond of human flesh, numbers of people, especially such as were fat and fleshy, were murdered and cut into bits, which were then used as bait.' To this circumstance, coupled with the fact that the inhabitants were accustomed to fish on Sundays, the worthy man attributed the absence of the picked dog-fish from the coast. The flesh of this species of shark is perfectly white, and is eaten both fresh and salted, and dried, in which latter state it at times forms an article of commerce."

The black shark (*S. spinax*) is sometimes seen in southern Norway, and there are altogether no less than nine or ten different kinds of sharks to be met with upon the coasts of Scandinavia, which would hardly be credited in these northern seas. All, or most of these fish, are worth something when captured; but the most valuable quarry is perhaps the basking-shark, for which I believe a regularly established fishery has been carried on off the northern and north-western coasts of Norway for considerably more than a hundred years. The late Mr. Lloyd, whose long residence in Scandinavia so eminently qualified him to afford reliable information upon all subjects connected with natural history and sport, tells us that the boats which are used for hunting the basking-sharks are large, being from thirty-six to forty feet in length, each boat having a well-trained crew of four men, all of whom are armed with harpoons.

"The fishing season," continues Mr. Lloyd, "usually commences in the beginning of August, when they cruise to and fro on such parts of the coast as are known to be the favourite haunts of the fish in question; and when they see one lying listlessly on the surface, as is its frequent habit (hence its English name), the harpooner, after the boat has approached it as nearly as possible, drives his weapon deep into its body."

"Subsequently operations are carried on in a similar manner, as when the whale is the object of attack. If the creature be lean, it at times can hold out for a whole day; but if it be fat, two or three hours usually suffice to tire it out, when it is hauled alongside the boat. Its tail is then partially severed to prevent its struggles, and afterwards it is stabbed with knives until quite dead. It is now turned over in the water, so that the belly lies uppermost, when it is secured by a rope to the mast. One of the men, provided with a long and sharp knife, then makes an incision in the fish sufficiently large to introduce his arm, upon which he severs the ligaments by which the liver is attached to the body. Finally the belly is ripped up, on which the liver floats to the surface, in like manner as a huge feather-bed, when the rope by which the fish is secured to the boat must be instantly severed, or the latter would be carried to the bottom with the creature."

It was nearly eleven o'clock p.m., when, after running through numerous clusters of tiny islets, swarming with noisy gulls, sea-swallows, and eider fowl, we at length cast anchor for a short time in the little harbour of Aalesund, where we remained until midnight, landing goods, amongst which were large bales of knives, forks, and other cutlery from Sheffield; and the "traveller" for this enterprising firm in England told me that he had just returned from the Arctic regions, where he had been receiving orders from the Hammerfest and Tromsö merchants for various steel articles, swan shot, Birmingham second-hand fowling-pieces, and other goods of a similar kind, for which it is hard to find a ready market at home. Such a statement rather does away with the romance of an Arctic tour!

Aalesund has a very sheltered harbour; and the little town, which carries on a great trade in dried cod and herrings with foreign countries, is prettily situated in a kind of half-circle upon the little bay, and the painted wooden houses peep out in every direction from amongst the bare patches of rock, which rise, in some cases almost perpendicularly, out of the water. This town is famed for its lobsters, which are caught in large numbers at the mouths of the fjords, and are mostly sent to London and Christiania. Crabs also are a favourite delicacy in Norway, and a baked crab-pie is a common dish for the supper-tables of the rich. Oysters, unlike the lobster or the crab, are by no means numerous on the Norwegian coast, and as expensive as is the case at home, the best oyster-bed being at Krageröe, situated between Christiansand and the entrance to the Christiania fjord.

The neighbourhood of Aalesund is rich in the romantic associations connected with the ancient Vikings, and the sea-pirates of the "good old days," when the innumerable fjords of this wild and rock-bound coast afforded a safe shelter to the daring spirits that manned the vessels of St. Olaf, and were the retreat of the gallant, but it must be added, somewhat unprincipled heroes of Norsk story and song. Looking upon the constantly winding and intricate channels of many of the fjords on this western coast, it is easy for the traveller to perceive how a large fleet of piratical ships could have anchored almost anywhere in perfect security, sheltered from storms by the masses of rocky islets, and quite ready at any moment to dart out into the open sea, and attack any passing merchant vessel, or bear down upon the ships of an approaching enemy. The fierce inhabitants of Norway in the seventh and eighth centuries were constantly at war with each other, and their descendants, when not engaged with attacking their neighbours at home, spent their time in scouring the seas and carrying war and desolation into France, Italy, Iceland, Spain, and other lands; and their especially favourite foraging-grounds seem to have been the opposite coasts of Scotland, and the Orkney and Shetland isles.

As we sit on deck in a dreamy mood, looking over these silent wild fjords, our thoughts wander back to times long gone by, and one half expects to see King Olaf's fleet suddenly dart round some rocky promontory, and to hear echoing amongst the surrounding mountains the lusty battle-shout of the Northern seamen, whom Longfellow has so well described in the "Saga of King Olaf," when speaking of the crew of the vessel christened the "Long Serpent." What a weird sight must have been presented, when,—

> "Safe at anchor in Throndhjem bay
> King Olaf's fleet assembled lay,
>   And, striped with white and blue,
> Downward flutter'd sail and banner,
> As alights the screaming lanner;
>   Lustily cheer'd, in their wild manner
>   The 'Long Serpent's' crew.

Her forecastle man was Ulf the Red;
Like a wolf's was his shaggy head,
 His teeth as large and white.
As standard-bearer he defended
 Olaf's flag in the fight.
By the bulkhead, tall and dark,
Stood Thrand Rame of Thelemark,
 A figure gaunt and grand.

Einar Tamberskelver, bare
To the winds his golden hair,
 By the mainmast stood;
Graceful was his form and slender,
And his eyes were deep and tender
As a woman's, in the splendour
 Of her maidenhood.

In the fore-hold Biorn and Bork
Watch'd the sailors at their work:
 Heavens! how they swore!
Thirty men they each commanded,
Iron-sinew'd, horny-handed,
Shoulders broad, and chests expanded,
 Tugging at the oar.

These, and many more like these,
With King Olaf sail'd the seas.
Never saw the wild North sea
Such a gallant company
 Sail its billows blue!

Never, while they cruised and quarrell'd,
Old King Gorm, or blue-tooth Harald,
Own'd a ship so well apparell'd,
 Boasted such a crew!"

FISHERMEN HAULING THEIR HERRING-NETS.

CHAPTER XIV.

"It is well through the rich wild woods to go,
And to pierce the haunts of the fawn and doe!
Joyous and far shall our wanderings be,
As the flight of birds o'er the wandering sea.
Come, while in freshness and dew it lies,
To the world that is under the free blue skies.
Come to the woods, in whose mossy dells
A light all made for the poet dwells,
And the voice of cool waters midst feathery fern,
Shedding sweet sounds from some hidden urn.
There is life, there is youth, there is tameless mirth,
Where the streams, with the lilies they wear, have birth.
                                        HEMANS.

Wednesday, July 5th.

NEAR the port of Aalesund, in the days of yore, stood, it is said, the strongly-built castle of Rollo "the walker," so named because he was a baron of such weight and so tall that no horse in the land was able to carry him. This hero was the conqueror and founder of the Duchy of Normandy, and was

the ancestor of our William the Conqueror.
He fought in numerous wars against France,
and at length Charles the Simple, who was at
that time King of the French, gave Rollo his
daughter Grizelle in marriage, as a reward for
Rollo's having consented to become a Christian.
He was then created Duke of Normandy, and
was called upon to pay the customary homage
to the king by kissing the royal toe, which
Rollo did by lifting the poor king's leg so high
for the purpose, that the monarch was thrown
down upon his back by the hardy Norseman!

At nine o'clock this morning the "Nordland"
steamed close inshore, as the wind had considerably gone down, and the sea also was
calmer, although there were heavy rollers from
the westward, and we passed below the grand
beetling cliff of Hornelen, the upper part of
which was unfortunately shrouded in a heavy
mist, but the lower ledges showed what a vast
mass of rock the cliff must appear when seen in
clear weather. Hornelen, which is some 2900
feet above the sea, is said to be the loftiest sea-precipice in Europe, and a huge cliff it truly is,

with black, bare, perpendicular sides, as far as our eyes could see, towering upwards into the misty sky; and in some places the cliff seems to actually overhang the ocean, and looks as if about to descend in one vast avalanche into the boiling sea below. Clouds of sea-gulls hovered around this dreary spot, making the scene doubly wild by their eerie screams, which, however, are most useful to the sailors on the dark winter nights, to guard them from this dangerous rock-bound coast.[1] A better idea of the height of Hornelen may be gained if I mention that it is stated to be even loftier than Skiddaw, near Derwentwater in our own country; and

[1] On our own coasts sea-gulls are of the greatest service to the mariner in the dark nights of winter, when his bark often may approach too near some dangerous rocky headland, when, though the danger cannot be seen by those on board, the warning cries of the birds are the means of saving many a vessel from disaster. On the Yorkshire coast—where, previously to the passing of the Sea-birds' Preservation Act a few years since (and which the author had the satisfaction of heartily supporting), parties of cockney "sporting" gentry were accustomed to shoot the poor sea-gulls in countless numbers during the breeding season—the fishermen are devoted to these useful birds, which have for ages been known as the "Flamborough pilots."

the mountain in question, it must be borne in mind, is a sheer, perpendicular precipice. I used to think some of the vast cliffs upon the rugged coasts of Sutherlandshire, and in the Orkneys, were marvellously grand; but if any one wishes to look upon the grandest sea-mountain in the whole of Europe, let him pay a visit to Hornelen.

We passed during the forenoon the entrance of the Nord fjord, which possesses some fine and very wild scenery; but without the traveller has the luck to have a yacht at his disposal, it will not be an easy matter to explore its beauties, as the accommodation to be obtained on its shores is bad. We saw from the deck several fine glaciers, and the summits of many ranges of snow-capped mountains; but what struck me most was the marked change in the formation of the clusters of islands through which we sailed to-day. Near Throndhjem, Molde, and Christiansund, we always saw a certain amount of bright green verdure upon the numerous islets; and, as a rule, they were low-lying and rugged on their shores, whereas most of those we passed between Hornelen and Bergen were rounded, as if by the action of ice, or by glacial formation, and in hardly a single instance (excepting quite close to Bergen) did we observe any grass or herbage of any sort, only bare, dreary rock on every side of the ship. Here and there a solitary fisher's cottage was to be seen, and the remark of the Rev. Robert Everest is very true, that "man, along this coast, is really like a great sea-coot, that makes its nest just above high-water mark; his neighbour is the diver, and both push out for the fishing-ground together every morning."

In the afternoon the "Nordland" steamed through a narrow passage betwixt the islands of Losmoë and Sulen, where, as the author I have just quoted remarks, the observer fancies that these two great masses have been at some previous date split asunder, leaving the channel between them; and "as we enter" it, "and look closer at the huge blocks that overhang us, we see that they are a compound of the remains of other rocks (grauwacke), a part of those foundations of the earth that 'as a vesture have been folded up, and changed.'"[2] Some hours before we sighted the town of Bergen, the entrance of the Sogne fjord was crossed, and here we passed a large number of small fish-laden vessels, called "jagts;" most of them, however, were returning empty to the Arctic regions, to fetch fresh cargoes of dried cod to Bergen and other of the ports upon this western coast. The peculiar rig of these vessels is extremely picturesque, and their sails are generally very white and clean-looking, which cannot be said of their decks, which have a disagreeable and very strong odour of fish.

It was very rough near the Sogne fjord, the white surf from the big rollers being dashed upwards to a great height, as it broke upon the rugged rocks lining the shores of the smaller islands, which were innumerable and on every side, making the channel to an inexperienced eye appear a very hazardous one.

The scenery of the province of Bergenstift, which we have now entered, is said by the

[2] "A Journey through Norway, Lapland, &c.," by the Rev. R. Everest, F.G.S. (1829), p. 216.

natives to be the most wild and lovely of any part of Norway; but opinions will probably differ upon this point. Many of its fjords and fosses are, however, undoubtedly very beautiful; and for the rugged picturesqueness of its coast views, it can vie, without fear of being surpassed, with any district in Scandinavia.

The Sogne fjord is of great length, being more than one hundred and twenty miles long; and besides its principal branch, it possesses numerous offshoots, all of which are famed for the beauties of their scenery, especially the Aardals fjord and the Lyster fjord. Excursions can also be made by the sportsman to the Sogne fjeld, where ptarmigan and reindeer will be met with; and wild flowers in great abundance will offer attractions to the botanist. Yachtsmen will delight in this grand fjord; but it is not absolutely necessary to bring a yacht, or large boat from England, as very fairly comfortable vessels are always to be hired from Bergen.

It was nearly eight o'clock in the evening, when the prettily-situated town of Bergen came into view; and as we steamed slowly into the little harbour, which was perfectly crowded with all kinds of shipping, a small, thick, but very wetting rain commenced to fall, and continued to do so throughout the evening. This place shows almost the heaviest rainfall of any European town; and since our return to England I have lit upon the following account of the climate of Bergen, which I extract from a very interesting work by Mr. W. M. Williams, F.R.A.S., the author of the familiar knapsack guide to Norway. Bergen "is the fatherland of drizzle; it receives above eighty-two inches of water per annum, nearly five times as much as falls in corresponding latitudes in Sweden; above three-and-a-half times the quantity that is poured upon equal areas of London, Edinburgh, Dublin, or even Glasgow, and more than four times as much as on St. Petersburg."[1] Amongst the shipping in the harbour were an immense number of the jagts for carrying the stock-fish, to which allusion has been previously made, and their quaint form and

[1] "Through Norway with Ladies," p. 7.

antiquated rig cannot fail to strike the attention of the traveller, their high prows especially giving them a very old-world appearance. The men who build these vessels, and the crews who navigate them are so conservative in their ideas, that I am told they will not allow the slightest alteration to be made in their shape or rig. "They will not," says Murray's Guide, "even avail themselves of the use of the windlass; and the huge square sail, therefore, still requires the same power to haul it to the mast-head as it did twelve hundred years since. They are clinker-built, and with great breadth of beam; but are not adapted for sailing, except in smooth water. It has been erroneously stated that these jagts are perfect models of those used by the old Norsemen in their piratical voyages. Their *Drage* and *Orm* were long galleys, with one or more banks of oars."

Our voyage of two days and nights from Throndhjem to Bergen has been very pleasant, and we were sorry to bid adieu to Captain Beck and his officers, who have on every possible occasion shown us the greatest attention; but, although the weather has on the whole been good during our southward passage, L—— was not sorry to be once more on dry land, and we were as glad to have arrived at our destination, as the northern sailors in Longfellow's poem of "Beowulf's Expedition to Heort," whose vessel—

"Went over the sea-waves,
Hurried by the wind
Most like a sea-fowl,
. . . . with foamy neck,
Till . . . . the second day
The curved prow
Had passed onward.
So that the sailors
The land saw
The shore-cliffs shining,
Mountains steep,
And broad sea-noses.
Then was the sea-sailing
Of the Earl at an end.
　Then . . . . the people
　On the land went,
The sea-bark moored,
God thanked they,
That to them the sea-journey
　Easy had been!"

On landing from the "Nordland" we walked from the harbour to Holdt's Hotel, which turned out to be a capital house, though expensive. When I was last in Bergen, in 1871, this hotel was not in existence, but Bergen has greatly improved in every way since my previous visit, there being a considerable number of new buildings to be seen in all directions. The Hotel Sontum, at which I found capital accommodation five years ago, has now greatly deteriorated. The good people of Bergen retire to bed betimes, as I found the streets quite deserted at 9.30 p.m., not more than two or three persons being met with during my walk of half an hour. A few firemen, who wear a curious old-fashioned uniform, were patrolling the highways, but there was hardly a light to be seen in any of the houses, and no lamps of any kind were visible. So strict are the regulations against fire in this city, that every householder is compelled by law to have a large pail, or rather cask, of water standing in front of his doors, so that plenty may be at once available on the outbreak of a conflagration.

On the firemen discovering an outbreak of fire, the guns from the fort at once give the alarm, and every one turns out to assist in subduing the fire. No one is allowed to smoke a pipe or cigar in the streets at night, and this regulation is very strictly enforced by the authorities; and this precaution is much needed, the principal part of the city being built of timber like most other Norwegian towns. Bergen has frequently suffered from terrible fires; in 1188, for instance, most of the city, and no less than eleven churches, were burnt down, and just twenty-one years ago nearly two hundred houses in the western quarter of the town were consumed. Whole streets are often burned to the ground in a few hours; indeed there was a fire of some extent near the harbour only three days ago, and we inspected the blackened ruins of the warehouses on our way from the steamer to our hotel.

Thursday, July 6th.

We were kept awake the greater part of the night by the horrible snoring of an individual in the next room to the one we occupied, and I should be sorry to say how many times I threw my shooting-boots against the wooden partition, but with no effect farther than to cause the old gentleman to cease his "music" for a few minutes, when it would recommence with increased energy. We this morning saw this disturber of our rest, and a fatter person we had never gazed upon; so possibly he could not help indulging in the entertainment of last night, for his puffings and red face were terrible to hear and see as he walked downstairs to the coffee-room.

It was a most glorious day and very hot, the rain of the past night having quite ceased, and the blue sky was cloudless. L—— and I walked up the steep hill, on the slope of which the large museum is built, and spent some time in inspecting its collection of northern antiquities, natural history, and ancient furniture, all of which is well worthy of a visit. The stuffed fishes, walrusses, and skeletons of whales, are especially worth attention; the coins, and stone and bronze implements, brought from all parts of Scandinavia, being also a very valuable collection. Whilst in one of the upper galleries at the museum, we were specially interested in looking at a most beautifully carved Dutch bedstead, the history of which is curious, and is given in Murray in these words:—" Upwards of two hundred years since this bedstead was brought to Bergen by a young English couple, just married. The husband was unfortunate in trade, and soon after died, leaving his widow *enceinte* with her first child. Norwegian hearts warmed to the young mourner and her fatherless infant, and when they at length sailed for England, the widow gave this only and valued relic of her happy days to a family here who had shown her the greatest kindness. Their descendants presented it to the museum, where it remains a token of British gratitude for Norwegian generosity."

One of the best general views of Bergen is to be obtained from the hill above the museum, the picturesque city looking from this point especially pretty, lying as it does snugly sheltered by the steep, rugged mountains which surround it. The harbour of Bergen is completely land-locked, and very commodious, the situation of the city being remarkably well chosen as long ago as the year 1070 by King Olaf Kyrre; and its foreign trade is, I believe, even greater than that of Christiania itself. Stock-fish, cod-liver oil, herrings, and wood, form the chief articles of commerce.

The English are stated to have been the first who opened up the trade of Bergen, but they were driven out of the town about the year 1436, their place being supplied by the Hanseatic League, which, in its turn, was abolished about 100 years ago, since which time the trade has been open to all nations.

Of course we visited the cathedral, the curious old German church, the art-union (where there are a few pictures worth seeing), the fortress of Bergenhuus, and other objects of interest, all of which will be found fully described in the guide-books. During the afternoon there was a grand parade of militiamen in the Eugen Square, but I did not form a very high opinion of their knowledge of drill. They were, however, a fine body of men; all of them are shopkeepers in the town, and these parades take place at frequent intervals.

Whilst talking of the Norwegian army I am reminded of the former existence of two corps of "skating-soldiers," but, I believe, there are none at the present day. In the times of the constant wars with Sweden there were two regiments of these troops, each man being armed with a rifle and a short sword, and supplied with a pair of "skie," or long pointed skates, to enable him to proceed over the frozen fjords, when the severity of the northern winters put a stop to all military evolutions upon land.

Before the union of Sweden with Norway, one corps of these "skielöbier" belonged to Throndhjem, and the other to the district of Aggerhuus. Their uniform was green, and, in fact, they exactly resembled our Rifle Brigade; and, on many occasions, they were found very useful when expeditious movements in time of war had to be undertaken. As these troops were able to march over the frozen snow, they were much dreaded by their foes, whose men and horses sunk deep into the snow-drifts over which the skating soldiers passed without inconvenience. They were especially useful in harassing the rear of a retreating army during winter, and in cutting off the baggage-trains of an enemy.

During the afternoon L—— and I rummaged in several of the shops in the Strandgarten, where old silver is sold, and succeeded in picking up some very good silver spoons of about 200 years old; but the prices asked for "gamle" silver have risen in Bergen to an alarming degree since I was last here. Some of the silver stores are well worth visiting, but let the traveller beware lest he be taken in by the officious merchants, who have a vast amount of rubbish for sale, as well as a certain quantity of *bona fide* goods.

Before retiring to rest I went on board the "Nordland" for the last time, and brought away in a small boat our two carrioles, which were then transferred to a tiny steamer called the "Voss," in which we sail to-morrow morning for Bolstadören, on our way to Christiania.

Friday, July 7th.

We were up by 5 a.m., and after a hasty breakfast we walked through the quiet streets of the sleeping city down to the quay where the "Voss" was lying, and at six o'clock the little vessel started, and the city of Bergen was soon hidden from our sight by a sudden bend of the fjord. We cannot take leave of Bergen without a few words on that well-worn subject, the sea-serpent, which, it is said, has often been seen in the immediate neighbourhood of the city. This wonderful and terrible monster has been popularly believed for hundreds of years to frequent the coasts of both Finland and Southern Norway, and so many credible persons have at various times borne witness to seeing the creature, that no unprejudiced traveller will in my opinion be justified in altogether disbelieving the statement.

That some sea-monster of huge dimensions exists in these northern seas there can be no doubt, but whether the so-called "serpent" is an enormous conger-eel, or some hitherto undescribed species, must for the present, at all events, remain a matter of doubt. Pontoppidan, the learned Bishop of Bergen, who was an excellent naturalist, gave credence to the reports of fishermen and others as to the appearance of a sea-monster on the Norwegian coasts, and this creature he calls the Kraken. In describing it, he says that, particularly in the North Sea, the creature keeps at the bottom, excepting in the months of July and August, at which seasons the spawning takes place, when the sea-serpent comes to the surface in calm weather, but at once disappears beneath the surface when the wind raises the least ripple.

Captain Brooke, in his "Travels to the North Cape," also gives a long *résumé* of his inquiries as to the existence of this wonderful creature. After reviewing the evidence for and against the Kraken, this author concludes by saying, "Taking, upon the whole, a fair view of the different accounts related respecting the sea-serpent, no reasonable person can doubt the fact of some marine animal of extraordinary dimensions, and, in all probability, of the serpent tribe, having been repeatedly seen by various persons along the Norway and Finmark coasts. These accounts, for the most part, have been given verbally from the mouths of the fishermen, an honest and artless class of men."

"Many of the informants, besides, were of superior rank and education" (and here follow the names of a bishop, a dean, various clergy, and the Governor of Finmark), "men who ought not to be disregarded. Ideas of the existence of some marine animal, far exceeding in bulk every other, have been entertained from the earliest times. The mention made of the monster in the book of Job is unquestionably the most curious and interesting."[1] Captain Brooke then proceeds to remark that the description of the creature given in Job is written in such minute and terribly sublime language, that everybody is enabled without difficulty to judge if this description is applicable to any of the large fish known to inhabit the deep. Why should not some Leviathan

[1] Job, ch. xli.

exist at the present day, is a question more easily asked than answered; but that some huge sea-monster occasionally appears upon the Norwegian coasts, is my sincere belief, and I fully believe that such will some day be ascertained as a certain fact.

The distance by water from Bergen to Bolstadören is about seventy miles, which took the little steamer—laden to the water's edge as she was with horses, goods, and crowds of peasants—some half-dozen hours to accomplish. The morning was chilly, the wind being north-easterly, but we sat upon deck throughout the voyage, as the scenery was very beautiful and extremely wild. Numerous water-falls were passed, some of the height of at least one thousand feet above the fjord; and many a snug cluster of farm-houses were nestled here and there beneath the grey cliffs, which loomed above these picturesque dwellings, often to an enormous height, some of the mountains literally overhanging the fjord beneath, into whose blue waters the winter avalanches are poured.

Before reaching our destination, as we were sitting quietly upon deck, admiring the glorious wildness of the ever-changing mountain views, we were suddenly startled by hearing a loud report, which was echoed a thousand times from the surrounding hills. It was occasioned by the blasting of the solid rock by the edge of the fjord, in spots where the engineers, now engaged in constructing the new line of railway from Bolstadören to Bergen, have decided to carry the works. The echo of the loud report of the gunpowder was repeated from the wild mountain gorges for nearly four minutes, till

> "Faint and more faint, its failing din
> Return'd from cavern, cliff, and linn,
> And silence settled, wide and still,
> On the lone wood and mighty hill."

During our voyage up the Bergen fjord, we noticed several curious traps for salmon, which consisted of a large net set in a semi-circular manner, with one end attached to the shore. A ladder, roughly constructed of ropes and fir poles, led to a kind of platform on which the owner of the "trap" reclines all day long

smoking his pipe and lazily gazing into the
blue depths of the fjord beneath his perch, which
is so built that it overhangs the water. When
a fish enters the net the peasant from aloft at
once sees it, as the waters of these fjords are
so transparent that the eye can penetrate to a
great depth beneath the surface. Before descending, the man pulls a long rope which
closes all exit from the net, and then he takes
to his small boat, gathers in the net to the
shore and knocks the unfortunate salmon on
the head with a short thick stick. We noticed
several peasants thus engaged, and the quantity
of salmon thus destroyed during a favourable
season is very large.

Bolstadören was reached at noon, and we at
once proceeded in our carrioles along a pretty
road to the western end of the lake of some
four miles in length, called the Evanger Vand,
where the road ended, and we were obliged
to embark in two large boats together with our
carrioles, the wheels of which had to be taken
off in order to get the vehicles into the largest
of the boats. The scenery of the Evanger

Vand is very wild and beautiful, and we saw many a little farm perched high up on the mountain-side overhanging the lake, and the peasants were hard at work at their hay-making, and so high were they above us, that the men and women looked like pigmies. On reaching Evanger we found we had to wait three hours for ponies, so we took our lunch in the station there to pass the time. The people of this country, whether rich or poor, are remarkable for their courtesy. When visiting at a house in Norway, it is usual, at the conclusion of a repast, to thank the host for the dinner or breakfast of which one has partaken. This is done by the guest shaking his entertainer heartily by the hand, and saying to him "Tak for mad," literally "thanks for the repast," to which he generally replies, "Velbecommen," or "may it agree with you."

If you pass a peasant upon the high road, you will often observe that he either respectfully touches his cap to you, or removes it altogether, and he expects his salute to be acknowledged. Many of our fellow-countrymen, I fear, do not take the trouble to do this, and are consequently thought very wanting in courteous manners by the good people of Norway. It is also usual, if the traveller enters a shop in a town, to remove the hat, and not to put it on again until leaving.

At Evanger, we found the station occupied by English sportsmen, who had just arrived there for salmon-fishing in the river which runs into the lake near the village, and has a fair repute as a salmon stream. From Evanger a charming excursion may be made to the summit of a mountain called Mykletveitveten, which is about 3650 feet in height; and whence, in clear weather, a magnificent panorama over the interior of the Hardanger is obtained.

It was very hot when we quitted Evanger, and a dusty, but most enjoyable drive of some eleven miles through lovely scenery, brought us to the pretty little village of Vossevangen. During this drive we noticed, for the first time since we have been in the country, some green woodpeckers and turtle-doves, and clouds of

magpies were to be seen on all sides; whilst
the grey crows, as mischievous here as they
are at home, were busy as usual foraging in
every farm-yard and in every cultivated field.

The valley near Vossevangen presented a
beautiful appearance, and was more like
summer than anything we have as yet seen.
Crowds of sturdy sunburnt peasants were hay-
making by the side of the lake near the village;
the little cows and goats were lying lazily under
the cool shelter of the birch-trees; the whole of
the valley was a lovely mass of the brightest
green grass, relieved here and there by extensive patches of wild flowers of every colour
imaginable, and clumps of the grey-stemmed
birch or the dusky pine were scattered in
picturesque profusion around the placid lake
in whose deep-blue waters the white and red
wooden houses of Vossevangen, each with its
little garden, were vividly reflected.

We drove to Herr Fleisher's hotel, where I
put up in 1871, and spent some pleasant days
in this valley, shooting; and he gave us a very
cordial welcome. The only thing in this truly

summer landscape that can remind us of winter is the small patch of glistening snow upon the summits of the lofty mountains upon the opposite side of the lake; but the evening was so bright and warm, that L—— and I went out fishing after supper, and spent several hours very pleasantly in wandering along the river-banks, and exploring the forest through which the stream runs before entering the lake.

We did not capture very many fish, but a few trout were brought home in the creel for breakfast to-morrow; there being no wind, the fish would not rise well to the fly. The woods were redolent of the pine-trees, and were carpetted with the most lovely wild flowers in all directions; bilberries, juniper, wild strawberries, raspberries, and other fruits being also in rich profusion. As we stood by the river-bank at 11 p.m., watching the sunset, which was a most glorious one, a woodcock flew across the stream and passed over our heads. There are a great number of cocks in these woods now, as they are engaged in breeding, and the observer may often see them flying about the open glades of the forest during the night. These birds breed in the vast woods of Norway and Sweden in comparative security, being seldom molested by man; and indeed, were it not so, the breed would speedily die out, and when the chill autumn winds and the first fall of snow came to tell the birds it is time to depart for England and other warmer climes, there would be but few woodcocks to obey the summons of instinct.

The Norwegian peasant is a terrible poacher, and the quantities of ptarmigan, woodcock, snipe, black-game, wild ducks, &c., captured by means of snares during autumn and spring is amazingly large. As long, however, as the grand old forests of Scandinavia escape destruction by the axe of the woodman, we need never fear but that year after year flights of cocks will arrive in Great Britain from over the North Sea. The present chapter cannot be more aptly closed than by the quotation of the following pretty poem, which I take from Lloyd's "Game Birds of Sweden and Norway," and which is translated from the Swedish of Stagnelius, originally appearing in "Chambers' Journal."

These lines are intended to indicate the love of the migratory birds for the land of their birth, and the sorrow the natives of Norway suppose them to feel, when the near approach of winter threatens a speedy failure of their usual food supply, and hastens their departure for more genial climes. It is called the

LAMENT OF THE BIRDS OF PASSAGE.

Behold! the birds fly
  From Gouthiod's strand,
And seek with a sigh
  Some far foreign land.
The sounds of their woe
  With hollow winds blend:
" Where now must we go?
  Our flight whither tend?"
'Tis thus unto heaven that their wailings ascend.

" The Scandian shore
  We leave in despair;
Our days glided o'er
  So blissfully there.

We there built our nest
   Among bright blooming trees,
There rock'd us to rest
   The balm-bearing breeze;
But now to far lands we must traverse the seas.

" With rose-crown all bright
   On tresses of gold,
The Midsummer night,
   It was sweet to behold.
The calm was so deep,
   So lovely the ray,
We could not then sleep;
   But were tranced on the spray,
'Till waken'd by beams from the bright car of Day.

" The trees gently bent
   O'er the plains in repose,
With snow-drops besprent
   Was the tremulous rose.
The oaks *now* are bare,
   The rose is no more;
The Zephyr's light air
   Is exchanged for the roar
Of storms, and the May-fields have mantles of hoar.

" Then why do we stay
   In the North, where the sun
More dimly each day
   His brief course will run?
And why need we sigh?
   We leave but a grave
To cleave through the sky
   On the wings which God gave;
Then, Ocean, be welcome the roar of thy waves."

When earth's joys are o'er,
   And the days darkly roll,
When autumn winds roar,
   Weep not, O my soul!
Fair lands o'er the sea
   For the birds brightly bloom,
A land smiles for thee
   Beyond the dark tomb,
Where beams never-fading its beauties illume.

CHAPTER XV.

"The gay green wood! 'tis a lovely world,
    With a beauty that's all its own;
And pleasant it is in the summer time
    To roam through that world alone."

*   *   *   *   *

"—— Oh to lie down in wilds apart,
    Where man is seldom seen or heard;
In still and ancient forests where
Mows not his scythe, ploughs not his share,
    With the shy deer and cooing bird!"

Saturday, July 8th.

I WAS up soon after five o'clock, and walking quickly past the few picturesque wooden houses that constitute the village of Vossevangen, I soon found myself in the large forest of pine-trees that extends from the shores of the lake to a considerable distance to the northward. After a pleasant walk by the riverside, I reached a large piece of water; and here, by wading in for some yards, as the water was very shallow, I managed to kill some nice trout with the fly. The woods were lovely at this early hour, one mass of dark green trees over one's head, and a perfect carpet of the brightest grass and wild flowers beneath one's feet; ferns of much beauty grew along the river-banks in great profusion, a gentle shower caused the forest to be sweetly redolent of the pines, and the silvery rain-drops upon every bough glistened in the sun. The redwing, aptly called in Norway "the northern nightingale," filled the air with song, whilst the tapping of the great black woodpecker (*Picus martius*), which is fairly common near this spot, sounded now and again from the opposite side of the stream, which dashed trembling and foaming over its rocky bed at a great rate in the wild glen; and the deep silent pools, where I managed to move some large and cunning trout, were overhung with the weeping birches, whilst the yellow broom and the juniper thickly clothed the rocky banks.

Upon the lakes near Vossevangen there are often to be seen various rare water-fowl, and I well remember the chases after some fine black-throated divers that I had here in the spring of 1871, when the ice on the fjord was just beginning to break up. I then supposed that this comparatively scarce bird would be found breeding on the shores of the lakes, but as far as I am now enabled to ascertain such is not the case. A few golden-eye ducks and little grebes, together with the common wild duck (*Anas boschas*) were the only species we met with during our present visit.

I have shot many golden-eyes on these pieces of water, especially upon the large lake near the village, and they seem to be very common here in spring and autumn. Just now most of these birds are away in the north, breeding. The golden-eye (*Anas clangula*) is fond of nesting in a hole in a low-growing tree, such as the pollard-willow; and the Laplanders, aware of this habit, turn it to account by constructing boxes, which they place upon poles, and erect in lines wherever the golden-eyes come to breed. The birds, year after year, will occupy these boxes, and the Lap rewards himself for his trouble by taking for his own consumption what eggs he requires.

One of the grandest water-falls in Norway can be visited from Vossevangen; it is called the Vöring-foss, and consists of a vast body of water precipitated from the giddy height of about 600 feet down a wall of rock, which, however, it never touches.

At midday we were once more in our carrioles, and bidding good-bye to Herr Fleisher (whose house I can most strongly recommend), we soon found ourselves at the next station, called Tvinde, a distance of seven miles. Here L—— was pleased to see the people of this station (which is very dirty and miserably bad) engaged in making *fläd bröd*, which is a kind of flat round-shaped cake, something like the Scotch oat-cake, but much larger; and it is used by the Norwegian peasants instead of bread, and is made as thin as a wafer.

At Tvinde there is a very fine water-fall, the mass of water not being very large, but the foss is of great breadth, and of considerable height. When I last saw it, the forest was deep in heavy snow, and as I stopped my sledge to change ponies I went to look at the foss, which was then falling within a huge canopy of ice, and had a very different appearance from the beautiful stream of clear water we saw to-day.

A pretty stage of six and a half miles took us speedily to Vinje, whence a good road, but mostly uphill, led to the next station, Stalheim, situated in a very wild and solitary spot, and where we were kept a long time waiting for fresh ponies. From this station to Gudvangen, the traveller passes through some of the most glorious scenery in Norway; the road from Stalheim, whence a beautiful view of the valley far below is obtained, being probably one of the grandest highways in the whole of Europe.

A little to the northward of the station at Stalheim an immense mountain seems to form an abrupt termination to the road, but on arriving at the top of this hill a beautifully engineered, winding road will be found to conduct the traveller to the valley of the Nærödal, a thousand feet below. This grand mountain is known as the Stalheimscleft. This winding pathway is one of the finest works of a celebrated Norwegian engineer, and the descent is easy: the road is carried *en échelle* down the face of this stupendous cliff, the zigzags being of a very easy gradient, and about twenty-four in number.

Two fine water-falls, each nearly 1000 feet in height, are passed, one to the right of the road and the other to the left, as one descends this road into the valley, through which we drove by the side of a pretty little river for several miles. This valley of the Nærödal is so deep that it is only at about midday that the rays of the sun penetrate to the road which runs along the bottom of the glen, whose sides are very precipitous, and the path is in many places almost blocked up with the *débris* of numerous avalanches of the past spring.

After a lovely drive through this romantic glen, in which the principal object was a picturesque mountain with a rounded summit, called the Justedalsnut, we reached the tiny village of Gudvangen, where we were glad to find comfortable quarters and a good dinner, as it was nearly ten o'clock, and we had been much delayed on the road.

Sunday, July 9th.

We were told last night that the little coasting steamer for Lærdalsören would call at this place before 5 a.m., so L—— and I were up by four o'clock, and after a weary waiting of five hours, during most of which time we sat upon the landing-stage so as not to miss the boat, we returned in despair to our inn. No sooner, however, had we ordered our second breakfast than the long-wished-for whistle of the approaching vessel was heard echoing amongst the mountains.

We at once went on board, and were very glad to see on deck the faces of T—— and W——, from whom we had last parted a month ago at Dombaas on the Dovre fjeld. We left Gudvangen at 10 a.m., and had a good view of the little place, which is very beautifully situated at the end of the Næröfjord, which is here very narrow, and bordered by two huge mountain cliffs of about 5000 feet high on either side, and from our hotel-door we were able to count no less than nineteen waterfalls, each of about *three thousand feet in height*, and this will give some idea of the grandeur and sublime magnificence of Gudvangen. Most of these fosses fell sheer down into the blue waters of the fjord, and were of varying breadth, some being mere silver threads, and others large volumes of water, all of them coming off the snowy fjelds above us.

Several hours were occupied in reaching the port of Lærdalsören, where we left the steamer and again took to our carrioles, T—— and W—— accompanying us. Our route lay along the pretty banks of the Lærdals river, where good salmon and sea-trout fishing is to be had, and we continued to drive alongside this stream until we reached the old church of Borgund, a distance of about twenty-three miles from Lærdalsören.

This church of Borgund is one of the most curious and interesting in Norway, and we left our carrioles in charge of the post-boys while Mr. T——, who is a clergyman, read a

portion of the English service to L——, Mr.
W——, and myself, as it was Sunday, which in
travelling I fear one is sometimes too apt to
forget. We wondered if the English Church-
service had ever been heard within these
ancient walls before: most probably not.

This church is said to have been built about

THE OLD CHURCH OF BORGUND.

the eleventh or twelfth century, and is constructed entirely of wood. There is a remarkable passage, roofed with wood, surrounding the church, the object of which I suppose is to give shelter to the congregation in bad weather, whilst waiting for the arrival of the clergyman. The edifice more resembles a Chinese pagoda than anything else, and has the effect of a toy-church, such as a child would play with in a box of wooden houses. The building is painted with pitch every few years, in order to keep out the wet, and the wood has consequently become very dark in colour, which gives the church a quaint, old-fashioned appearance, and it is a striking feature in the wild landscape.

The peasants do not use this old church now, but a new one is being erected in close proximity to it, and when this is finished it is feared the more ancient and interesting building may be taken to pieces, and bodily removed, as was the case with another curious wooden church from Wang, not far from Throndhjem.

This edifice was removed in carts to the coast, and then shipped off to Silesia, having been purchased by the King of Prussia, who caused it to be re-erected upon its arrival in that country.

We said adieu to our friends at the old belfry-gate of Borgund church-yard, as they return to-night to Lærdalsören, on their way to England. Our road still continued uphill to Hæg i Lærdal, at which station we again changed our horses, and a fresh pair soon took our carrioles at a good pace up the steep road by the side of the Lærdals River, through a magnificent rocky gorge, with towering masses of mountains on every side, which leads to Maristuen.

Maristuen is a good and commodious station, and the people were anxious for us to stay the night with them, but as there were sounds of revelry within, and as moreover I had some trouble with a tipsy peasant, who chose to sit upon the door-step, we decided, late though it was, to push on to the next halting-place. Maristuen is a capital head-quarters for the sportsman, reindeer being found on the neighbouring fjelds, and even bears being by no means rare. Indeed it is said that a peasant very narrowly escaped being killed by a bear close to the station a few winters ago; and our post-boy pointed out to us, between Maristuen and the next station, Nystuen, a spot where bears had been seen several times during the past winter.

Some skulls of bears are nailed up over the door at Maristuen station-house, and they are met with every year in some numbers in the neighbouring woods, and often pay a passing visit to a wayside "sæter," from which they are generally able to carry off a calf, a goat, or some such trophy.

Maristuen, being about 3000 feet above the level of the sea, is in a very bleak situation, and here may be said to commence the plateau of the Fille fjeld, which continues for the next twenty miles of our route. Our drive to Nystuen was a long one of nearly eleven miles, and so cold and biting was the north-east wind that we almost regretted that we had not stayed at Maristuen. Before arriving at Nystuen, which is about 3170 feet above the level of the sea, we passed through a most desolate region; nothing but grim, grey rocks were to be seen on every side of the road, with here and there a dreary-looking lake, and we were quite surrounded with snow-clad mountains of great altitude, from which a bitter wind was blowing, and the sole inhabitants of this dismal fjeld seemed to be the little lemmings, of which we saw a great many as they constantly scuttled away across the road, or sat up upon their hind legs in an inquisitive manner, to see who were the intruders upon their solitude.

That the traveller in Norway should be always provided with plenty of warm clothing, was proved to us to-day; as at Lærdalsören, at breakfast-time this morning we were nearly roasted by the burning sun, whilst at 10 p.m. this evening we were shivering in our carrioles, which now and then were driven through snow lying by the side of the high road. It must, however, be borne in mind that the altitude of the plateau of the Fille fjeld, at its highest point, is some 3900 feet above the level of the fjord at Lærdal-ören, which is of course sufficient reason to account for this great change in the temperature.

On our arrival at Nystuen we found the people of the station all in bed, but after they had been awakened they prepared comfortable rooms for us, and a capital supper, served up at midnight, at which excellent red-fleshed trout from the neighbouring lake were conspicuous.

The costume of the peasants upon the eastern side of the Filie fjeld, will strike the traveller as being entirely different from that worn by the people who dwell between the summit of the fjeld and Lærdalsören, and some of the women in this latter district are really pretty, having, says Murray, " fair hair, oval faces, and soft grey eyes. Their dress is a tight bodice of dark cloth, buttoned up to the throat, and with long sleeves; cloth petticoat, generally dark green, buttons and ornaments of silver. The married women wear a white cap of very singular form. Those women who have had a child without being married, wear a cap peculiar to themselves, and are called ' half-wives.' The maidens wear their hair in a most becoming manner; it is braided with narrow bands of red worsted, and wound round the head—the Norwegian snood."

Throughout this country the traveller cannot fail to notice that the wooden floors of the

houses are often strewed over with the fresh
green top-shoots of the juniper and spruce fir.
The peasants renew these about once a week,
and the branches help, to a great extent, to
prevent the disagreeable smell and closeness
arising from the rooms being heated by stoves.
This, of course, is more necessary in the winter
months, when firing is indispensable; but to
my mind even in summer-time it makes the clean
little fir-panelled apartments of the Norwegian
"station" look fresh and neat, and when the
foot of the passer-by presses the tender
branches a refreshingly sweet forest odour fills
the rooms.

Monday, July 10th.

There are great attractions at Nystuen if
the weather be fine, amongst which are several
interesting excursions which can be made thence
to the various mountains in the vicinity, from
some of which most magnificent panoramas can
be obtained. Capital trout-fishing is to be had
in some of the lakes and streams close to the
station, and the reindeer-stalking and ptarmigan-
shooting are well spoken of. Trout are often

caught near Nystuen, up to three pounds' weight; but in the large lake near the station the fish are very shy, and seldom rise well to the fly, the people at the station catching what they want either in nets or by means of night-lines baited with worms; there is a great abundance of ground feeding in some of these mountain lakes, which makes the fish keep near the bottom.

It was a bright sunny morning, so after breakfast we left Nystuen, and had a pretty drive through a wild part of the Fille fjeld, where nothing was to be seen but towering mountains on every side, whose peaks were all snow-capped, and the country looked desolate and dreary in the extreme. Masses of stunted juniper and flowering shrubs, however, brightened up the weirdness of the landscape to a certain extent, and vast quantities of beautiful wild flowers strewed the stony surface of the fjeld as far as the eye could reach. Little pools of stagnant water here and there gleamed in the sun, and a solitary pair of wild ducks, a few small chatts, and an odd lemming were the only signs of animal life we saw upon the fjeld.

There is, nevertheless, beauty in this very wildness, for

> "Fen, marshes, bog, and heath all intervene;
> There are deep pits, with watery bases, found,
> And curious plants enrich the shady ground,
> There are the feathery grass, the flowery rush,
> The gale's rich balm, the sundew's crimson blush,
> Whose velvet leaf, with radiant beauty drest,
> Forms a gay pillow for the plover's breast."

Just before we reached Skogstad, twelve miles distant from Nystuen, we thought we saw some reindeer upon the summit of a mountain, about three miles to the southward of the road, but the atmosphere was too hazy to enable us to judge with certainty.

At Skogstad the station-master told us that several large herds of reindeer had frequented, throughout the past winter, that part of the Fille fjeld near where we imagined we had seen them.

The whole of the scenery that will be passed, from the plateau of this fjeld to Christiania, has been so frequently described, that I shall do little more than record the special incidents that occurred on our southward drive. The weather, although so bitterly cold upon the top of the Fille fjeld, became charming after we had descended the very precipitous road from the plateau to Skogstad, where the warmth of the sun quickly made us throw aside the coats and wraps in which we had started from Nystuen. From hence a capital pair of fresh little horses rapidly took us along the still-descending road to Thune, where we had to wait some time before our new steeds were forthcoming. A pretty drive through a pine forest of great beauty, and in whose recesses the tapping of the woodpecker and cheery cry of the cuckoo made themselves heard, soon brought us to Oiloe, where good ptarmigan and grouse-shooting is to be had in the autumn.

Here we lunched; and that the trout from the river, which runs close to the station, are of large size and excellent quality was proved by some splendid fish which were set before us. Some of these trout must certainly be as heavy as four pounds in weight; but, alas! they were caught upon the night-line, as usual, and indeed the setting of lines, and worm-fishing seems to be the only portion of the angler's art carried on to any extent by the peasantry in this country.

A drive of nearly eight miles further southward landed us at Stee, near which place there are said to be a few bears in winter, and wolves are also common during severe weather. A story is told of a peasant who was sledging, in the hard winter of 1846, on one of the large frozen fjords not far from Stee, when a pack of half-a-dozen large wolves, fierce with hunger, attacked him. He had, however, fortunately for himself, his woodman's axe in the sledge beside him, and with this weapon he was enabled to cripple three of his savage assailants, whose bodies were at once eaten by the remaining three unwounded animals; and before they had finished their repast, horse and man had reached a place of safety.

After leaving Stee our road passed a fine water-fall, and was still gradually descending whilst we skirted the large piece of water called the Mjös Vand, or Little Mjö-en, which is some 1580 feet above the sea, and the scenery of which is exceedingly wild and grand. Part of the road by the Little Mjösen passes so close under the overhanging rocks that it is roofed over with a kind of hut for some little distance, the wooden planking being necessary to prevent avalanches of snow and stones being hurled upon the road from the precipices above. The station of Reien is very beautifully situated, but the evening was getting late; so we pushed on to Fagernæs, than which there is no better or more charming house to put up at throughout the length and breadth of the land.

L—— was rather tired, as our drive from Nystuen has covered a distance of nearly sixty-one miles, so she did not accompany me to the river, where I had the pleasure of getting wetted to the skin by a sudden thunder-shower, which also prevented the trout from rising to the fly as they should have done.

Tuesday, July 11th.

Mosquitoes—and truly their name must have been "legion"—kept us awake the greater part of the night, and we subsequently found out that Fagernæs is celebrated as a favourite head-quarters of these annoying little pests. The station of Fagernæs is a capitally built modern house, with plenty of accommodation for travellers, and we were made most comfortable by the landlord and Miss Thora, his sister, who may fairly be congratulated upon having one of the pleasantest stations in Norway. Situated upon the banks of the lovely Strand fjord, which is full of trout, sheltered by a vast pine forest, and backed by fine hills, with capital shooting and river-fishing to be obtained within easy distance, it would indeed be surprising were this not a favourite resort. Indeed, so great is the jealousy of the two station-masters on the road both to the north and south of Fagernæs, that they do all they can to induce travellers to stay with them, but generally without avail, so widely known and justly appreciated is this pleasant spot.

We did not leave Fagernæs till the afternoon, and our next stoppage was at Frydenlund, about seven miles distant, and here we had to

wait a couple of hours for horses, so L——
and I spent the time in fishing. The scenery
by the river at this spot was beautiful, and
there were plenty of large trout, but we only
succeeded in catching about a dozen, the sun
being too bright for much success.

From Frydenlund to Sveen station our road
was very picturesque, leading through a wildly
wooded country, and over a steep mountain,
from which the views were splendid. This
hill separates the Bægna valley from the
Etnadal.

Tomlevolden was next reached, whence a
very long drive of more than two hours
brought us at length to Odnæs, at the head of
the extensive sheet of water called the Randsfjord, which is more than fifty miles in length.
Soon after leaving Tomlevolden the sun disappeared, and for the first time since leaving
Bergen, we noticed how quickly the evenings
are beginning to close in compared with what
was the case farther north.

The woods looked very dark as our carrioles
rolled merrily along the level road; the tapping

of the woodpecker and the cooing of the doves were no longer heard, and—

> "The shades of eve came slowly down,
> The woods are wrapp'd in deeper brown,
> The owl awakens from her dell,
> The fox is heard upon the fell."

We did not reach Odnæs until 11.30 p.m., when it was quite dark; but during the latter part of our drive a full moon shone out from a cloudy sky, and its effect upon the grey, twisted stems of the ancient birch-trees in the forest through which our road lay was very beautiful. There are some splendid old trees near the head of the Randsfjord, of a size that is not often equalled in Norway; and this is especially the case with the birches and willows, and there are also magnificently grown specimens of spruce firs close to the roadside not far from the station.

At midnight a cold supper was placed before us, and so hungry were we that I forget the exact number of birds that we ate bodily, but luckily they were not very big ones, being redwings and fieldfares, and most excellent eating they proved.

The fieldfare (*Turdus pilaris*) is a very abundant species in all the wooded districts of both Sweden and Norway, extending almost up to the North Cape itself. During the summer its principal resorts are the vast pine forests, where its nest is often to be seen by the passing traveller. It is sometimes placed low down in a tree overhanging the high road, indeed in one or two spots near Engen i Stören, the eggs could have been taken from the nests by a person standing up in his carriole. It generally breeds in colonies, after the manner of the common rook. These birds are such excellent eating that the peasants shoot and trap them in large numbers.

Wednesday, July 12*th*.

The steamer, which plys once daily up and down the Randsfjord, commenced a series of noisy whistlings at an early hour this morning, and, fearing that we should be late, we hurried across the fields which separate the station at Odnaes from the lake, and got on board by

8 a.m.; our carrioles were hoisted on deck, and the little vessel sailed merrily away down the fjord, the scenery of which was pretty, though scarcely to be called wild or very fine.

There are very large pike and perch in this lake, and the trout-fishing is said to be good, and the fish are of a large size. The day was lovely, and multitudes of swallows were to be seen on all sides chasing the flies that danced over the water in the glancing sun. These birds are looked upon throughout Norway and the north of Europe generally with love and veneration, for it is said by the peasants that when our Saviour was crucified a small bird flew down from the skies, and, perching upon the cross, looked into the Lord's face, sang sorrowfully the words, " Hugsvala, svala, svala Honom," which meant, " Console, console, console Him," and ever afterwards the bird was named the " svala." In return for its commiseration to our Saviour, Heaven is said to have promised the bird that prosperity should in future attend those who protected the swallow, its nest, and its young ones.

It is believed by many in Norway that these birds pass the winter at the bottom of the rivers and fjords, where they lie in a happy state of torpor until the warmth of approaching spring tells them it is once more time to leave their watery home, and take to their wings again! Many, even among the most educated classes in this country, implicitly believe in this strange theory.

The legends connected with animals and birds are endless among the inhabitants of Scandinavia, and there are several other versions of the story of the swallow, which vied with the crossbill (whose plumage bears the blood-stains from the cross to this day!) and the turtle-dove in ministering to the dying Lord, whereas the green plover (*Vanellus cristatus*), on the other hand, reviled Him. The peewit is stated to have flown round and round the cross, and Golgotha resounded with its dreary, mocking cries, "Pee-wit; pee-weet."

There is, again, yet another version of this legend, given by Lloyd,[1] who remarks that the

[1] "Scandinavian Adventures," vol. ii. p. 345.

people "say that this bird was a handmaiden of the Blessed Virgin, and whilst in servitude purloined its mistress's silver scissors, and that, as a judgment, the transformation took place. Moreover that, as a brand for the theft, its tail was forked in the manner of scissors, and that it was doomed for ever to fly from tussock to tussock, uttering its plaintive *tyvil, tyvil*, that is, 'I stole them, I stole them.'"

There is good accommodation on the Randsfjord steamers, and the food is excellent, and the fresh wild strawberries with which we were supplied on board were very good and cheap. We reached the southern end of the lake at about 2 p.m., and, landing at once, I had our carrioles taken to the little railway-station near the Hadelands Glasværk, where they were placed on trucks, and after some delay the train was taking us very slowly on our way towards Christiania.

Part of this line of railway from the Randsfjord to the capital is pretty, passing through large pine forests; Hönefos, Haugsund, and Drammen being the chief places of interest upon this route. At Hönefos, where I spent some time in 1871 very pleasantly, there is good trout-fishing to be obtained, and a few elk are said to exist in the neighbouring forests; but its chief interest consists of the part this village played in Norwegian history. When Norway was invaded by the Swedes in 1716 the parish priest of Hönefos was very ill, and a party of some two hundred of the enemy's cavalry were quartered at his house. His wife, however, managed to ply the Swedish soldiery with drink to such an extent that most of them were soon helplessly tipsy, when she privately despatched one of her servants to the captain of a small body of Norwegians, who were not far off, and who at once fell upon the Swedes and slew the greater part of them.

After a long and tiring journey by the miserably slow train, we were delighted by at length seeing in the distance the spires of the churches of Christiania, and by 8 p.m. L—— and I were once more back in our old quarters in the Victoria Hotel.

Thursday, July 13th.

The morning of this, our last day in Norway, was fine, and there was a very hot sun, but a strong wind from the south tempered the atmosphere, which would otherwise have been unbearably warm. L—— and I spent the morning in packing up our various treasures, and the afternoon was occupied in being photographed, sitting in our carrioles, to which we are very sorry to have to bid adieu, and we almost decided to buy them and take them with us, but the price asked for them was too high to make it worth our while to do so.

Having completed our preparations, at 3.15 p.m., we went on board the "Albion" steamer, which is to convey us to England; and a few minutes after we had embarked, the anchor was up, and Christiania soon faded from our sight as we steamed away down the fjord.

Soon after leaving the capital, we noticed upon the eastern shores of the fjord a large number of wooden storehouses, whose use was not at first quite apparent. On inquiring, however, of Captain Langlands of the "Albion," who is a first-rate officer and has a ready fund of information, we ascertained that these buildings were used as stores for the vast quantity of ice which is obtained every winter from a large lake, situated at the distance of about half a mile from the fjord. This lake being, I believe, shallow, freezes very rapidly, and the ice is of most excellent quality, and is cut into large square masses, which are then placed on sledges, which (as the lake is at a much higher level than the fjord) easily travel down the hillside to the stores, where the ships are ready waiting to take in cargoes of ice for England, France, and other parts of the Continent. This lake was originally called by some Norwegian name which I forget, but it has been lately purchased by an Englishman, who rechristened it "Lake Wenham;" and from here comes the best ice to be obtained in the London market. Few people, probably, are aware that the "Wenham ice," which they fondly imagine has crossed the broad Atlantic ocean, in reality has made no longer a journey than from the shores of Christiania fjord.

The view to the northward on leaving the city was very beautiful; the wooded mountains towering above the church towers, the massive outline of the new palace, the numerous islets, covered with waving birches and pretty country-houses, painted red, green, or blue, and the rays of a brilliant sun shining upon the bright waters of the fjord, made up a picture on which the eye delighted to dwell. The prettiest feature of this view was, perhaps, the passing peep that was obtained of Oscarshal, the summer palace of the king.

During the afternoon the wind rose very considerably, and by the time we passed the Færder Island, with its lighthouse, at the exit of the Christiania fjord, the sea had become so boisterous that L—— was obliged to go below, and by 11.30 p.m. the seas were running very high, and a bright moon was shining over the stormy waters as I turned into my berth.

Friday, July 14th.

We reached the port of Christiansand at 7 a.m., and stayed there long enough to enable us to take on board a large quantity of lobsters and other fish for the London markets, and by the time I went on deck we were about ten miles distant from the Norwegian coast. By mid-day we were in the open sea, and the last we saw of old Norway was the distant headland of the Naze.

The quantities of mackerel boats that we saw to-day reminded me of a horrible anecdote, which was told currently in Christiania, of some poor sailor who had been shipwrecked in the fjord, and whose body was afterwards found half eaten by mackerel! For this reason this excellent fish, and the whiting also, are very unpopular, and are only eaten by the poorest in the land.

Rather before 2 p.m. the sea suddenly went down, and the "Albion" slowly steamed from the bright sunshine into what at first seemed to be a heavy cloud resting on the water, but it turned out to be a very dense fog, and our steam-whistle had to be kept going throughout the rest of the day, and the fog-horns of the sailing-vessels had a most dreary sound coming constantly out of the dusky thickness.

After it became dark there was a great deal of phosphorescence in the sea, and I amused myself for some time in watching the thousands of brilliant sparks thrown up by the bows of the steamer into the dark air, for there was no moon, and the fog had not cleared off. At midnight the fog-cloud seemed to suddenly roll itself upwards, and the eastern sky was already tinged with the red hue which betokened the rising sun as I went below.

Saturday, July 15th.

The North Sea, so rough and turbulent as a rule, was calm to-day as a mill-pond, and there was not a ripple upon its surface. L—— and I sat on deck watching the countless thousands of jelly-fish which were floating near the top of the water, and we noticed one of them with a big star-fish, almost as large as himself, inside his transparent body. Great shoals of herrings and mackerel also were seen during the afternoon; and of the former fish we must have passed countless thousands, as they continually showed their presence by rising to the surface in vast numbers, the mackerel often leaping clear out of the sea.

Towards evening we entered another thick fog, for which the North Sea, in calm weather, has such a questionable celebrity. The whistle was blown every two minutes, in order that the vessel should not run down any ships or fishing-boats, of which there were several lying becalmed, whose fog-horns were heard during the night.

Sunday, July 16th.

At 3 a.m. we found ourselves suddenly in the very midst of the English fleet of trawlers from Yarmouth, and by the merest chance one of the boats escaped being run down by the "Albion," as the fog was still very thick, and the crew on board of the boat only rang a small bell by way of a danger-signal.

At 10 a.m. the sun shone out gloriously, as if to welcome us back to England, whose flat shores we soon sighted, and by mid-day we were steaming up the Thames, and at 5 p.m. we landed at the Isle of Dogs, having drunk to the health of Norway before we left the ship in a flowing bumper. I cannot do better than conclude this simple record of our tour by quoting one of the patriotic songs, for which the Norwegians are so famed.

1.

Minstrel, awaken the harp from its slumbers,
   Strike for Old Norway, the land of the free!
High and heroic, in soul-stirring numbers,
   Clime of our fathers! we strike it for thee.
      Old recollections
      Awake our affections;
They hallow the name of the land of our birth:
Each heart beats its loudest, each cheek glows its proudest,
For Norway the ancient, the throne of the earth.

2.

Spirit! look back on her far-flashing glory,
   The far-flashing meteor that bursts on thy glance;
On chieftain and hero, immortal in story,
   They press to the battle like maids to the dance.
      The blood flows before them,
      The wave dashes o'er them;
They reap with the sword what they plough with the keel,
Enough that they leave to the country that bore them,
Bosoms to bleed for her freedom and weal.

3.

The shrine of the Northman, the temple of freedom,
　Stands like a rock, where the stormy wind breaks:
The tempests howl round it, but little he'll heed them;
　Freely he thinks, and as freely he speaks.
　　　　The bird in its motion,
　　　　The wave in its ocean,
Scantly can rival his liberty's voice;
Yet he obeys, with a willing devotion,
Laws of his making, and kings of his choice.

4.

Land of the forest, the fell, and the fountain,
　Blest with the wealth of the field and the flood,
Steady and trustful, the sons of thy mountain
　Pay the glad price of thy rights with their blood.
　　　　Ocean hath bound thee!
　　　　Freedom hath found thee!
Then flourish, Old Norway! thy flag be unfurl'd!
As free as the breezes and breakers around thee,
The pride of thy children, the front of the world.

And let us also, not ungrateful to the glorious land where we have passed so many happy days, pay our last tribute of esteem and love for her fjords, fosses, and fjelds, and exclaim, with her own sons and daughters, "Flourish, Gamle Norge!" And, before we part from those indulgent friends who have accompanied us in this imperfectly written record of our wanderings in the far North, let us advise all who are in search of health, pleasure, sport, splendid scenery, or variety, to leave the beaten track of Continental travel, for one summer at least, and to try Norway and Lapland, and they will then agree with us, that no more charming trip could be undertaken than a tour to

"THE ARCTIC REGIONS AND BACK IN SIX WEEKS."

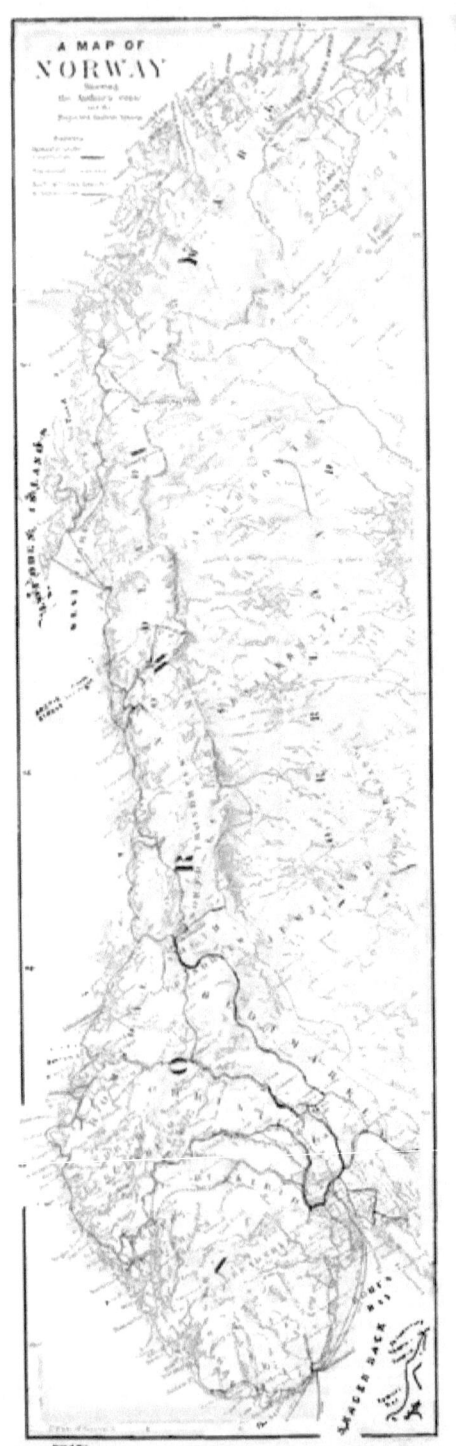

APPENDIX.

The following summary of our expenses may, I think, be found useful to any one who may decide upon taking a tour somewhat similar to that described in the previous pages. Our total expenses were not large, altogether amounting to £83 6s. 7d., and this sum includes board, lodging, presents to hotel and other servants, postboys, and boatmen, the entire posting and railway and steamer travelling expenses of two persons, and the hire of two carrioles, with harness, etc.

For one person travelling alone the expenses would, of course, be slightly in excess of the half of the sum here named for two; for there are many ways in which two people can economize, such as in use of the same apartment, the same table at meals, and in various other minor matters of detail.

The total expenses in the following list were incurred during a period of six weeks (from June 9th to July 16th), that is, from London to Tromsö, and from Tromsö back again to the English capital.

I may observe that many, probably, would have expended far less, and some much more money; but I think I may reasonably say that as we invariably took first-class tickets on the steamers and in the trains, and had the best rooms in hotels and roadside stations, combined with good food, and

very fair wine, our total expenditure of £83 6s. 7d., during
our six weeks' tour, will prove Norway and those parts of
Lapland that we visited to be by no means extravagant
countries in which to travel.

Our total expenses were as follows, and I have thought it
best to give the items in English money, as showing the
more readily, at a glance, what was charged us:—

	£	s.	d.
June 9th: two first-class tickets from London to Hull, £2 15s. 6d., dinners at Hull, 11s. 6d.	3	7	0
Two tickets for steamer, Hull to Christiania (half of the return fare of £6 0s. 0d. for one person here charged)	6	0	0
Three days' food on steamer, steward's fees, and porters at Christiania	2	10	6
Bill, including excellent wine, beer, etc., and good rooms at Victoria Hotel, Christiania, for two days	3	7	6
Driving to Oscarshal with two horses; fees at Oscarshal, to driver, etc.	0	7	5
Two first-class tickets, Christiania to Lillehammer, and fare of two carrioles (forty miles train, and seventy miles by steamer on the Mjösen)	1	18	6
Our sitting-room and bedroom accommodation, breakfasts, lunches, dinners, etc., and fees to servants at "stations" during eleven days	6	18	3
Paid for two horses for the carrioles for a distance of about 223 miles, from Lillehammer to Engen i Stören	5	6	0
Fees (called "drikkepenge") to postboys for the same distance	0	6	8

Two first-class fares, and charge for two carrioles from Storen to Throndhjem (forty miles)	£0	9	10
Two tickets for saloon and best cabins on steamer from Throndhjem to Tromsö and back (eight days)	6	6	0
Food for two persons (consisting of three good meals) wine, beer, and steward's fees, during the above period of eight days on the steamer	4	8	0
Hotel bill for one and a half days at Tromsö	1	8	0
Paid for boat and two rowers at Tromsö for rowing twenty miles to visit the Laps; a boat for fishing; and extra small fees to fishermen and others	1	0	0
Hotel bill at Throndhjem, including good wine, beer, three meals per diem, etc., for three days	2	16	0
Two tickets for saloon and best cabins on steamer, and charge for our two carrioles, from Throndhjem to Bergen	3	16	6
Two persons' food, wine, beer, and steward's fees, for two days, Throndhjem to Bergen	1	3	6
Hotel bill for one and a half days at Bergen	1	11	6
Two tickets, first class, and fare of our carrioles by steamer "Voss," from Bergen to Bolstadören (seventy-five miles)	1	0	1
Posting with two horses from Bolstadören to the head of the Randsfjord, about 188 miles, including first-class fares and freight of our carrioles on steamer from Gudvangen to Laerdalsören (thirty-five miles)	5	8	0
Fees to postboys for the same distance	0	6	9

	£	s.	d.
Hire of two carrioles and harness during our tour	8	0	0
Our accommodation at "stations," breakfasts, lunches, dinners, wine, beer, fees to servants, etc., during six days	2	8	8
Two first-class fares, and freight of our two carrioles down the Randsfjord (fifty miles)	0	13	3
From the southern end of the Randsfjord by train, two first-class fares and two carrioles, to Christiania	0	16	6
One and a half days at the Victoria Hotel, Christiania, board, lodging, etc.,	1	19	6
Various small incidental expenses	2	2	6
Two first-class fares by "Albion" steamer from Christiania to London	6	0	0
Three days' food on board for two persons, steward's fees, wine, beer, etc.,	3	0	0
Total expenditure for six weeks	£83	6	7

I will not go so far as to guarantee that every separate item of the above account of our expenditure is *perfectly correct*, but it certainly is so within a few pence; and it may be relied upon as a fair estimate of the ordinary cost of a similar trip for two persons.

The distance we covered during the tour described in these pages was as nearly as possible (including, of course, the numerous windings of the fjords which the steamers visited) five thousand English miles.

GENERAL INDEX.

Aak hotel, 335.
Aalesund, 313.
Aardals fjord, 356.
Above the clouds, in bed, 98.
Accidents frequent at the walrus hunting, 258.
Acerbi quoted, 279.
Action of the ice upon islands north of Throndhjem, 155.
Advice as to carriole driving, 16.
——————— civility to inferiors in Norway, 11.
——————— driving the "station-horses," 76.
——————— harness and reins, 46.
——————— luggage for the traveller, 13.
——————— medicines to take with one, 15.
——————— packing curiosities and skins, 14.
——————— sheets and pillow-cases, 21.
——————— waterproof-coats for the carriole journey, 80.
Agershuus, the castle of, 51.
"Albion," we embark for England on the, 409.
Aldershot, 19.
Ale, Norwegian, 41.
Amateur whaler, an, 294, 295.
America, emigrants for, 323.
American travellers in Norway, 100.
And fjord, abundance of sea fowl on the, 184.
——————— an ornithological treat on the, 186.
Anglers, attractions of Norway for, 2.
Apelvær islands, abundance of sea birds at, 158.

Apelvær, dried cod fish on, 150.
Apples near the Arctic circle, 322.
Apricots, 322.
Arctic Circle, we cross the, 164, 291.
——— scenery near the, 165, 291.
——— fox, habits of the, 275.
——— method of capturing the, 277.
——— price of their skins, 145.
——— nights, brightness of the, 262.
——— regions, shopping in the, 246.
——— scenery in Tromsö fjord, 186.
——— seas, sights of the, 251.
Arvika, 9.
Attractions of Norway to the angler, 2.
——————————— to the artist, 3.
——————————— to ladies, 4.
——————————— to the sportsman, 2.
——————————— general, 1.
Aufin's Bridge, 115.
——————— trout and grayling fishing at, 116.
Auk, the extinction of the Great, 301.
——— little, 301.
——— as food, 302.
——— "red snow" caused by, 303.
Aune station, 129.
——————— good shooting near, 129.
Austbjerg, 130.
——————— sport near, 132.

B.

Babies and cradles of the Laps, 211.
Baggage, our, 20.
Barometer, a Laplander's, 266.
Barley, rapidity of its growth in Lapland, 222.
Basking shark, fishery for the, 342.

Baths, scarce in Norway, 71.
Bears, 391.
Bearskins, price of white, 115.
Bear, the polar, 252.
———————— increasing scarcity of, 253.
———————— its digestive powers, 253, 255.
———————— description of shooting one, 253.
———————— immense size and weight of, 254.
Beauclerk, Lady Di, quoted, 70, 77.
Beauties of Norway cannot be seen hurriedly, 16.
Beautiful appearance of jelly-fish, 153.
———— scenery of the Christiania fjord, 36.
Beds, Mr. Bennett's remedy against shortness of Norwegian, 57.
—— discomfort of Norwegian, 57.
—— of the Laps, 216.
Bedstead, history of a, 363.
Beian, 152.
Bennett, we visit Mr., and engage carrioles, 45.
———— his handbook for travellers, 13, 15.
Bergen and the sea-serpent, 367.
———— hotels, 359.
———— museum of, 362.
———— old silver articles at, 366.
———— precautions against fire at, 360.
———— situation and trade of, 363.
Bergen fjord, salmon-traps on the, 371.
Bergenstift, scenery of the, 355.
Besaker, boats manned by women at, 152.
———— vast quantities of jelly-fish near, 153.
Birds at sea, 29.
—— rare on the Mjösen lake, 66.
—— immense numbers of, in the Arctic ocean, 271.
Bird-life, absence of, in Gudbrandsdal, 88.
———— abundance of, near Apelvær, 158.
Bjerkager station, 133.
———— sad accident to a quarryman near, 133.

Black and white exhibition, a scene fit for the, 182.
Black guillemots at sea, 29.
Blackthroated divers, 383.
Boats at sea, English fishing, 29.
—— for walrus hunting, 257.
Bodö, 168, 286.
—— good shooting near, 170.
Bolstadören, 372.
Boots for ladies in Norway, advice as to, 20.
Borgund church, 388.
Botanists' paradise, a, 122.
Botany of the Dovre fjeld, 122.
Bottle-nosed whales, 155, 156, 204.
Brœndhaugen i Dovre, fine scenery near, 93.
Bredevangen station, 90.
Breakfast on board ship, our first, 24.
Brightness of the summer nights, 97, 118.
Breeding cliffs of sea fowl in the Loffodens, 272.
Bronö, 162.
Bull, we meet a, 95.
" Bushman, the old," quoted, 131.
Byhre station, 87.

C.

Capercailzie on Hitteren island, 326.
———— shooting at Dahl in 1871, 62.
Carriole driving, freedom of, 4.
———— not unsociable, 75.
———— our first day's, 73.
Carrioles, we engage our, 15.
———— necessaries for a journey in, 48.
———— advice as to provisions to take in the, 81.
———— smart appearance of our, 47.
Carlstad, 9, 10.
Cattle on the way to a fair, 87.
Cathedral of Throndhjem, the, 308.

Cheese, an ancient, 42.
Cherries, wild, 138, 322.
Chilblains, the Lap cure for, 281.
Christiania, our arrival at, 38.
——— great heat at, 39.
——— hotels in, 40.
——— sights of and excursions from, 56.
Christiania fjord, absence of bird-life on the, 37.
——————— entrance to the, 35.
——————— scenery of the, 36.
Christiansand, 31, 411.
——————— picturesqueness of its situation, 31.
——————— salmon fishing near, 32.
——————— shooting to be obtained at, 32.
Christiansund, abundance of fish near, 329.
——————— abundance of flowers at, 328.
——————— fishing at, 327.
——————— prosperity and trade of, 328.
——————— romantic approach to, 327.
Church, ancient at Throndhjem, 306.
——— behaviour of the Laplanders at, 227.
Churchyard of Throndhjem cathedral, 307.
——————— the beauty of a Norwegian, 308.
Circle, we cross the Polar, 164.
Civility to inferiors, advice on, 11.
Cliff of Hornelen and its sea-fowl, 351.
Climate of Lapland, 224.
——— on the coast, mildness of the, 223.
Cloudberry jam, 82.
Coal-fish, 177, 189.
Cod fish, dried at Apelvær islands, 159.
——— a large one caught, 301.
——— fishery of the Loffoden, 160.
——————— men and boats employed at the, 159.
——— fishing, 29, 267.
——————— in Tromsö harbour, 267.
Coffee in Norway, excellency of, 44.

Colour of the Logen river, remarkable, 78.
Como, the lake of, compared with the Mjösen, 65.
Cormorants, 37.
——— curious appearance of a cliff occupied by, 161.
Copenhagen, 9.
Courtesy of all classes in Norway, 373.
Cowberry jam, 83.
Cows, Kerry, in the Arctic regions, 200.
——— Norwegian, 65, 87, 126.
——— price of in Norway, 112.
Cradles of the Laps, 214, 215.
Crossbill, the, 406.
Cuckoo in the Arctic regions, 190, 261.
Curiosities, how to take care of, 14.
Custom-house officers, civility of, 39.

D.

Dahl, a day's sport near in 1871, 62.
——— capercailzie shooting at, 61.
Danger from fire in Norway, 53.
Day, change in the length of when proceeding northward, 28, 14.
Deep-sea lines for cod, great length of, 29.
Delay in sailing from Hull, 22.
Denmark, 9.
——— the route by Germany and, 12.
" Devil's passage," the, 82.
Dinner on board the " Hero," a select, 27.
Disregard of time in Scandinavia, 11.
Diver, the great northern, 37, 179, 186.
——— the blackthroated, 383.
Docks, busy appearance of Hull, at night, 23.
Doctors in Norway, scarcity of, 15.
——— in Lapland, non-existence of, 15.
Dogs of the Lap encampment, 208.

General Index.

Dog-fish, the picked, 310.
Dolls, Lapland, 264.
Dombaas, our arrival at, 96.
——— wild situation of, 97.
——— wolves near, 101.
——— we leave, for the north, 102.
Dover and Ostend, the route to Norway by, 8, 12.
Dovre, 94.
Dovre fjeld, abundance of reindeer moss on the, 121.
——— ascent to the plateau of the, 94.
——— as a field for the botanist, 122.
——— game to be found on the, 118, 125.
——— great cold on the, 118.
——— highest part of the road over the, 118.
——— sand on the, 102, 120.
——— scarce flowers found on the, 123.
——— wildness of its scenery, 119.
Driv river, trout fishing in the, 121.
——— wild flowers on its banks, 123.
Drive through snow, we, 113.
——— a hot, in the Guul valley, 139.
——— to Oscarshal, a pretty, 49.
Driving, the freedom of carriole, 4.
——— our first day's carriole, 73.
Drivstuen station, 127.
Dröbak, the straits of, 38.
Droski, the carriage of the cities, 49.
Drunkenness in Throndhjem, 317.

E.

Eagle on the Dovre fjeld, 121.
——— golden, 245.
——— killed by a salmon, 331.
——— the sea, 185, 329.
——— ——— abundance of, near Christiansand, 329.

Eagle, the sea, drowned by large fish, 350.
—— owl, the, 110, 121.
Eider down, 145, 180, 199, 201.
————————— production of and value of, 199.
————————— quilts from Greenland, 146.
Eggs of the eider duck, 198.
Eider ducks, 37, 154, 179, 186, 195, 271, 33?.
————————— habits of the, 195, 196, 197, 200, 204.
————————— in Iceland, 202.
————————— nests, we visit their, 197.
————————— Pontoppidan's description of habits of, 203.
Eidsvold, 63.
————————— fishing to be obtained near, 66.
————————— rare water-birds at, 66.
————————— scenery of, in summer and winter, 64.
Emigrants for the new world, 323.
Encampment of soldiers, we pass an, 78.
Engen i Stören, we arrive at, 135.
————————— great heat at, 136.
————————— salmon fishing at, 136.
England, we leave, 21.
———— back again in, 414.
Ermine skins, cheapness of, 115.
Euphemia of Rugen, Queen, 51.
Evanger, 373.
———— Vand, fine scenery of the, 372.
Exorcism against lemmings, an ancient, 111.

F.

Fagernæs, 400.
————————— attractions of, and picturesqueness of, 401.
Fashion, travellers ruled by the, 6.
Færder island and its lighthouse, 35, 411.
Fieldfares, habits of the, 104.
Fille fjeld, 392.
———— great cold upon the, 392.
———— wildness of the, 396.

"Finkel," 261.
Fir-trees in Norway, 86.
Fire, danger from, in Norway, 53, 191, 262.
First breakfast on board the "Hero," 24.
—— train from Stockholm to Christiania, 9.
Fish, abundance of, in the Mäelström, 174.
Fish-supper, a grand, 41.
Fishing at Lillehammer, 72.
—— in Gudbrausdal, 79.
—— near Christiansand, salmon, 32.
—— near Eidsvold and Minde 66.
—— in the Guul river, salmon, 136, 139.
—— with hand-lines from the steamer, 176
—— in Tromsö harbour, 267.
—— at midnight in Tromsö fjord, 189.
—— for mackerel off Frederikstad, 37.
Fishery, account of the cod, 159.
Fishing-boats at sea, 29.
—— rods, best mode of carrying on a carriole, 74.
"Fisk Lappar," 236.
Five thousand miles in six weeks, 16.
Fjord, the scenery of the Christiania, 36.
"Fläd-bröd," 384.
Flakstad island, 175.
Flowers, abundance of, at Lillehammer, 72.
—— —— —— on the Dovre fjeld, 120, 122.
—— —— —— on the Fille fjeld, 393.
—— —— in the Loffoden islands, 183.
—— —— in the Guul valley, 136.
Fokstuen-on-Dovre, 113.
—— —— —— wild drive to Hjerdkin from, 115.
Food of the Laps, 229.
Formokampen mountain, 93.
Fossegarden, 79.
Fox, a Norwegian, 80.
—— Arctic, habits of the, 275.
—— —— modes of capturing the, 277.

Fox, Arctic, price of skins of, 145.
—— silver, great value of the, 278.
Frederikstad, 37, 56.
Frogneraasen, view from the, 56.
Frydenlund, 101.
Fur-stores at Throndhjem, 111, 318.

G.

Game to be found on the Dovre fjeld, 118.
"Gamle Norge," 5.
Garlic, 133.
Geology of the Loffodens, 290.
—— — of the Mjösen lake, 70.
Glacial action upon mountains near the polar circle, 161.
—— ————— islands north of Throndhjem, 155.
Glaciers, 66, 165, 183.
Glutton, the, 145, 235.
Goldeneye ducks, 186, 283.
—————— — habits of the, 383.
Gooseberries, wild, 138.
Grass, "rein," 265.
Grayling fishing at Minde, 66.
———— —— on the Dovre fjeld, 116.
Grebes, 66.
Greenlander's method of catching Arctic foxes, 277.
Grieffenfeld, history of Count von, 150.
Gudbransdal, fishing and shooting of, 79.
————— fine scenery of, 86.
Guillemots, 186, 271.
Guide-books for Norway and Lapland, 13.
Gudvangen, picturesqueness of, 386.
Gulf stream, its effect on the climate of Norway, 223.
Gulls, 26, 154, 179, 185, 271.
Guul, abundance of wild flowers in the valley of the, 136.
—— fertility of the valley of the, 137.
—— salmon fishing in the, 138.

H.

Hæg, 391.
Habits of eider fowl, 195, 200.
———————— in Iceland, 202.
Haerstadt, 273.
Hadeland glasverk, 407.
Haddocks, 267.
Halfdan the black, 61.
Hammer, 68.
Happy life of the Laps, 218.
Harness for the tame reindeer, 240.
—— hints as to carriole, 46.
Harvest in Lapland, 222.
Hawk-owl, habits and nesting of the, 130.
Heat, great at Christiania, 39.
"Hero," the, 22.
Herrings, 413.
———— a species of fresh water, 67.
Hestemando island, 166, 291.
Hints as to driving hired horses in Norway, 76.
———— provisions for a carriole journey, 81.
———— waterproof coats, 80.
Hitteren, red-deer of, 326.
Hjerdkin, 117.
"Hog's back," railway accident in the tunnel of the, 18.
Holiday, where to take a, 1.
Hönefos, 407.
———— the massacre of the Swedes at, 408.
Hop-gardens in the Guul valley, 137.
Hornelen, cliff of, 351.
Horses, advice as to driving hired, 76.
———— excellency of the Norwegian, 75.
Horten, 38.
Hoyland the robber, history of, 53.
Hull, busy appearance of the docks, 23.
—— routes to Norway from, 8.
Humber, we sail from the, 24.

F f

Hunting the Walrus described, 258.
"Hush-a-bye, baby, upon the tree top!" 215.

I.

Ice, the Wenham lake, 410.
Iced water in Norwegian railway carriages, 60.
Iceland, habits of eider fowl in, 202.
Irrigation in Gudbrunsdal, 85.
Isle of Dogs, we land at the, 414.

J.

Jagts, 170, 300, 355.
——— description of their rig, 358.
Jams, Norwegian, 82.
Jelly-fish, vast number of, near Besaker, 153.

K.

Kerry cows in the Arctic seas, 290.
King eider ducks, 219.
Kirkestuen, 82.
Klipper-cod-fish, 159.
Knapsack guide to Norway, Murray's, 15.
"Komager" of the Laplanders, 225, 247.
Kongsvold, 119, 121, 127.
——————— a good place for botanists, 122.
——————— great cold at, 125.
——————— snow-storm at, 125.
——————— variety of wild flowers at, 120, 123.
——————— wildness of its scenery, 119.
Kringelen, the massacre of the Scotch at, 90.
Kvaloe island, 194, 206, 260.
——————— Lap camp on, 206.

L.

Lærdalsören, 388.
Ladies, attractions of Norway to, 4.
——— walking-boots for, 20.
" Lament of the birds of passage," the, 378.
Lamont's works quoted, 253, 254.
Landing in Norway, absence of bustle on, 40.
Lapland, abundance of mosquitoes in, 221.
——— harvest in, 222.
——— rapid growth of crops in, 222.
——— variation of its climate, great, 221.
Laps, babies of the, 214.
——— beds of the family, 216.
——— behaviour of, in church, 227.
——— cures for diseases, 280.
——— description of a family meal, 216.
——— ——— their tents, 211.
——— ——— the children's cradles, 214.
——— ——— their sledges, 238.
——— drunkenness of the, 227, 261.
——— encampment of, on Kvaloe island, 206.
——— family on the move, a, 239.
——— food of the, 229.
——— funerals of the, 282.
——— greediness of the, 226.
——— larder of a family, 235.
——— Linnæus on their happy life, 218.
——— manufactures of the, 224.
——— out shopping, 247.
——— strong aroma of their tents, 211.
——— ugliness of the, 210.
——— uncleanliness of the, 212, 216.
——— vocal accomplishments of the, 280.
——— women are well treated by the men, 234.
Leathern reins for carriole-driving, 46.
Lemming, we see our first, 103.
——— abundance of, on the Dovre fjeld, 103.

Lemming, abundance of, on the Fille fjeld,
——— as food, 106.
——— appearance of the country after a migration of, 108.
——— description and habits of the, 104.
——— migrations of the, 104.
——— perseverance of, on the march, 108.
——— prayer used in olden days against the, 111.
——— probable causes of the migrations of the, 105.
——— prolificness of the, 106.
Length of days, change in the, 28.
Lierfossen, the, 319.
Lillehammer, 70.
——— fine scenery near, 69.
——— wild flowers at, 71.
Listad station, 87.
Lobsters at Aalesund, 344.
Lodingen, 273.
Logen river, fishing in the, 79.
——— immense trout in the, 78.
——— milky colour of the, 78.
London to Norway, the route from, 8.
Loffoden islands, breeding cliffs of sea birds in the, 272.
——— cod-fishery of the, 160.
——— first view of the, our, 172.
——— fishing from the steamer amongst the, 176.
——— midnight scenery of the, 182.
——— wild grandeur of the, 181, 273.
Longfellow's Saga of King Olaf, 324.
Losmöe island, 354.
Luggage, what to take from England, 13.
——— how to pack it on a carriole, 74.
Lyster fjord, 356.
Lythe fishing, 177, 189.

M.

Mäelström, the, 173.
——— its danger exaggerated, 173.

Mäelström, abundance of fish in the, 174.
Mackerel, large shoals of, 37, 185.
——— bloodthirsty, 412.
Magpies in Gudbransdal, 89.
——— mode of capturing, 89.
Maristuen, 391.
——— bears at, 391.
Medicines for the traveller, advice as to, 15.
Mergansers, 186.
Midnight fishing at Tromsö, 189.
——— in the Arctic seas, 166.
——— beauty of the scene in Arctic seas at, 167.
——— scene in the Loffodens, 182.
——— sun invisible at Tromsö, 267.
——— our first view of the, 167.
——— our last view of the, 285.
——— put out, 191.
——— sunshine, a table of the, 270.
Midsummer's night at Throndhjem, 141.
Minde, fishing near, 66.
Mjösen lake, the, 63.
——— the "Little," 399.
——— compared with the lake of Como, 65.
——— fresh-water herrings found in the, 67.
——— great depth of the, 70.
——— picturesqueness of the, 69.
Mjös Vand, the, 399.
Moen station, delayed at, 92.
Moltelser jam, 82.
Molde, abundance of fruit-trees at, 334.
——— situation of, 333.
——— fjord, abundance of fish in the, 338.
——— a rough entrance to the, 332.
Monkholm, the legend of, 150.
Moskenæs, 173.
Mosquitoes, abundance of, in Lapland, 221.
——— at Hagernæs, 409.

Mosquitoes, veils for protection against, 19.
Moss, reindeer, 124, 231.
Murray's guides, usefulness of, 13.
Mykletveitveten, 374.

N.

Naes, 335.
Nærödal, the, 385.
Namsen river, abundance of seals near the, 157.
——— excellency of, for salmon fishing, 156.
——— fjord, beautiful scenery of, 156.
Namsos, 157.
Naze, the, 30.
Nest of the eider duck described, 201.
Nesting haunts of eider fowl at Tromsö, 197.
Nid, the river, 321.
Nights, brightness of the summer, 97.
Night in the North sea, a rough, 28.
Nord fjord, 353.
"Nordland," we embark on the, for the Arctic regions, 148.
——— civility of officers of the, 151.
Norway, chief attractions of, 1.
——— healthiness of its climate, 5.
——— compared with the Continent, 6.
——— various routes to, 7.
Norwegian civility, 373.
——— jams, 82.
——— peasants contrasted with Egyptians, 85.
North sea, frequency of storms in the, 25.
——— roughness of the, 25, 28.
——— shallowness of, 25.
Nystuen, 392.

O.

Object of this book, the, 16.
Odnæs, 402.

Oiloe, large trout at, 398.
Olaf, St., history and death of, 310.
——— and the wizard, legend of, 312.
——— Longfellow's saga of, 324, 347.
——— shrine of, 311.
——— birthplace of, 88.
"Old Bushman" quoted, the, 131.
Old silver at Dombaas, 99.
Officers, courtesy of the Norwegian naval, 151.
Ormsrnd's hotel at Lillehammer, 71.
Oscarshal, we visit, 49.
——— history of, 51.
——— interior of, 50.
Ostend, the route by Dover and, 8, 12.
Owl, eagle, 110.
——— hawk, habits of the, 130.
——— nesting of the, 131.
——— snowy, 110.
Oyster-catchers, breeding haunts of, 197.

P.

Passports not required in Norway, 39.
Peas, rapid growth of, in Lapland, 222.
Peewit, legend of the, 106.
Pipe cleaner, a Laplander's, 228.
Plover, the legend of the green, 406.
Poachers in Norway, 377.
Polar bear, the, 252.
——— its powers of digestion, 253.
——— Lamont's description of shooting the, 253.
——— price of skins of the, 145.
Ponies, excellency of the Norwegian, 75.
Porpoises, 38, 154, 185, 293.
Præsthuus, 133.
Ptarmigan, 245.
Puffins, 271.

Q.

Queen of Sweden and Norway, funeral of the late, 9.
Quilts of eiders-down from Greenland, 116.

R.

Railway travelling in Norway, slowness of, 10, 60, 140.
Randsfjord, the, 102.
Raspberries, wild, 138.
Rauma river, the, 335.
Razorbills, 271.
Red deer on Hitteren Island, 326.
Redwings, 382.
——————— a supper of, 403.
Reien, 400.
" Rein " grass as a barometer, 265.
Reindeer, courage of the tame, 243.
——————— as a steed, 240.
——————— described by Mary Howitt, 237.
——————— ferocity of the tame, 241.
——————— fondness for its master of the tame, 242.
——————— foot of, compared with that of the moose, 237.
——————— habits of, in summer, 231.
——————— harness used for the tame, 240.
——————— hams and tongues, 233.
——————— large horns of, 231.
——————— milking the tame, 234.
——————— moss, 124, 231.
——————— stalking the wild, 125.
——————— uses of the tame, 229.
——————— uses of their horns and skins, 232.
——————— weight of a good fat, 232.
——————— wild, 397.
Reindeer's horns, a shopful of, 248.
——————— price of, at Tromsö, 256.

Reins for carriole driving, leathern, 46.
Rise, sport to be got near, 128.
Rivers, subterranean, 165.
Robber, Hoyland the, 53.
Rogstad, 137.
Rollo " the walker," legend of, 350.
Romsdal mountains, 333.
——————sport in the, 335.
Romsdalshorn, the, 337.
Rorqual, Sibbald's, 293.
Routes to Norway, 7.
Russian whalers at Tromsö, 256.

S.

Sæters on the Dovre fjeld, 112.
Salmon fishing in the Guul, 136.
—————————— excellency of, in the Namsen, 156.
Salmon traps, curious, 371.
Sand on the Dovre fjeld, 102, 120.
Sandtorv, 184, 273.
Sannossöen, 163.
Scandinavia, attractions of, 6.
——————— disregard of time throughout, 11.
Scotch, massacre of, at Kringelen, 90.
Scotch fir, height at which it grows above sea level, 86.
Scotland, route from, 8.
Sea serpent, the, 367.
——————— Captain Brooke's description of, 368.
Seagulls leading boats to the fishing-ground, 30.
Sea fowl in the Vest fjord, 171.
Seal, an inquisitive, 39.
Seals, 157, 179, 252.
Seven sisters mountains, 163.
Shallowness of the North Sea, 25.
Shark, the basking, fishery for, 312.

Shark, various species of, on the Norwegian coasts, 340.
——— fishing in the olden times in Norway, 341.
Shooting near Christiansand, 32.
Shopping in the Arctic regions, 246.
Silver, great rise in the price of old, 100.
Sinclair's defeat at Kringelen, 90.
Skager Rack, the, 30.
Skating soldiers of Norway, 365.
Skogstad, 397.
Skjæggestad, 82.
Skua-gulls, 185.
Slowness of railway travelling in Scandinavia, 10, 60, 140.
Snechætten mountain, 119, 122.
Snowstorm at Kongsvold, 125.
Snowy owl, 110, 121.
Sogne fjord, the, 355.
Soldiers, the skating, 365.
Stalheim, 385.
Steamer on the Mjösen, the, 67.
Stockmarknaes, 177.
Storklevstad, 87.
Storthing, 42.
St. Olaf, the history of, 310.
——— the saga of, 324, 347.
Stee, 399.
Sunsets, splendour of, on the west coast, 162.
Sunshine, a table of the midnight, 270.
Sveen, 402.
Svolvær, 273.
Swallow, legends of the, 405.
Sweden, a distant view of, 35.

T.

Temperature in Scandinavia, discrepancy of, 223.
Tents of the Laps, 207.
Terns, 158, 179, 186, 197, 271, 292.

General Index.

Threnen islands, 165.
Throndhjem cathedral, 308.
——————————— churchyard, 309.
——————————— service at, 316.
————— fireworks on midsummer's eve at, 150.
————— great heat at, 143.
Tiedman's paintings at Oscarshal, 50.
Time, disregard of, throughout Norway, 11
Toftemoen and Herr Tofte, 94.
Toothache, a Laplander's cure for, 280.
Torghatten, 162, 297.
Torget island, scenery near, 299.
Torrisdal river, salmon fishing in the, 32.
Trees in Norway, 86.
Trout fishing on the Dovre fjeld, 116.
————— near Lillehammer, 72.
———— immense in the Logen, 78.
Tromsö, absence of bird-life near, 189.
———— midnight fishing at, 189.
———— precautions against fire at, 262.
———— trade and population of, 268.
———— fjord, Arctic scenery of, 186.
Tvinde, 384.

U.

Ugliness of the Laps, 210.
Uncleanliness of the Laps, 212, 216.
Usefulness of sea-fowl to the mariner, 352.

V.

Valdersund, 152.
Veb ungsnæset, 335.
Vefsen, 163.
Verüe island, 173, 175.
Vest fjord, 170, 285.
———— splendid scenery of, 172.

Vest fjord, vast flocks of birds on the, 171.
"Victoria" hotel at Christiania, 40.
Vikings, associations of the, 346.
Vinge, 385.
Vöring-foss, 384.
Vossevangen, 374.
————— pretty situation of, 375.
————— early morning in the woods of, 381.

W.

Walrus, accidents frequent at the hunting of the, 258.
————— hunting described, 257.
————— increasing scarcity of, 250.
————— solicitude of mother for their young, 259.
————— tusks, 248, 249.
————— value of their tusks and oil, 250.
Weasel on deck, a, 274.
Wedding in low life at Throndhjem, 305.
————— procession, we join a, 133.
"Wenham lake" ice, 410.
Whales, 252, 292, 338.
Whale, the bottle-nosed, 155, 156.
————— the "finner" or razor-backed, 292.
————— large one in sight, 293.
————— seen in Molde fjord, 338.
————— stranded at Flakstad, 175.
Whalers in Tromsö harbour, Russian, 256.
White fox, habits of the, 275.
Wild flowers at Lillehammer, 71.
Wild fowl near Tromsö, abundance of, 245.
Wintry scenery near Tromsö, 195.
Women crews for boats, 152.
Wolves, a peasant attacked by, 399.
————— on the Dovre fjeld, 101.
Wood in Norway, great altitude at which it grows, 86.
Woodcocks, 376.
Woodpecker, the great black, 382.

INDEX TO SCIENTIFIC NAMES

OF

ANIMALS, BIRDS, FISH, AND FLOWERS MENTIONED IN THE WORK.

A.
Alca impennis, 301.
Anas boschas, 383.
—— clangula, 383.

B.
Balænoptera musculus, 293.
———— Sibbaldii, 293.
Bubo maximus, 110.

C.
Canis lagopus, 275.
Carex sylvatica, 239.
Cenomyce rangiferina, 231.
Colymbus glacialis, 37.
Cuculus canorus, 261.

D.
Delphinus tersio, 156, 294.

E.
Epilobium origanifolium, 123.

F.
Felis lynx, 49.

G.
Gadus carbonarius, 177, 273.
Gulo borealis, 145, 235.

H.
Haliætus albicilla, 185, 329.

L.
Larus canus, 196.
—— Islandicus, 185.
—— marinus, 185.

M.
Mallotus Grœnlandicus, 277.
Medusidæ, 153.
Mergulus alle, 301.
Mustela erminea, 275.

O.
Orca gladiator, 296.

P.

Picus martius, 382.
Prunus avium, 138.

R.

Ranunculus glacialis, 124.
Ribes rubrum, 138.
Rubus idæus, 138.

S.

Salmo ferox, 78.
Squalus acanthias, 340.
——— borealis, 340.
——— maximus, 340.
——— spinax, 342.
Stellaria alpestris, 123.
Sterna hirundo, 158.

Strix funerea, 130.
——— nyctea, 110, 121.

T.

Trichechus rosmarus, 248.
Triticum violaceum, 123.
Trollius Europeus, 72.

U.

Uria grylle, 29.
Ursus maritimus, 252.

V.

Vanellus cristatus, 106.
V. vitis Idæa, 83.

W.

Woodsia hyperborea, 123.
——— ilvensis, 123.

GILBERT AND RIVINGTON, PRINTERS, ST. JOHN'S SQUARE, LONDON.

www.ingramcontent.com/pod-product-compliance
Lightning Source LLC
Chambersburg PA
CBHW022113300426
44117CB00007B/692